Blue Moon Rare Fire

The extraordinary true story of a woman's rise
when darkness fell

By
Helena Jayne Bryant

The story you are about to read is a true story based on actual events. I have done my best to recreate memories and past conversations accurately. Names, dates, and places have been changed to protect the innocent, who are worthy of this consideration. The guilty benefit vicariously. Therefore, any similarities to any persons living or dead are purely coincidental.

My truth comes alive on these pages. My story is no one's but my own.

*To Sparrow—Yours are the wings
that carried me home.*

FOREWORD

I'm blessed to be a reader and an editor. In fact, I'm pretty sure I was born to be both. And after a lifetime spent with words, there are two things that I know in my bones to be true:

1. As a society and as individuals, our stories are our most precious possessions.

2. The right story will find you at the right time.

Our stories explain where we've been, and they show us the way forward.

I'm not talking about just fairy tales or the classics—although they're certainly treasures. I'm talking about the life stories that speak to us. The kind we read far into the night, and the kind we tell our girlfriends over coffee (or wine).

These are the stories that make us think and help us learn. They mirror our own experiences, expose us to new ideas about old topics, help us find the similarities among the differences, teach us lessons, and help us figure out life.

Women are amazing storytellers. It's in our blood.

We share our books and experiences with one another, and then we pass them on. Because stories—whether truth or fiction—are textbooks for life. They're lessons that help us navigate relationships, parenting, aging, loss, and all the other experiences that we struggle to understand.

We learn from knowing how others have coped and triumphed. And where they've fallen down. What they've figured out.

What's amazing is that often, the stories that find us are exactly the stories we need at that very moment.

I have always had a knack—or maybe it's a very clever spirit guide—for walking into a bookstore and picking up exactly the book I need at that time. Many times I've even bought a book, not knowing why I needed it. Then, after it sat on my shelf, unread, for months or even years, I'd feel a nudge to pull it down. And it would be about the very issues I was experiencing at that moment.

Freaking weird. And wonderful.

Meeting Helena was exactly like that. We found each other at exactly the right time—and it was definitely the universe at work.

She had a story to tell. And I have a passion for helping people get their stories out into the world.

The first time we talked on the phone, I was so engrossed in her and her story that I totally ignored my corgi puppy, who had turned a rain-filled flowerpot on my deck into his own personal splash pool. As Helena and I got deeper into our conversation, he ran around my kitchen, flinging dirty water everywhere with a big, corgi smile on his tiny face.

But all I cared about was hearing Helena's story.

She said she'd written a memoir in the form of letters to her adult daughter about her experience being stalked for thirteen years. She'd written about losing herself. About being abused. About surviving rape. About being homeless.

She'd become a long-haul truck driver just to stay ahead of the stalker. She'd experienced epiphanies and miracles. And she'd overcome. In the end, she'd emerged stronger and better for the experience.

She had, she said, been through some shit. And she'd learned some shit.

Now, she wanted to share her story with other women who could use some of the wisdom and hope that she'd found.

She wanted to know if I would help her.

"Oh, hell yes," I said.

I hung up wanting to cheer. Partly because I'd just found another member of my tribe. But also because I'd met a woman who embraced and owned her story as her truth.

And it's badass, to borrow Helena's term, to own your own truth. To claim your own story.

The stories we live are just as valuable as the ones we read in books. And it's so important to own them. If we don't like the story we're living, we can't change it until we accept the truth of the story itself.

No matter how valuable the lessons are that you read and hear in others' stories, they don't do you any good if you aren't telling yourself the truth about your own story. You can't change what's fake, and you can't change what you run from. You can only change what you admit to be true.

In *Blue Moon, Rare Fire*, Helena tells you her story. She dives deep into her truths. What surfaces is often painful, violent and weird. But it's also beautiful and inspiring.

And it's always honest. That's what makes it powerful and magical. Facing her truth and sharing her story is also what empowered her to change it.

It was brave of her to put it all down on paper and offer it to the world. And she did it because she hopes her story will help others. She walked through mud and pain and fear, and she learned some shit.

Now she's doing what storytellers have always done: She's sharing it with the world.

And God bless her for it, because stories like hers—like all the stories we tell each other—show us the way forward.

Blue Moon, Rare Fire found its way to me at the perfect time. And now it has found its way to you because something in it can help you.

The universe knows what you need when you need it.

I hope that Helena's book has the amazing impact on your life that it has had on mine.

Kristy Phillips

Mill Creek, Washington

January 2020

BLUE MOON
RARE FIRE

ONE

Dear Sparrow,

I'm home. Finally.

Breathe, I tell myself. *Breathe.*

There's a difference between breathing and just taking in air.

I'm making a conscious effort to inhale the beauty of the gathering sunrise, hoping the refreshing scenery will let the road slip further and further from my mind. Staring out at the Gulf of Mexico feels like the perfect way to welcome myself home—the harmony of earth, water, and sky makes me feel as though I can channel Bob Ross into a peaceful shade of Zen.

As soon as I stepped out of my truck, I was eager to rid myself of the road I'd just left behind. The road of my travels came to feel like an angry ex-boyfriend, its frantic energy coursed through my veins, attaching itself to my psyche as if it had every right to invade my personal space.

1

A few hundred thousand miles or so later, I could no longer tell where the whole of me ended and the road began. But now that I face the water, with my back leaning into a comfortable beach chair, the inspiring view feels like I'm experiencing the road's exact opposite; I've stepped out of the din and into the sublime.

My thick leather boots feel like concrete slippers and look ridiculously out of place among the seashells and driftwood, even though they've been a natural extension of my body for years now. I can't quite remember how long I've made my toes wait to feel the sand again, but I guess it doesn't really matter because they don't have to wait anymore.

I suppose it will come as no surprise to you that I headed to the water before even setting foot through my front door. I grabbed my trusty thermos, a pad of writing paper from the glove box, and walked directly toward one of my favorite spots on the beach.

Now I'm nestled just beyond the sand dune covered in tall beach grass that forms a protective barrier between the scenic highway behind me and the sea in front of me. The palm tree marking this spot— whose trunk curves at a curious right angle, making it look like the tree is perpetually inspecting the sand—serves as my finish line. To anyone else it would look like a tree shaped by the will of the wind. To me it looks like a welcome-home mat on the front porch of everything safe and familiar.

I was eager to return home. I'd spent too long out on the road this time around. The experience weathered me. I feel drained. For months it felt like I was holding my breath. After the fire, all I wanted was home. Then came your phone call, making the want turn into a need, which fit my mind beautifully—the road doesn't satisfy me the way it used to, no longer my sanctuary on wheels.

For a very long time, I needed the road. It was my cocoon—its resonance quieted me, satisfying my wanderlust, letting me touch the face of complete freedom for the first time in my life. But as the years wore on, the road stopped feeling like my happy place. Once the sparkle was gone, it started to feel like I was placing a fortified barrier between me and the real world.

I suppose my eyes have now seen enough mountains, deserts, canyons, and rainbows to feed my imagination for a lifetime. It's time to leave the road behind. It's time to decompress, rejuvenate, and step back into life again. In that order—with no room for bullshit in the spaces in between.

It feels good to see the Gulf of Mexico again. I've come to realize that she and I are kindred in a peculiar sort of way. Beneath her silvery calm lies an enigma that moves with the spirit of a black cat: fierce and serene, methodical and unpredictable, spiritual and bewitching. Like most of us, the Gulf is a mystery wrapped in the ribbons of beauty and chaos. Also like most of us, she's a force to be reckoned with as much as she's an energy longing to be embraced.

The Gulf seems rather sentimental today. Only a slight breeze encircles me, and the waves lapping at the shore seem relaxed and thoughtful, allowing me to settle into myself while the morning eases its way into the night sky like a shot of cream eases its way into coffee. The retreating darkness relinquishes its shades of midnight, making room for the colorful bursts of morning. I watch as the butterscotch sunrise announces itself, blending seamlessly into a lavender halo. As the darkness surrenders itself to the magnificence of light, I can't help but feel as though the sky is trying to tell the story of my life.

Speaking of, I tell you this with unabashed certainty: I came here this morning with the singular intention of telling you the secrets of my heart.

Of course, that declaration sounds rather lofty and dumb, but it's true.

I've known for years that one day I'd share my journey with you, partly because you deserve some answers and partly because denying what I've been through doesn't make sense anymore. I've put this moment off as long as I could, always believing the universe would guide me to a giving place like a soul to a Sunday. I trusted that when the time was right, life would offer me the perfect words in the perfect setting so I could feel safe talking about messy things. My Pandora's box used to be so heavy. I'm here today to talk about the memories I stuffed for so long, until I finally learned the healing art of how to set them free.

I suppose we all have a Pandora's box, a secret chamber within us that serves as our trauma vault, encasing our fear and sadness so we don't have to look at them every day. Life has some heat to it, spawning ghosts, shadows, and scars we try hard to forget. Everyone needs a quiet place to store private pain. And we do our best to keep it under lock and key for the sake of *Keep Calm and Carry On*. But boxes can get cumbersome, and hidden feelings can't sleep forever. Some of us are able to move forward in spite of our pain, while others struggle to move forward at all. I guess the success of our liberation comes down to the size of the box each of us needs to keep our ghosts silent and numb. And to our willingness to release buried sadness when the time is right to do so.

But we'll talk about hidden chambers later. For now, I'm glad to be home, awake, and alive.

Fiat lux, I say to the sky.

Fiat lux, my thankful heart sings.

Actually, I'm pretty sure good fortune is sitting right next to me because here I am, with pen in hand, in a setting that helps season my thoughts so I feel comfortable beginning the process of telling my life story. I've longed for this moment for years. And here it is. I'm ready to begin.

4

Breathe, I tell myself again. *Breathe*.

I don't suppose you understand what all this breathing is about. You won't feel this moment quite as big as I do, but that's only because you have no idea what I'm about to say. Through my letters, you will come to have a better understanding of the woman I am, and more importantly, the road I traveled to get here. Now that you're a young woman making your own way in this world, maybe it's time I offer you the sacred keepsakes of my journey, hoping you might find some wisdom and inspiration.

Sometimes, when we learn of others' mistakes, it helps us see our own mistakes in a healthier light, like a lamppost illuminating the stepping stones on the magical road we call *life*.

Before I get started, let me begin by speaking the highest thought in my personal pyramid of truth: Your love and friendship are the greatest gifts I've ever received.

You and I have been a team since before you were born. I suppose it felt natural for you—the only child of a single mother—to reach for my hand. Yet, we gravitate toward one another for reasons that go beyond just parent/child bonds. We are like two interlocking puzzle pieces, separate yet joined, creating a picture that flows with symmetry and color, adorned with humor and irrepressible warmth.

Maybe we were sisters in another life, or maybe the universe just needed another helping of uncomplicated bliss. Either way, you're delightfully quirky and I've been told that I'm the interesting side of strange, but it works somehow, doesn't it?

I have to smile when I think of the many people who have scratched their heads trying to explain our closeness. Operating from a place that is both ethereal and grounded, we stumbled upon our remarkable fellowship by sheer instinct, I suppose. I didn't know how to be any other kind of mother, and you didn't know how to be any other kind of child.

But a child can't separate the woman from the person she sends Mother's Day cards to, even when the mother is incapable of being conventional. It's not until we step into our own womanhood that we begin to understand that our mothers were women before they were mothers. Even though we've always enjoyed a special bond, there are many things I've never told you, mostly because I didn't know how. But the fruit seems ripe now. Maybe it's time I answer some of the questions you've had the compassion to never ask.

After you called to tell me you were expecting a baby, my mind drifted to places it had never been before. The idea of becoming a grandmother forces a woman to consider what she has to offer such a momentous occasion. Since the beginning of time, the role of the grandmother has been carved into the totem pole of humanity as the matriarch of the herd, the keeper of the fire, the lighthouse for the tribe. I hope to honor the grandmothers before me by offering my grandchild the gift of a mother at peace with her past. I hope my letters will help cleanse your headspace by leveling some bumpy terrain so you can step into your future feeling loved and lighthearted, at one with your most beautiful self. I suppose I could give my grandchild a tummy-time mat or a plush koala bear toy, but somehow, an emotionally nourished mother seems like the best gift of all.

I was in the Pacific Northwest when you called to tell me about the baby—northern Idaho to be specific. After we got off the phone, I pulled off to the side of the road and walked into the woods. I felt compelled to be alone for a while, the kind of alone that inspires calm reflection, welcoming an intimate connection with the cosmic and the spiritual. I sat staring at a glistening waterfall embellishing the side of a lush, green mountain, letting the scenery seep into my pores, fill my lungs, delight my eyes.

Lost in the wonder of all things steady and true, the core of me embraced a fantastic sort of knowing: I didn't need to run anymore. I'd seen enough beauty, experienced enough life, and worked my way through enough La Brea Tar Pits to consider myself ready to make a difference in this world. My future didn't lie in tumbling around on the asphalt rollercoasters of America, my future was right where I'd left it when I first set out on the open road.

I left the woods that day understanding the purpose of my travels: I believe now that I'd needed to see a wider world so I could better appreciate my own. I'd needed space to roam so I could discover the strength that had been inside me all along.

I stepped back into my truck that day knowing it was time to un-pack the experiences of my life so you could walk toward your future with more clarity and insight. I felt a sudden hunger to share my story so you could experience your own kind of healing. Only when my heart began calling me home did I finally understand that home was where my story was always meant to unfold. I'd always imagined my journey would tell itself somewhere out in the wild spaces known only to hermits and mountain lions. But now I know it's here—in the still-ness of the water, with the scent and feel of home, that the lessons of my life will untangle themselves and finally speak their truth.

For starters, please know this: Mine is the story of the idiot and the sage. But instead of the idiot and the sage being the neighbors across the street, they're the energies living within me—within all of us. My idiot has walked a very crooked mile, but sometimes a crooked mile can lead to the straightest path.

As you know, I've always been a "run with scissors" and "color outside the lines" sort of spirit. As you will see, I've never made life easy on myself—I tend to float when I should march and march when I should float. For much of my life, I felt like a Salvador Dali painting trying its best to walk in sensible shoes. And whenever you try to walk in shoes that don't fit, you tend to fall down a lot. And fall I did.

I now find it incredibly ridiculous that I spent so much of my younger years trying to mute the vivid colors within me, hoping to fit into a world that seemed so insufferably beige. I've never even liked beige, always considering it the color a good idea turns when no one comes to claim it. Why I ever wanted to blend in to the point of invisible makes little sense to me now. I'm finally wise enough to understand that a soul becomes restless when it's suppressed because by design we're intended to be explosions of light, color, and imagination. We manifest poetically when we're free to express ourselves as uniquely, as radiantly, as a Chihuly glass sculpture.

I guess I had to learn the hard way that when you deny yourself the right to live authentically, you find yourself heading down every wrong road in search of something you already own. When you starve yourself of your own individuality, you lead your mind into dark waters. And dark waters suck.

Please know from the onset that my story is the onward progression of a soul who has seen some shit, has been through some shit, and as a result, has learned some shit. I've lived the life of the beggar, the fool, the shamed, and the harlot. I've known blinding darkness and the pain of a wicked man's cage. I've lied, I've imploded, and I've denied myself the gift of a meaningful life. But through my experiences, I've felt the grace of compassion, the fever of grit, and the freedom of self-love and forgiveness. I've learned how to tap into my inner Athena, feed the white wolf, and bring forth my own brand of brave.

I've also learned that you'll never find peace, the elusive kind of peace all men search for, until first you learn how to free your mind.

Life has taught me this, sweet child: The battles in life are not futile, they're fertile. No wise oak ever grew without the wind and rain.

Even though you will find that many of my experiences are completely mystifying, teetering on the brink of insanity, I'm not revealing myself so that you can feel my pain. I've already defeated the sadness, tamed the madness, so there's no reason for you to shed a tear for me. I am a woman who has been elevated. And my story isn't about the darkness, anyway.

My story is about the light.

As I began to formulate the idea of telling my story through a series of letters, I felt I had to distance myself from the expectation that my words needed to be polite or flowery all the time so they seemed less shocking. My story is intensely personal. I'll have to travel through mud in order to bring it up from the ground. And mud is dirty. Mud screams and curses and makes a fool of itself sometimes. So bear with me when you get to the organic parts, I'm telling my story the way I feel it needs to be told.

I decided to write letters so you can pick them up and set them down when it feels most comfortable. Just because I'm willing to speak my truth doesn't mean you're obligated to listen.

For years, I've sent letters from all over America telling you of my travels. You once told me that you like to read them just before bed. I liked picturing you snuggled beneath your purple-and-blue comforter with my letters in your hand, as if we were sharing the events of our day before saying goodnight the way we had before.

Now that my letters will cover a very different subject matter, I think it's important for you to choose when to read them. Some letters might take you a while to get through. Some might feel more honest than honest needs to be, but transparency is safe in the hands of those who know you really well and have decided to love you anyway.

And I don't know a better way to honor the warrior within me than letting you know the battles she's fought and the wars she's won.

Hopefully, tucked somewhere inside my journey you'll find a link to your own self-discovery. I'm not asking you to adopt my beliefs—how we see the world is influenced by how we experience the world, so I understand if my truths don't fit you as comfortably as they do me. You'll certainly uncover your own truths in the years to come. And few gems are more precious than the ones we mine from our own inner earth. That being said, I look forward to the opportunity to talk to you about the art of living well, as defined by a woman who's unapologetically human.

I guess I've been writing these letters in my head for years; considering my pitfalls and blunders, and the situations thrown at me like a surprise party in hell. It took some time and perspective—some going deep and reaching high—but I think I'm finally able to articulate the value of all my twists and turns.

I now believe I traveled the roads I had to so I could learn powerful truths in a way that felt meaningful to me. Truth reveals herself in a manner that feels relevant to our life quest. Our subtle yet prolific connection with the universe handcrafts a personalized assortment of aha moments, never quite in the way we want, but usually in a way that gathers the most attention.

Within each of us burns the heart of a fighter, a dreamer, a dignitary, and a shaman. A person speaks her truth in the way she thinks, the way she loves, and the way she carries her flame. Each of us taps into our living essence differently, but first we have to discover it.

And sometimes, back roads are the ones with the most realistic view. But when we find a pathway to wholeness, when a new stream of consciousness turns rust to glitter, when the soul finally has something worth talking about, then the road we took to get there was the one we needed most.

So let's talk about stuff. It's time.

Let's share, let's heal, let's grow.

My mind returns to the water with its surface glistening like a blanket of crystals. The pale-blue horizon is dusted with clouds of pink cotton candy—the day has declared herself fully awake. I hear cars whizzing by on the road behind me. The solitude of my morning has given way to the sights and sounds of everyone else's ordinary Tuesday.

I'm no longer alone on the beach. An elderly man with hair like snow and skin like a weathered saddle walks quietly along the shoreline, slicing the air with a stick. He carefully examines the jellyfish the tide left behind, poking them like puddles of egg whites. I watch as he moves along the water's edge with the spirit of one who, just like the jellyfish, longs to return to the sea. I wish I could talk with him for a minute. I bet he knows a thing or two.

I've been lost inside my writing for hours. My legs are stiff and cramped, my eyes are missing my sunglasses. I didn't really plan on staying so long this morning. The act of writing feels like a purge; I guess I let it carry me away. It may seem like I'm throwing up all over this letter, but sometimes mental vomit can feel like intensified sanity. It can also sound a lot like rambling. We both know I ramble pretty well. I hope I write with more intention.

Joan of Arc said, "I am not afraid. I was born to do this." Obviously, I'm no Joan of Arc, if she weren't already dead she'd die laughing at the suggestion that I feel a connection to her words. But I believe I was born to walk my path so I could completely experience all the layers of me and then share what I learned.

I used to be afraid, but I'm not anymore. I've come home to claim my Eden.

They say the pen is mightier than the sword. If that's true, then please consider me armed and dangerous, because my pen has things it needs to say. My journey taught me the nature of greed, lust, lies, and betrayal. More importantly, it also taught me the nature of kindness, strength, meaning, and love. I'm an ordinary person who fell into an extraordinary life. My story is the stuff of nightmares and fairy tales.

But unlike nightmares and fairy tales, my story is true.

I think I'll set down my thoughts for the day. The heat has found me. I probably should've put on something more comfortable before I headed down here this morning. My boots lie sprawled out in the sand looking like a bad idea with good intentions—I guess I'll walk home barefoot. I doubt my feet will mind. I plan on taking a long, hot shower, then savoring the simple pleasure of sleeping in my own bed. I can't quite remember how long it's been since I slept in my own bed, but I guess it doesn't really matter because I don't have to wait anymore.

I'm home, I must remind myself. *I'm finally home.*

It's time for life to begin.

Sending positive energy across the miles and holding you close in thought,

Your Loving Mother

TWO

Dear Sparrow,

I'm sitting in my favorite chair tucked in the corner of my favorite room—my bedroom. I can't stop looking at my new curtains. I love the way they embellish the morning sunlight streaming through the window. They have that Moroccan flair that speaks to me, in swirls of orange, turquoise, and green on a backdrop of buttercream.

I know we've laughed about it, but I firmly believe you can never have too many lanterns hanging from your ceiling, too many exotic throw pillows on a couch, or too many layers of colorful fabric draped around the room. Add some books and plants and whimsy, then suddenly, your house turns into a home.

I'm pretty sure my sense of style got its inspiration from the inside of Jeannie's bottle from the show *I Dream of Jeannie*. I mean, who wouldn't want to live there? As you know, I've always allowed color to run amok in my house, giving the impression that a box of crayons with an overactive imagination was hired to cover everything in anything but white. I suppose that interior design, in its most pleasing form, is really just a snapshot of the soul.

The crystals I've collected lie scattered about, and my prisms are casting rainbows. I've seen their wonder countless times, yet it never grows old. I'm convinced that every politician in Washington, D.C., should be required to keep a crystal on their desk and a prism in their window. And of course, a piece of obsidian—the stone of truth—in their pocket. Maybe even in their mouth.

I lit a candle and heated some essential oils—spearmint, orange, and lemon with a dash of vanilla. Soon, my room will fill with the scent of Fruity Pebbles, as you've described it. I have George Winston's album *December* playing softly in the background. You remember that CD, don't you? We always listened to it on Christmas morning while we sipped marshmallows with a dollop of hot chocolate and opened our gifts.

I suppose music's ability to set a relaxing tone is rivaled only by that of a good view. If you combine the two, it creates a touching memory you can run to whenever you need to warm an inner blue.

But I'm not feeling blue today. I'm feeling nostalgic. Nostalgia feels like amber.

I moved that old dresser you never liked (what's wrong with a few scratches?) into the guest room to make space for a writing area now that I've declared myself a storyteller, a wordsmith of riddles and sagas. An old dresser may not be beautiful, but it holds special things better than a new dresser ever could.

There's an African proverb that says, "A new broom sweeps very well, but an old broom knows the corners." Once upon a time, just like you, I loved shiny and new best of all—until I realized that shiny and new has no story to tell, like a page with no words or a door with no handle. To me, old things hold their history like an oyster holds its pearl. I tend to favor items that have been passed on or passed through because they've found their mojo, sending a spirited energy into the air.

I set up this workstation in my bedroom so my surroundings would feel warm and inviting as I write. I run my hands over my favorite shawl—the one that begged me to take it home when I found it in a thrift store. I look at the painting you made with the haiku you wrote. I gaze at the metal stars dangling above my vanity and the herbs that hang in bunches from my grandmother's drying rack. Family photos are everywhere. Each of these items creates a sensation that is beautifully alive within me.

I feel safe.

I feel creative.

I feel like remembering.

I suppose every story has a beginning. Milestones mark the chapters of our lives. Starting school, graduating college, buying a home, and getting married are predictable doorways we pass through, neatly separating *before* from *after*. These special moments gather certificates, photos, and mementos—memories we can touch.

But some chapters don't have an obvious beginning. Some beginnings are obscured, hidden beneath the busy layers of life, making it difficult to pinpoint what came first: Was it the seed or the soil, the need or the desire, the lesson or the belief? Sometimes, it can be difficult to put a journey into a perspective that sounds logical and orderly because there isn't always a bookmark to define where some chapters truly begin.

Some stories begin to write themselves long before anything remarkable happens. Yet even the subtle nuances of our existence matters, shaping our reality brick by brick, thought by thought, one experience at a time. Most thoughts and experiences are hand-selected, but others are tossed at us like a water balloon, a sack of what-the-fuck, sometimes even a hand grenade. Can we ever be certain which bricks were laid by choice and which were laid by fate? And more importantly, which bricks mark the beginning of a road we have yet to travel?

I guess our story truly begins as soon as our soul has consciousness, because the wiring of our framework is the spark that produces light. Does that moment happen at birth, in the womb, or further back at a place in time we haven't found yet?

I tend to lean heavily toward the latter. I feel comfortable believing that long before the soul began its earthly flight, it existed in a realm beyond our knowing—I've met far too many old souls to believe otherwise. Maybe knowing where my story began doesn't really matter anyway. It wasn't the beginning that threw hand grenades at me, but it did have an impact on how I perceived moments of pain and darkness.

Understanding that the future stands on the shoulders of the past, I realize the texture of our lives is greatly determined by the fabric of our childhoods. Our core strengths, the ethos that sustains us, the birthplace of our worldviews are woven into the tapestry of our youth. Some may run toward it, and some may run from it, but our family and our history are as relevant to our life experiences as the tides' experience with the sea.

I've often told you stories from my childhood, like the time when I was three and used a picnic table as a diving board, jumped into a baby pool, and broke my leg, or the time I accidentally swallowed a four-inch darning needle (who does that?).

But a childhood carries more substance than the moments we talk about during long road trips or while looking through old photo albums.

In case I never said it out loud, let me reassure you that my childhood was probably the closest thing to a fairy tale I will ever know. I grew up in a better-than-average-home, with a better-than-average family, in a better-than-average city, nestled in the sweetness of innocence and favor. I didn't realize until I was an adult how idyllic my childhood really had been. Back when I was a kid, my world tasted like an ice cream sundae with a cherry on top; it felt like a warm, cobalt-blue towel on a white, sandy beach; it sang the song of bicycles in a parade, a screen door slamming on an evening filled with fireflies, and Christmas carols under a canopy of falling snow. My earliest childhood memories hold the scent of homemade bread pudding on a table with plenty of food to go around.

My family was like the Weebles that wobbled but never fell down.

Growing up in Ohio in the seventies was a gift any kid would want. Plus, your grandparents were young, hip, and full of life. Their parenting philosophy was pretty simple: Read more, speak clearly, work hard, spend wisely, find yourself, but don't be rude.

Even though I experienced the sunny side of childhood, I was never able to convince myself that my family was cool and I was blessed. Instead, I saw my life as painfully vanilla. To me, we were a vanilla-flavored family living a vanilla-flavored life in a town overrun by vanilla. Vanilla can feel stifling. Predictable. Unimaginative. I was certain that our bowl full of cherries needed some sprinkles, like an elephant I could ride to school, a cave I could explore, maybe even a Woodstock revival in our back yard.

As far back as I can remember I hungered for something fantastic, something dipped in supercalifragilisticexpialidocious. I held a wild thirst and a need for something more. I was often lost in the world inside my head. I suppose I still am. I used to dream that one day I would move away from my bubblegum hometown, change my name to Sassafras, buy a monkey, and live in a tree house. I thought I would spend my days righting wrongs, exploring the oceans, saving the rainforests, and solving the mysteries of space. I dreamed of having the personal style of Cher, the activism of Jane Fonda, the poise of Audrey Hepburn, and the determination of Scarlett O'Hara. I wanted to leave an imprint, convinced that I could be a powerful crusader for social justice and still look good in feathers.

Of course, dreaming was easy back then because life felt safe. A soul needs to feel safe before it can dream. The people in my neighborhood were who they said they were. As a result, I felt confident that life was good, people were transparent, and the world was capable of fulfilling a girl's most outrageous dreams.

I grew up believing that everything was possible. The seventies were a revolutionary time in our nation's history. Even though what played out on the nightly news didn't seem to directly shape the tempered rhythms in the heartland of America, the energy cruising through the atmosphere felt charged with new ideas and the battle cry of change. America was waking up, and even as a child, I longed to be a part of it.

My restlessness caused me a lot of internal grief—I was supposed to be happy for cryin' out loud! (Said in the voice of your grandfather.) So I read a lot, escaping to the land of unlikely heroines and girls who lived on the edge. Thankfully, my family collected books (and cats) like charms on a bracelet. I fell in love with the adventures of Pippi Longstocking, certain that I needed her for a next-door neighbor, a confidant, a friend. Pippi knew how to shake up the establishment and make every day seem like a reason to eat cake. What's not to love?

I went to dance class until I got bored. I went to Girl Scouts until I got bored. I took ice skating lessons until I got a concussion. Meanwhile, I dreamed about motocross and women marching in Washington.

When I was young, my favorite playmate was my older brother, Vince. I admired him endlessly. That hasn't changed, even though the miles between us keep me from seeing him as often as I'd like. I was especially drawn to him because he was always so sure of himself, an *I am what I am* kind of person. He had more friends than a library has words, and as he got older, that list of friends kept getting longer.

Growing up with three sisters, surrounded by Barbies and mood swings, Vince always remained centered in who he was as a person, as if he'd dropped from the womb fully defined, indifferent to the flow around him. I envied his ability to feel like his skin fit just right. It was a stark contrast to my introverted awkwardness, which was always painfully on display. Sometimes I would wake up in the morning and tell myself I was going to be like Vince all day long. Until I started crying for no reason, then I knew I wasn't like Vince at all.

Vince and Pippi were trying to show me how to love myself unconditionally, but unfortunately, I didn't grasp their handle on self-acceptance until many years later.

I don't remember a time when I didn't feel different. I was out of place, like a January stuck inside the month of June. I never felt like I meshed with my siblings—I wanted to, I just didn't know how. I was nothing like them. They were blue-eyed and breezy with confident smiles and talented minds. I was green-eyed and complicated—more like a trombone than a tambourine. They earned a lot of gold stars. I earned a lot of lectures.

I knew I was peculiar, but I didn't know why. Or how to fix it. Or how to embrace it. I was simply too weird for my own liking. My

Aquarian nature was always searching for something I couldn't find and couldn't name.

I had unusual skills, like finding four-leaf clovers, which to those around me seemed kind of weird. As you know, I've found dozens and dozens of four-leaf clovers. Even at this writing, with my eyesight far from perfect, I can still spot them easily. I've always had the ability to quickly identify a pattern and see the mutation within it, never finding *Where's Waldo?* or *I Spy* to be much of a challenge. This talent is virtually useless, like being able to tie a cherry stem in a knot with your tongue, but it was enough to set me apart from those who couldn't do it. It's difficult to explain the look a person gets in their eyes when you hand them a freshly picked four-leaf clover—it's one part excitement, one part disbelief, and one part *Is there something wrong with you?*

And the knowing. That's kind of weird, too. I've always been tuned into the energy field around me as if its volume were set on high. I receive vibrations from people, animals, and trees, which are often followed by a strange sense of awareness, like knowing where a lost dog lives or what song will play next on the radio. (I don't always know, but it happens often enough to feel strange.)

Nothing gets you laughed off the playground faster than saying dumb things like, "That tree is sad. His feet hurt."

We all have gifts. Some are just more mainstream than others. I remember the first time I was troubled by **my** gift. When I was 10 my family and I visited my aunt and uncle—the ones who live on a dairy farm near the Ozark Mountains. One evening, while my brother and I sat with our cousins in a bedroom cast in the murky shades of twilight, the cousins brought out a Ouija board. I'd never seen one before. We formed a tight circle, watching as the pointer glided across the board, answering each of our questions. Before long, I began to feel a prickling sensation on the back of my neck, like a fly that keeps returning to the same spot. At first, it was only annoying, but soon, I began to feel uneasy. The feeling grew stronger until it was as if someone were standing directly behind me. The energy felt very heavy, like a wet towel draped over a balloon. I'd never felt anything like it before. I kept looking over my shoulder to see if someone was standing behind me, but no one was there.

Each time I tried to refocus my attention on the game, it felt as though the energy took one step closer to me. I searched the faces of my brother and cousins, but none of them seemed aware of the ominous presence. I couldn't take the ghostly feeling one second longer, running down the stairs into the living room where my parents sat talking, plopping myself between them on the couch. The mysterious energy immediately dissipated as if acknowledging the couch was base and I'd safely reached it.

My brother and cousins followed me down the stairs, laughing in delight that I'd been so frightened, boasting that they had been the ones moving the pointer. I smiled a weak smile as if I were glad to be in on the joke, but my uneasiness hadn't come from the movement of the pointer. It had come from the invisible energy that had stood directly behind me.

Not wanting to be laughed at or told I was silly, I didn't mention my experience, but I felt out of sorts for the rest of the evening. I slept with the lights on.

I never played with a Ouija board again. Some may say it's just a silly game, and sometimes it is, but when it's used to call up the darkness, the darkness is eager to play along.

I'm not suggesting I'm psychic. I can only report that there is a state of knowing that lies somewhere between obvious and opaque, a sixth sense that channels energy and information invisible to the naked eye. Perhaps these vibrations are stronger in some people, or maybe it's like a muscle: The longer you ignore it, the more it fades away. I've never been able to explain my sense of intuition, I only know it's a part of me, like the restlessness is a part of me. Today, people may say this gift makes me special. But as a child, my heightened sense of observation and discernment didn't make me feel special, it only solidified my overall feeling of oddness.

Odd can feel heavy. Odd can feel painful. Odd can make you color your internal canvas in shades of lonely and gray. If I'd realized that my thoughts about myself were painting my very essence, maybe I would have figured out a way to calm my sensitive nature by choosing colors that better matched the warmth of my blessings.

No one wants to feel odd, yet many of us do, convinced that everyone around us is living inside a Lisa Frank poster while we're doing our best to escape a Jackson Pollock maze. And since being is a state of mind, it's easy to let abstract feelings get in the way of simple joy.

Sometimes, you have to live a little before you realize that your darker shades actually complement your lighter ones—violet never looks more passionate than when it's sitting next to yellow.

I wouldn't say I was an unhappy child. But happiness is fleeting, only lasting a little while before it moves on so someone else can have a turn. Being happy is like riding a Ferris wheel: If you wait in line, you're sure to get a turn—and the view is great—but when the ride's over, you pass your seat on to the next person.

Happy makes you feel good when everything is going well. But happy is hard to manage when life feels like a paint-by-number set with all the numbers rubbed off. So, happy isn't what I was searching for—I was too intense for happy alone to fix.

I would go on to search most of my life for the inner peace that seemed to elude me. It would be years before I discovered that inner peace isn't something you buy, something you take, or something you're given. And it doesn't come quickly. Having inner peace is a skill you perfect over time, like a potter's hand against a mound of eager clay. It begins as just a blob on a spinning wheel, but with dedication and patience, the potter's hand forms it into something that can withstand heat, carry water, and be the quiet you cling to when all around you is noise.

So maybe this is where my story really began. Maybe the feeling of not fitting in, like my insides were wired wrong, was the first step toward the road I would travel one day. If I had a chance to go back and feel it all over again, able to make changes in all the right places, I probably wouldn't, because through the process, I became.

By the eighth grade, I was asking for Friedrich Nietzsche's book *Beyond Good and Evil* for Christmas. In my free time, I studied philosophers like Kant, Descartes, Buddha, and Jung. I was cerebral to a fault, and if left to my own devices, I could overthink things as simple as Cracker Jack prizes and carefree girls on roller skates.

I entered high school in the eighties, covered in acne and too much hair spray. At an age when it's so important for a young woman to feel pretty, I felt no one would ever use the word *pretty* to describe me. It was almost unbearable when someone stared at my face. I felt ashamed, like I was damaged goods. Inside, I became angry.

I hated school, certain that no one noticed anything below my neck. I had once felt fearless, but after the acne came, I didn't feel so fearless anymore. I hated the pretty girls, mostly because I wasn't one of them.

Adding to my misery, I was selected for my high school's first gifted and talented class, but I didn't see myself as either gifted or talented. The students in the class were a collection of square wheels, not unlike the misfits from The Island of Misfit Toys in *Rudolph the Red-Nosed Reindeer*. We were the cowboy who rides an ostrich, the bird that swims, the gun that squirts grape jelly. We weren't the cool kids, and if any of us had any aspirations of becoming cool, enrollment in the gifted and talented class sent that dream spiraling over an intellectual cliff.

Most of the students were math geniuses, which to me was the first requirement for being called "gifted." I, on the other hand, was horrible at math. Math is a concept so foreign to me that reading Greek upside down in the dark seems easier. I still firmly believe that any equation with a letter in it is the work of someone who should've spent more time playing outdoors.

In a classroom filled with students bound for Harvard or MIT, I felt like I didn't belong, escaping to a place in my head that welcomed the feeling of numb, hoping I'd make it through that reputation-killing class without screaming, "Math is fucking boring! How 'bout you put away your calculators and let's talk about real shit for a while!"

My parents often called me *creative* and *unique*, but I just knew those were code words for *strange*.

I remember little about high school other than being frustrated and bored. I suppose many people can relate to the feeling of passing through high school feeling like a toadstool on a conveyer belt. I'd convinced myself that school was a waste of time. So I didn't blink an eye when I found out I didn't have enough credits to graduate.

But it wasn't math that was my downfall, it was gym.

Please read this very slowly so the ridiculousness of it has time to sink in: I failed high school because of gggyyyymmmm.

I failed gym because I never went. I thought to myself, *Who needs to learn how to run an obstacle course?* Turns out, the obstacle course had the last laugh because I needed that credit to graduate. I didn't have the sense back then to care. I was too busy playing mental hopscotch and planning a grand escape.

This would be the first time, but unfortunately not the last, that I found myself stuck. Staring at an empty frame designed to hold my diploma should have been the wake-up call I needed to begin taking my future more seriously. But it wasn't.

At the time, I believed that a high school diploma could never define me. Perhaps there's some truth to that idea—we are more than our certificates and our degrees. But let's be real. In order to really shine—the "kick the shit out of life" kind of shine—you need to unleash your true potential.

Dreams are great, but without hard work, they're nothing more than fortune cookie clichés. An education gives you the backing you need. A person looking to forge a new path better have a good pair of shoes, and a person wanting a better life will need a decent car.

Dreamers need tools, too.

I understand that you needed to take a few semesters off so you could focus on the baby, but I encourage you to get back into school as soon as possible—and before your commitment to yourself gets lost in a sea of Fisher-Price toys, play dates, and baskets of unfolded laundry.

I speak from experience when I tell you this: Next to good health, an education is the best gift you can give yourself. It takes you where you want to go, reducing the impact of landslides along the way. Because landslides do happen. And when you didn't arm yourself with the tools you need to lessen a landslide's impact, then the only ass you can kick is your own.

Please remember this, sweet Sparrow: The only person holding you back from your destiny is you. It's unfortunate when the hardest roads we will ever travel are the ones we paved ourselves.

I looked up to discover the evening sun is setting. I've hardly eaten anything beyond my breakfast of a buttered English muffin, avocado slices, and a few cherry tomatoes. My green tea with sprigs of sweet mint sits untouched in the mug beside me.

I can't wait for your baby shower next Saturday, especially now that we know you're having a girl. When you called me after the ultrasound, I held the phone in stunned amazement, waiting for the euphoria to sink in. If I had the ability to make magic like Jeannie did in *I Dream of Jeannie*, my life would look exactly as it does right now. Thank you so much for the gift of a granddaughter. I know you had nothing to do with the sex of the child, but in my heart, I choose to believe you did.

I'm so glad your grandmother is making the long drive to see us. Three generations of women joined together in celebration is a beautiful beginning to your love story. It sure feels like happy showed its face again, doesn't it? Welcoming a child is the greatest joy a family can experience. We gather around you because we believe in you. And we believe your child will help shape the future in colors of silver and gold.

Here's to family, togetherness, and possibilities.

Here's to life when it tastes like strawberry cake.

Sending positive energy across the miles and holding you close in thought,

Your Loving Mother

THREE

Spring 2019

In the kitchen

Dear Sparrow,

I'm relaxing at the kitchen table this morning. The vase of pink roses and white chrysanthemums left over from your baby shower sits proudly in the center. Their cheerful disposition makes me feel as though they're winking at me.

I added to the vase a few sprigs of spearmint and lemon balm from the plants I have on the porch. The scent of lemon and mint fills the air. Delicious. The herbs have grown wildly since we planted them. They need a good haircut, yet I can't seem to take scissors to them. Shaping things that don't want to be shaped is always such a chore.

I decided to eat a light breakfast then take a walk just as the sun was beginning to rise. Though I was eager to begin writing as soon as my feet hit the floor, I decided to welcome the day more slowly, knowing I'd be sheltered in place for the remainder of the day once the writing began.

Time doesn't seem to exist when I'm alone with my letters to you, the hands on the clock have no power over me anymore. Writing makes me feel calm and focused even though I know the deeper I get into my story, the darkness is sure to come.

For now, though, I enjoy the process of stepping back in time, seeing things with fresh eyes, allowing myself to gather perspective for the journey I will speak of soon enough.

Before pain came to silence me, I felt young and hopeful. My fairy tale continued. My daydreams sustained me.

My mind slips to my first husband, Jeffrey. I haven't thought of him in years. Our marriage was both short and unimaginative, so any memory of him has to be dusted off.

I married young—at nineteen. We met when I was seventeen and quickly fell in love, although more accurately, it was probably just a deeper shade of like. I can't remember ever loving Jeffrey the way I loved your father. I think Jeffrey was only a one-way ticket away from childhood and my feelings of incompleteness.

He was a nice young man. Although he was a few years older, we shared similar backgrounds. On the surface it appeared we had much in common. He was an all-American kind of person—that old advertising jingle, "Baseball, hot dogs, apple pie, and Chevrolet" describes him pretty well.

We were both virgins, passing through the doorway of sexual beings late one night while lying on my parents' couch watching a *Saturday Night Live* skit called "The Coneheads."

It was a pathetic foray into my own sexuality. I doubt three minutes passed from the time we started until the time it was over. I remember thinking, *This is what all the fuss is about? People actually write songs about this?* We both felt ridiculous. He made an excuse to leave. We never spoke of the experience again and tabled sex for several months. Clearly, the motto "If at first you don't succeed, try, try again" wasn't in his personal repertoire.

The marriage was doomed from the beginning. I had no inclination to be a conventional wife, couldn't cook, and had little interest in playing house. I grew bored quickly.

Though Jeffrey had a gregarious personality, his zest for life never registered past zero. The highlight of his week was playing slow-pitch softball on the weekends. I grew bored of this, too. I simply couldn't see the point of sitting on hot, metal bleachers merely so I could clap occasionally. It didn't take long before he came to represent the living embodiment of the vanilla life I was trying to escape.

Jeffrey was a bookkeeper. The fact that he understood math—and actually wanted to work with it every day—should've been my first clue we were ill-suited companions. But I probably would've stuck the marriage out a little longer had he not developed two annoying habits: drinking too much and gambling too much.

I remember the night he woke me from a deep sleep to confess he'd just blown the rent money betting on horses. He was crying uncontrollably, snot dripping from his nose. He smelled like whiskey and regret. Babbling incoherently and slurring his words, he promised over and over he would never do it again, but I knew he would.

He'd gambled before, but never to the point of using money we'd set aside for bills. His drinking had become a habit, too. I realized he'd turned a corner somehow.

I was now married to an addict.

I had no experience with addiction at that time. Your grandparents drank socially, but I don't remember seeing them drunk. And I'd never seen snot drip from my father's nose while he sat in a puddle of his own tears. I knew that Jeffrey's father was a recovering alcoholic, but I wasn't aware that alcoholism is a genetic disease. I began to wonder if Jeffrey had some ghosts he wasn't telling me about. I began to ask myself how in the world I was supposed to make a life with someone I no longer trusted, and more importantly, no longer liked.

Please understand: Jeffrey's addiction didn't make him a bad person—his addiction made him a bad husband. I didn't know what to do. So just a year after I'd married him, I left and never looked back.

Years later, Jeffrey reached out from my past and asked for a quick divorce so he could marry a woman he'd been dating. I showed up at his attorney's office at the appointed time, and thankfully, Jeffrey wasn't there. I signed my name on the dotted line and walked out the door.

I never saw him again.

It's been said that everything that casts a light also casts a shadow. I know this to be one of the guarantees of life, a universal truth that begs consideration. Everything under the sun will experience its exact opposite, the duality of yin and yang. What's good and right in the world will come to know its counterbalance.

This collaboration of contrasting energy awakens insight and deepens understanding, opening a doorway to oneness, where light and shadow merge into a comprehensive wonder that celebrates the fullness of all living things. The quicker you accept the art of balance, the dynamics of synergy and flow, the sooner the exterior forces pressing against you will begin to make more sense.

In retrospect, I realize I sashayed into adulthood with a set of unrealistic expectations. My upbringing was Mayberry, USA. But sadly, the world isn't an episode of *The Andy Griffith Show*. I was wise beyond my years, or so I'd been told, but I lacked the critical awareness that the world can be a scary place, even close to home.

Until you find out differently, it's easy to believe that everything you've ever known is a glimpse of how the rest of the world works. I'd never once considered that the safe bubble of my youth might not follow me beyond my parent's front gate, having no reason to believe that people could be less than sincere. The beauty of my upbringing cast a bright light, but it also cast a wide shadow. I wasn't prepared when I learned that ordinary people can be sinister and cunning just for shits and giggles. I thought bad guys would look like bad guys. I had no idea that walking among us are predators and barbarians with ulterior motives slithering inside the shell of a handsome face.

The next chapter in my life taught me that seeing things how you want them to be instead of how they really are can lead you down a treacherous road, that your version of reality can become victim to the ugliness of another person's mind. It's foolish to try to convince yourself that everyone around you is mentally sound, that weirdos exist only in another part of town, or on TV, or somewhere you've never been.

By nature, each of us has a calling toward personal integrity, but not everyone seeks this path. Unfortunately, some people are stuck in a place of extreme shadows. And just like expanding fog on a dangerous mountain, the shadows eventually consume them.

After leaving Jeffrey when I was 20, I moved in with a close girlfriend. Stacey was an energetic person with an easy laugh, baby-doll eyes, and silky blonde hair that fell from her ponytail like jingle bells. She loved the music of the B-52s and snacked on bowls of buttered lima beans like some people snack on popcorn. She and I were at the same place in our lives: killing time, making friends, sharing secrets, and shopping for cute clothes at affordable prices.

The nightclub where we both worked as cocktail waitresses was the "in" place to see and be seen. It was upscale and trendy, with plush leather couches; a sea of polished chrome; and a spacious, multi-level dance floor. On any given evening, the line to get in spilled out into the parking lot. Women stood waiting in line wearing sequin miniskirts and too much perfume, while men flexed their muscles in the mirrored glass that covered the outside of the building.

One particular Saturday night's soup du jour was a large group of college-age hockey players who had descended upon our city from parts around America. They'd been in town all week competing in a tournament, and this was their final hurrah in Columbus. They tipped well and seemed like a group of down-to-earth guys, so I did my best to keep their drinks filled and their wallets empty.

Midway through the evening, a small group of them invited all of us employees to an after-hours party they were throwing at their hotel. Several of the teams had reserved an entire floor of a rather pricey hotel located in the heart of downtown, overlooking the Scioto River. My co-workers and I were impressed and looked forward to attending the party as soon as our shifts ended.

After closing out my station, I rushed back to my place to change clothes. Another cocktail waitress, Lisbeth—a slim beauty with raven hair and light-green eyes—went with me. Thoroughly excited about the party, we quickly drove to the hotel, meeting up with several of our co-workers in the lobby.

The hotel party was in full swing by the time we arrived on the hockey players' floor. A sea of people drifted from room to room and gathered in the floor's hallway. Music was coming from every direction, and fragments of conversations drifted in the air. It was overwhelming, like the energy in Times Square at midnight on New Year's Eve.

My girlfriends and I caught up with the small group of hockey players who had invited us. We stuck close by them as they led us into a room that had a marijuana bong sitting on a coffee table. They offered us a sample. We declined. A cloud of smoke hung thick in the air, making it impossible for me to gauge how many hockey players and young women were in the room. I became slightly uncomfortable—the pervasive smoke made me feel like eyes were watching me from behind a mask. Perhaps sensing my discomfort, the men steered us out of the room and back into the lively hallway.

One of the hockey players in our group had taken a particular interest in me earlier that evening at the nightclub. He reminded me of one of Vince's friends—a guy I'd always had a crush on—so I quickly felt comfortable with him. I held his hand as he led me into another room where perhaps half a dozen people were sitting in small groups trying to escape the noise and commotion. I can't be certain where my girlfriends went after I left them standing in the hallway. I probably assumed they'd be lingering nearby after I'd had a moment of quiet conversation with the hockey player who held my attention.

After we entered the room, we sat down on the couch. Seated next to us was a couple who appeared to be arguing. Before long, they got up and left, heading back out into the hallway. At that point I was able to relax a bit more because I was no longer sitting back to back with a stranger. The hockey player, who I thought was my new friend, asked me if I wanted a drink. I settled on a whiskey sour.

He smiled and said, "I think I'll have one, too." He disappeared into the wall of bodies out in the hallway and soon returned with our drinks.

We sat making small talk. I can't remember what we talked about, but I do remember that fairly quickly into our conversation I began feeling slightly nauseated and lightheaded. I figured the sensation was due to a strong drink combined with an empty stomach. A few minutes later, I felt like my body was swaying slightly.

Before long, I began to feel like I might throw up. Or pass out. I remember wondering if my sudden sickness was from all the smoke in the air, or perhaps something I'd eaten earlier that day. When my eyesight started to become blurry and my dizziness escalated, I was pretty certain that my body was drifting from side to side like a rowboat riding a wake.

"Mr. I Look Like Your Brother's Friend But I'm Not" showed no signs of alarm, which confused me. He just kept on talking as if everything were fine. *He hasn't noticed*, I thought. *He must be an idiot. He has no idea I'm about to throw up on his perfectly ironed jeans.*

I decided I needed to find Lisbeth, but I could hardly get up from the couch. My ankles felt weak—there was no way I could walk in my high heels. I considered taking them off. Maybe I even tried. The room began to morph into a funhouse mirror—everything looked warped and strange. I knew something was wrong. The last thing I remember seeing was the spinning white ceiling as I fell back onto the couch. And then, quite strangely, I remember nothing more.

Everything surrendered to black.

I came back to consciousness lying naked in a bed with a man I'd never seen before. Another man stood next to the bed, staring down at me while holding his penis. It was hard. The room was completely silent.

I didn't know how long I'd been there, but clearly the rambunctious party was over. I could see the faint glow of dawn streaming through the side of the closed curtains and asked myself, *It's morning?*

Where am I? I wondered, trying to make sense of my surroundings. I tried to lift myself from the bed, until I realized I couldn't move my arms or legs. My body felt like dead weight. "This isn't real," I said as I closed my eyes, thinking I was locked inside a bad dream, hoping that when I opened my eyes again, I'd find myself lying in my own bed, in my own room, wearing my favorite *Little House on the Prairie*-style pajamas. My eyelids felt heavy, my brain churned slowly. It felt like my entire being was stuck inside a Pink Floyd song.

I began piecing together my last fragments of memory: I remembered the party, the man who looked like my brother's friend, and the whiskey sour. But that's all the further my memory would take me.

Why am I naked? Where's Lisbeth? How long have I been here? Who are these two strange men?

The blackness returned.

I fell back into the void.

The next memory I have is of Lisbeth barging into the room. To this day I don't know how she found me, where she'd been during my ordeal, or how she got into the room. But the shock of her noisy entrance parted the stillness and brought me back to reality. I heard her gasp.

"Helena, get the fuck up!" she screamed, making her way toward the bed.

I lay motionless but found the energy to whisper through parched lips, "I can't move." A look of horror flashed across her face. I saw the realization come alive in her eyes that I hadn't asked for this encounter.

She pulled the sheet over me and, summoning the strength of a gladiator, pulled me from the bed. The sheet fell loosely over me and did little to conceal my nakedness. We inched our way past the two men who had somehow become my lovers.

My mind hadn't used the word *rape* yet. I was still too confused and too sluggish, everything happening around me seemed so cartoonish and out of sync. My only clear thought was that I desperately wanted out of that room and away from those two strange men.

Lisbeth began half-carrying me, half-dragging me toward the door. It was only then, as we made our way across the room, that my eyes began scanning my surroundings. What I saw mortified me.

The hotel room was filled with men in various states of undress. They lined the walls in the portion of the room designed to be a sitting area. Many of the men were standing in the darkness, just outside the thin beam of light coming from the bathroom. I couldn't see their faces, but I clearly saw that some were fully dressed, others had their pants around their knees, and some were completely naked.

For the first time, I began to understand the weight of what had gone on that night. A wave of nausea spread through me. It felt like I was witnessing the aftermath of an uninvited evil, surreal and frightening and mean.

As my eyes searched the room in utter disbelief, I wondered if the men would let us leave. The door to the hallway was shut. The latch was locked. Someone must have relocked the door after Lisbeth had entered. I held my breath, keeping my eyes focused on the door, knowing it held the key to our fate. Completely vulnerable and outnumbered, I feared the men's lust was untethered to reason.

A heart can beat so loudly when fear claws the mind. It seemed as though the only sound in that room was the rhythmic pounding of a drum beating deep inside my chest.

Time stood completely still. The countless men stood staring, but they didn't say a single word. They watched as we made our slow progress toward the door. As soon as we were close enough, Lisbeth reached out to open the latch. It seemed like it took forever for the door to open wide enough for both of us to fit through. I kept waiting for a hand to slam it shut. I'd never before heard a door tell a story more slowly.

After we finally made it through the doorway, I did my best to hold on to the sheet covering my body, suddenly hyperaware of my own nakedness. Sensation was beginning to return to my limbs, yet it still felt like I was trying to walk using someone else's legs. I allowed the air to rush from my lungs. *Thank you, Jesus,* I remember saying to myself. I repeated it over and over.

Sometimes in life, those are the only words left to say.

I looked back over my shoulder one last time just as Lisbeth was moving away from the door. I don't know why I looked back, I've never been one to look back. Perhaps I wanted to make sure no one was following us or maybe I wanted to take in the scene one last time to convince myself that all of it was real.

Once the light from the hallway spilled into the room, it lit up the corners and layers of darkness. It was only with this wider, clearer view that I noticed the video camera sitting on a tripod in the farthest corner of the room. It was pointed toward the bed. Its lens cap was off, dangling from a string. The light was still blinking.

They'd videotaped everything.

My mind froze. Reality hit me like a sucker punch to the gut. I stared at the video camera as if it were a snake, coiled and hissing. As the door closed behind us, the video camera was the last thing I saw.

We left the hotel through a side entrance with only the sheet still around me. Lisbeth drove home in silence. Neither of us said anything because words were of no use. I remember seeing her hands clenching the steering wheel until her knuckles turned white. I stared out the window, but nothing registered. I was completely vacant.

Lisbeth dropped me off at my front door. I think I stumbled upstairs to my room, I don't remember. I think I showered, I don't remember. I think I stared up at my ceiling for a very long time before sleep came to save me, but I really don't remember.

I have no idea what became of my clothes from that night, my shoes, my purse, or the men who raped me. I never went searching for answers, and answers never came searching for me. I didn't call the police. I didn't file a report with the hotel. I was ashamed—deeply, deeply ashamed. I told myself that I must've done something to deserve my fate.

I now know that my reaction was typical for a rape victim, but back then I wasn't considering whether my reaction was normal, I only saw my experience as a revolting secret I must never, ever share. It was a secret that made me feel ugly inside. A secret that separated the nice girls from the broken ones.

There are certain parts of this nightmare that still elude me. I've always considered this a blessing. Sometimes the weight of knowing something for certain is a greater burden to carry than knowing nothing at all. I know I was drugged and raped, possibly even gang-raped, but I have no memory of the event. My body certainly remembered, though. Soon, bruises appeared on my buttocks, hips, and inner thighs. My joints ached. It seemed to take several days for my mind to return to normal. I felt splintered.

In the days following, everything seemed to move in slow motion. I felt disconnected from everything around me. I was constantly thirsty. Even now, I clearly remember the thirst. Perhaps I hoped water would cleanse the filth from my body and wash away the woman screaming inside me. But on the outside I didn't scream. I didn't even cry. I was in a state of shock, I suppose.

I quit my job. I never told my friends about the hotel or the rape. I never told my family. I could imagine my father somehow blaming me for my lapse in judgment in attending a hotel party with a large group of testosterone-driven men. "Child, what were you thinking?" I could hear him saying. And he would have been justified in asking that very question.

What had I been thinking? Innocence is one thing, but blind stupidity is quite another. Just because it's my right to go to a party and feel safe doesn't mean others are obligated to respect that right.

There's a Chinese proverb that says, "Pay no attention to where you fell, but where you first tripped, instead." Most of us will trip many times, as if tripping is what we do best. I realize now that I made multiple mistakes that night.

Please understand that I'm not blaming myself for the choices those idiots made—the weight of guilt is a burden they carry alone. However, I have to recognize the things I could've done differently that could have led to a different outcome:

1. I tripped when I knew I would be drinking but arrived at the party with an empty stomach anyway. This allowed the alcohol and drugs to enter my system too quickly, reducing the chance that I could get help before I was unable to help myself.

2. I tripped when I willingly allowed myself to be separated from my friends. There is safety in numbers. Just as in nature, the first one removed from the protection of the herd is the first to be devoured by lions.

3. I tripped when I allowed myself to believe that bad things don't happen in nice places and that someone's good looks mean they are good. The man who made me feel comfortable because he looked like someone I knew was the same man who slipped drugs into my drink.

4. I tripped when I didn't listen to my inner voice. Something felt off and I remember feeling uneasy, but I disabled my inner radar because I wanted to mingle and have fun. Your inner voice is the voice of truth—it's your greatest advocate. There were many warning signs that night that showed me the situation could get out of control, but I ignored all of them. When your

hunch tells you that something is wrong, listen and believe. The voice inside you is there to guide you. You may choose to ignore it, but you'll seldom be glad you did.

The bruises faded. I allowed the memory of that night to fade as well. I forced my mind to stop thinking about it, and, thankfully, my mind willingly complied. I stuffed the memory and the pain. I swallowed it whole. Staring down a demon takes an enormous amount of grit. At the time, I simply didn't have the necessary fortitude to process the rape in a way my mind could deal with.

My shame was deep, so deep, but the part that troubled me the most was knowing they'd filmed the whole thing. They could watch my humiliation over and over again, they could share it with friends, laugh about it over pizza. I'd never before heard of something like that happening. I felt certain no one would believe me. But mostly, I worried that if I told someone, they would begin to see me as ugly as I now saw myself. It simply wasn't worth the risk.

My silence held.

For years.

One day I would find my inner Athena—the mythological goddess of war and wisdom. Every woman has an Athena living inside her, but I hadn't met mine yet. So, I stuffed my ordeal into the hidden chamber where things we can't handle go to dwell. The fragments of memory I have from that night easily allowed me to move from a state of shock to a state of numb. Numbness felt safe because it didn't require any strength. Numbness doesn't require anything at all.

I let myself move past it. I let myself move on. Not by dealing with it in a healthy way, but by denying its corrosive existence.

Night has fallen. The house has grown dark without my attention, only the soft glow of candlelight kept me company as I finished this letter. My eyes ache. My brain begs for sleep. Perhaps I'll stop remembering for the day.

To relive this part of my past is unsettling. In order to bring it forward, I forced myself to touch every detail once again. Mental trauma is often packed away, not because it isn't important, but because the scars remember the lesson so the heart doesn't have to.

Though that event was very painful, it certainly wasn't the last time I would confront the evil of a twisted mind. As I look back on it now, I see that evil was just getting started. Darkness likes it when we believe the worst is behind us; darkness laughs when we let down our guard and convince ourselves that darkness has moved on.

Thankfully, the next time darkness came toward me I would wage a counterattack. I wouldn't take its presence as passively as I had before. Rape has a way of triggering the fighter. One day, the call of a child would stir me, and the strength of Athena would serve me very well.

We live, we learn, we evolve.

Sending positive energy across the miles and holding you close in thought,

Your Loving Mother

FOUR

Dear Sparrow,

Some time has passed since I last put pen to paper. I felt mentally drained after my last letter.

For years, I allowed myself to forget about that night. It's strange those feelings would still be so raw, especially considering all the experiences I've lived through since. Remembering all the details brought them closer to the surface, so now I feel like I need to lose them all over again.

I spent some time these last few days processing that night. I don't suppose I'd ever tried to before, always seeing the event as a whole rather than the individual pieces that linked together to form a single block of carbon in the interior spaces of my mind.

Looking back, with the distance of over thirty years to cushion me, I realize that not only did I trip that night, I kept tripping long after it was over. I share these thoughts with you now because I feel they're lessons you should consider in case you ever feel the need to swallow a pain like I did.

1. I tripped when I allowed the fear of not being believed to stand taller in my mind than my need for help and support. I can't say how my family and friends would have reacted because I never gave them the chance. So I denied myself the ability to move through the experience in a healthier way. Keeping a painful secret close to your heart is far more difficult, and more destructive, than the act of setting it free.

2. I tripped when I didn't file a report with the hotel or the police. Maybe they would've been able to help, or maybe they wouldn't. But not even trying gave those men far more freedom than they deserved. It also made me feel like I was the one with something to hide. Truthfully, I never needed to feel ashamed—I held on to my sanity in the face of adversity while the men fell victim to the weakness in their minds.

3. I tripped when I stuffed the experience and pain all these years. I didn't need to. Our society has many options for help when you need it, even if you just need to talk. Talking about something helps release its hold over you. There's no shame in admitting you've been through some shit, there's strength and healing in speaking your truth. If you ever find yourself up to your ass in alligators, sweet child, please love yourself enough to let someone else care.

After the night in the hotel, I changed. It wasn't a conscious decision, like a resolution or a promise, but an altered state of being that viscerally reshaped how I saw myself and the world around me. The innocence of my childhood was gone. I began to grow apart from everyone, especially my family. Needing quiet and hating sound, I retreated into myself. I became easily agitated, more argumentative, and had trouble focusing. I spent far more time alone. I came to have trust issues. I felt dirty inside for a very long time.

I remember spending a great deal of my free time in the woods, drawn to the solitude. As you know, I've always loved nature, I've always been one to run with the moon. I've lost count of how many raccoons I've befriended throughout my life, feeding them marshmallows directly from my hand. I guess nature is where I feel the most centered and alive.

The trees and the animals of the forest never seemed to mind my presence, allowing me to feel at one with something relevant and green and thriving. The tragedies of human warfare experience a cleaner truth when they stand in the presence a timeless, living energy that asks no questions and tells no lies. Lost in the flora and fauna, I didn't feel so numb inside.

I spent many evenings gazing up at the stars from the roof of an old building near my apartment. I never invited anyone else along—companionship felt like broken glass. I would climb the fire escape stairs, spread out a blanket, turn my eyes skyward, and empty out my mind.

I would lie there for hours, snacking on grapes and crackers, tracking the constellations as they moved across the sky, hoping the universe would send a secret message I might be able to understand. The sky's compelling beauty felt kind and generous, softening the edges of my hidden secret one quiet evening at a time.

Stacey and her new boyfriend, who would later become her husband, moved on. I did too. I rented an apartment inside a huge house resting on the edge of the Ohio State University district. Rent was cheap, houses were old, and the area was culturally diverse. It was the kind of neighborhood with front porches outfitted in plaid couches, gnomes with faded smiles, and beer cans stacked like trophies on milk-crate tables.

It was the first time I'd ever lived alone. The prospect both thrilled and concerned me. I had no idea how I would afford living on my own. I made decent money as a server at a family-style restaurant, but spending money on bills was something I was allergic to for longer than I care to admit.

Anyone driving by my new place would have declared it a dump. The house was so old it was well past the age of retirement, painted in a nauseating shade of baby-puke green, with windows blackened by thick sheets of street grime. Everything about the house screamed, *I've been ignored.* Yet, I found it charming, like an old woman dressed in curious fashion hiding bright orange socks inside boots laced with yarn.

The inside of the house felt like suppressed magic. It became my oasis. It had tall windows, arched doorways, and high ceilings that made me feel like it was hungry for some candlelight and creativity. Cracks in the plaster walls looked like roadmaps. The woodwork was scratched and thirsty, but felt wonderful each time I ran my hands along the boards. The wood seemed to sigh whenever I touched it.

I lucked out in finding multiple sets of thick, brocade draperies that a church was selling at a great price. Their rich merlot color and scalloped valances with gold threading really enhanced the overall look of the place. Ancient doorknobs and lighting fixtures, and the heavy velvet hanging from the windows made the house look more like a castle than a rental home in need of repairs.

I rarely had anyone over, so the living room was a living room in name only. It mostly stored my art supplies, my endless assortment of beads, and one long buffet table covered with a lace tablecloth I'd found at a second-hand store. I set a bouquet of silk sunflowers in front of the sealed-up fireplace and a tarnished candelabra on the mantle. The room felt cheerful and cozy, like a cup of homemade soup or a slice of pumpkin pie.

What had once been a large, formal dining room served as my bedroom—it was my favorite room in the house. Adorned with the music box from my mother, the seashells I'd collected as a child, and the black-and-white photographs I'd taken in the woods, the room felt sentimental and special. I loved being there. Even at this writing, I can still remember the feeling of wanting to hug myself every time I spent a day tucked inside my bedroom.

I had a nice stereo system and a beat-up TV that offered only three channels. For the most part, I ignored the TV. It sat gathering dust for weeks at a time while the music of Jackson Brown, Tracey Chapman, or the Indigo Girls filled the house, letting me hand select what I wanted my mood to sound like.

I bought a motorcycle and parked it in the large kitchen. I figured it could only help the kitchen's ruffled appearance. The floors were chipped and dingy, the metal cabinets were a sour shade of blue, and the Formica countertops had aged into a shade of urine that would make you call a doctor. After my motorcycle moved in, the kitchen came to have a *Rebel Without a Cause* meets *Alice's Restaurant* vibe to it. I liked it. Even toast tasted better.

The back door opened to a small yard overrun by weeds and neglect. I could easily push my Kawasaki 440 down the partially collapsed stairs, through the yard, and into the alley behind the house where everyone parked their cars. I didn't have a car. I simply couldn't see the need.

I felt safe inside that old house, like a turtle in its shell. The house wasn't much, but I didn't need much. I was thankful to have it as my cradle until I was ready to reconnect with the outside world.

I came to love living on my own. I adored living near the University—it was like a city within a city. Everything I needed was within walking distance. Around the perimeter of the campus were wonderful hippie shops, charming little restaurants offering every cuisine imaginable, and open-air bars sending music into the streets. Eclectic bookstores welcoming the pursuit of knowledge were as plentiful as parking spaces for bicycles.

Everything felt funky and interesting—even the laundromat, with its purple-and-red couches and walls covered in handwritten poetry. There was often a musician sitting on a tall stool in the corner, playing an acoustic guitar, or a violin, or a cello. An old brass spittoon sat on the floor welcoming tips. I never knew what to expect when I walked through the door with my basket of wash—a visit to the laundromat seemed less like a chore and more like a Saturday afternoon adventure.

Even though I wasn't a student, I felt right at home. The University attracted a wide range of people from all over the world, the glorious contrasts creating a mosaic of energy and ideas that felt open-minded and inclusive. It's hard to feel like you don't fit in when you're standing next to a person with dreadlocks dipped in grape Kool-Aid or someone wearing a Scottish kilt and flip flops. The counterculture of the sixties would be proud to know its message of *do your own thing* was still going strong smack dab in the middle of studious America.

As you read my letters, you probably imagine me with my hair in its usual style: one long braid (more gray than brown) falling down the center of my back. In your mind's eye, you see me wearing a loose-fitting tunic made of linen or gauze, hiding my robust German curves, with strands of colorful beads around my neck and wrists. This has been my unofficial uniform for years. I can't remember the last time I wore make-up, and you probably can't either. But I wasn't always so fond of shapeless simplicity. Now I dress for comfort, but when I was a young woman living on my own for the first time, I found a sense of satisfaction in decorating myself in the whispers of feminine ways.

It might surprise you to know that once upon a time, my hair knew the ways of hot rollers. My eyes knew the ways of emerald-green eye shadow. My favorite silver earrings were easily the length of my neck, sounding like wind chimes whenever the wind blew or I threw my head back in laughter. I favored long, flowing dresses paired with a man's suit vest and an antique brooch. And oh how I loved my cream-colored, lace-up boots. I wore them everywhere—even in the heat of summer. Even when riding my motorcycle, as if decorative footwear made the ride more appealing.

My personal style started to bloom once I was living on my own. Until then, I'd never known that I enjoyed feeling feminine. And I loved that my outward persona didn't feel so vanilla anymore. I suppose I was trying to channel my inner Rhiannon (after all, Stevie Nicks has always felt like a soul sister to me). Of course, no one can rock a shawl and top hat quite like Stevie Nicks, but I don't mind telling you that I spent a good deal of my life trying.

I've never once considered myself beautiful—my acne wouldn't allow it—but I came to feel like on a good hair day I might pass for pretty. My feelings of independence, combined with the exploration of my feminine self, began creating a clearer sense of definition in my head. Of the many things I discovered during this time of internal change, perhaps the feeling of being true to myself was what I cherished most.

Whenever I think about this period of my life, I consider it the season of bookstores. I fell in love with being able walk to the many options that seemed to be on every corner, each having its own, distinct personality. This was back when bookstores weren't owned by monopolies and didn't try so hard to emulate character through plastic novelties, commercialized displays, and eager smiles asking if you're a preferred customer. Back then, a warm body was considered a preferred customer. I would've once declared it impossible for a bookstore to feel like a hospital or an airport gift shop, but sadly, now I know it can be done.

Near my house stood a corner grocery store converted into a bookstore specializing in books on food, gardening, landscape design, and how-to books of all kinds. Its vibe was far different from the old church down the street, which had been refurbished into a bookstore specializing in ancient civilizations, philosophy, Greek mythology, medieval studies, and astronomy.

A person could choose a bookstore that best fit their interest as well as their mood. Whenever I found myself walking with no particular destination in mind (which was often), I would always end up at a bookstore, followed by a visit to a nearby coffeehouse. I would sip strong coffee from a heavy mug and thumb through the pages of books on astrology, earth science, and animal behavior. The whole experience of walking and wandering, ingesting books and coffee, felt euphoric to my soul.

Don't you just love the vibe of a good coffeehouse? With their interesting array of baklava and curious sandwiches, combined with the abstract art for sale hanging from their walls, they seem to ooze Jack Kerouac or *Zen and the Art of Motorcycle Maintenance*. They always have cool indie music playing quietly in the background, with the scent of cinnamon, basil, and mindfulness lingering in the air.

Reflecting on this time of solitude and femininity, candles and creativity, I realize that I was fully immersed in the purpose of being twenty-something: discovering who I was as an adult and what I liked now that I was free to choose for myself.

By then I'd experienced failing out of high school, failing at a marriage, failing at a few jobs, and the night in the hotel. That's a lot of failing for a young woman just starting out in life, so I began the process of self-discovery feeling like I was walking on crutches.

The hand writing this letter doesn't look as young as it did once, allowing me to see this part of my past differently than I saw it then. Now I know I wasn't busy failing at life, I was busy learning about life—even though it didn't feel much like learning back then. I was beginning to have a better understanding of myself in those beautiful, uncomplicated moments I spent trying on clothes in front of my mirror, dancing around my apartment to U2's album *The Joshua Tree*, browsing around the University, concerning myself with things that busy a soul.

Financially I struggled, but as I see it now, I was gathering rest and perspective in preparation for the coming storms. If ever there was a perfect way to restore and renew, that quiet, creative existence led me toward a path of enlightenment that became useful in my many battles to come.

Back then I thought I was busy getting over something. But I was really learning how to get through something. The universe was giving me the opportunity to learn the wisdom of bamboo.

Bamboo has perfected the art of how to face adversity without breaking. It gently bends with the howling winds, anchored by its roots until the storm has passed. Then, it stands tall again, adding another notch of victory on its journey toward the sun.

Sometimes the best way to learn how to love yourself is to first learn how to accept the things you're not. I believe there's a special plan for each of us, but we don't need to possess every talent ever given in order to get there. Some people are gifted in the arts, others in logic or leadership or math and science. We all have the talents we'll need to fulfill our life's mission, but they often look very different from the talents given to the person sitting next to us on the bus. Usually, we like theirs better.

I will admit, I spent the first part of my life wishing I was everything I wasn't. I was pretty certain that I could be more successful if I could only figure out how to be someone else. It seemed to me the gifts I'd been given were utterly useless. I suppose most people can relate to the feelings of inadequacy, since it's the error of human nature to feel as though we aren't good enough somehow. In reality, nothing could be further from the truth. Each of us has what we need to be remarkable in this world, but all too often our light is smothered beneath a mound of *I can't* or *I wish I had more*.

For a good chunk of my life, I would've sold my tongue to be exactly like your Aunt Savannah. With her chestnut hair, her crystal-blue eyes, and her craftsmanship with words, she is ambitious, poised, well educated, and sturdy. I am flowing water next to Savannah's finest wood. For years I equated this difference to my being less than and not equal to.

My feelings changed when I decided to step into Savannah's life and feel the world around me with her hands, hoping I could see it through her eyes. Once I tried to imagine what life would be like if I were her, I quickly discovered that I'd be overwhelmed if I were in her shoes. Savannah handles responsibility beautifully—it's her art. But it's not my art. While she's holding down boardrooms and juggling the demands of corporate success, I'm shopping for mood rings and boots with fringe on them. Savannah's the type that actually reads *The Wall Street Journal*, whereas I'm more likely to use it as a liner for my cat's litter box.

An epiphany struck me like the Stone of Duh when I realized that I wouldn't want her place in life because I couldn't handle the pressure of always doing and saying the right thing. Savannah *always* does the right thing—that's an enormous burden for anyone to carry.

I mention this for good reason: You are now the age I was back when I was living these memories. Thankfully, you're much more confident than I was, and you're much more grounded, too. But feelings are slippery, irreverent bursts of energy indifferent to reality or even practical advice, and life has a way of testing our view of ourselves. So if you should ever go through a spell where you feel like you don't measure up or as if your offerings look like peasant soup next to a queen's banquet, I offer my ideas on the matter, hoping you don't cannibalize your own value during periods of internal unrest.

I think people in general are ruled by either a sense duty or a sense of passion. This North Star is part of our physiology, untouched by conscious choice or intentional programming. Our guiding light rises from the mantle of our very existence, imprinted into our psyche by a maker who sees the grander plan.

Harriet Tubman, for example, was a woman clearly ruled by a tremendous sense of duty—an inner voice leading her to do incredible things. People who are inspired by a sense of duty are the adults of the world, leading us toward growth, accountability, global prosperity, and the art of humanity tamed. The adults of the world connect us to the importance of noble gestures for noble reasons.

Equally important are the people who are inspired by a sense of passion because they are the children of the world, leading us toward discovery, outside-the-box problem-solving, and expressions of our wild heart through music, art, dance, and literature. The children of the world connect us to the importance of unrestrained joy.

Without one, the other surely fails because balance couldn't exist if either duty or passion was forced to stand on its own.

So, if you ever start to believe that you'd be better off if you were someone else, remember that everyone has their own share of burdens, ones that might make their path seem a little less glamorous if you were forced to walk in their shoes.

I wish I would've learned how to appreciate myself sooner. I wasted a lot of time feeling like an ellipsis in a family filled with exclamation points. Thankfully, I'm now at a place in my life where I'm far removed from these feelings of inadequacy. And I've come to understand that being different isn't the absence of something. It's the presence of something.

Every soul floating through time and space has something worthwhile to contribute to the light within the circle. Our talents may seem strange, unimportant, even unwanted, but the stuff of our inner world is a unique love that longs to express itself. So maintain the courage to believe that even when you feel like you're a very small flame struggling to flicker in the darkness, you are still radiant to a universe that needs you.

I will close for the evening. All this thinking and reflecting has me in need of a good walk. I'm giving myself to these letters, but it feels right. It feels necessary somehow.

Your grandfather arrives tomorrow. I know he's eager to see you. I'll make a festive dinner of enchiladas and homemade salsa on Sunday, then maybe we can go to the beach at sunset and release our Chinese lanterns. He won't want any part of the Chinese lanterns because, as you know, your grandfather is a serious mind, a "look a man in the eye and give a firm handshake" sort of spirit. He doesn't find much value in blowing bubbles or sending wishes on rice paper into the sky. Maybe you could work your magic and bring out the silliness in him. After all, you've done it many times before.

Sending positive energy across the miles and holding you close in thought,

Your Loving Mother

FIVE

Dear Sparrow,

I woke early this morning to the enormous sound of a thunderstorm. Still in my nightgown, I stepped outside to watch the outrageous light show. A wall of rain fell from the roof, arching over the front porch, making me feel as though I were sitting behind a waterfall. Electric flashes of light scattered in a hundred directions, their energy piercing the air. It was exquisitely invigorating.

I've always considered a good thunderstorm to be Mother Nature's way of releasing her frustrations. She isn't the type to keep things bottled up inside—if she's feeling cantankerous, she isn't afraid to state her business and then move on.

I like that in a woman.

After the storm passed, I found myself thoroughly awake. I set my morning with coffee and candles, now I'm sitting in the glow of my room, ready to begin writing. This letter will touch on matters that speak the language of my spirit, reflecting on a moment in my life that became the cornerstone of my evolution. Enlightenment is the water that grows the seed. An unnourished seed is only a shell of an idea. It needs light to turn into something that can feed a mind.

I return to my early twenties, when I was a young woman trying to find herself. I got a few things right back then: I carefully selected the people in my life; I fueled my body with wholesome foods; I made it my habit to take a walk every day, consciously seeking opportunities to admire the trees, the sky, the moon. Once I gave myself permission to step off life's Tilt-a-Whirl for a while, pathways in my brain began to open.

I suppose it's a natural progression for one in search of herself to transition from questioning inner concepts like self-love and self-worth to global concepts like value and purpose, then extend these questions into the heavens by pondering concepts of divinity and spirituality.

It seems to me that our very existence is divided into three levels of experience—we experience the world alive within us, around us, and above us. We go deep, we go wide, and we go high.

In my quest for inner peace, I'd taken a lot of wrong turns. Whenever I went deep, I overdosed on thinking. When I tried to go wide, I ended up feeling like a bent fork in a field of cheerful daisies. I decided that going high might help me find the calm my heart seemed to need.

Let's talk about God for a minute. As I look back now, I realize I've always been drawn to spirituality. Not really religion, per se, but the intangible essence that's powerfully alive in every person, every moment, and everything that matters. I believe I was pondering Him long before I knew Him.

Of course, God is tricky like that—He's notorious for trying to form a relationship with you even when your mind is convinced that your spirit has no idea what it's talking about. When I didn't have a one-on-one connection with God, it felt like eating a favorite dish with an important spice omitted—I couldn't quite put my finger on it, but I knew something was missing.

When I was a child, people were moving further away from organized religion rather than closer to it. In the sixties and seventies, everything we'd been taught to believe no longer had a guaranteed seat at the table. America was beginning to question its own belief system, and as a result, people were no longer satisfied with shutting up and marching in a straight line. Furthermore, the Catholic Church—once the preeminent authority on all things God and godly—was beginning to show cracks in its exterior. The façade of absolute righteousness seemed a little less God-like once the world began to discover that all men truly are created equal—especially when it comes to greed and unimaginable sins.

It seems to me that issues of substance—like religion, politics, and ideology—usually follow the same predictable course: They swing wildly in one direction, then swing wildly in the other before settling somewhere in the middle. When I was growing up, the pendulum was swinging toward the absence of religion rather than its insistence. This movement helped establish freedoms from required prerequisites— you no longer had to openly practice your faith in order to be considered a decent person leading a decent life.

Each of my parents grew up in a religious household, but I get the feeling the dogma of their religion felt more confusing than liberating. And, like so many people of their generation, they were beginning to wonder if the invocations they'd been taught as children were truly inspired by God or were just a lot of rules to hide a lot of secrets. Since nothing can ruin a walk with God faster than a church with a knife behind its back, many people turned away from organized religion. Some even turned away from God.

I suppose your grandparents felt conflicted. How do you teach young minds about God when you're no longer sure what to believe yourself? So, I wasn't brought up in a home where we practiced the tenets of our faith ceremoniously. God's name was spoken—I knew the story of Jesus being born in a manger and the meaning of Easter—but God wasn't a regular topic of discussion. My parents quietly walked their beliefs instead. The golden rule of treating others how you would want to be treated was a regular theme in our home.

I had a playmate two doors down whose family went to church faithfully. I would watch her emerge from her house on Sunday morning wearing a fancy dress and white patent leather shoes, with big bows in her hair. Through her, I knew church was a very ritzy place—you couldn't climb a tree or drip ketchup down your shirt before going to church. As her family's car rolled down our street on its way to Sunday service, she always watched us neighborhood kids—riding our bikes, covered in dirt and Pop Rocks candy—with a sense of longing in her eyes. Her expression told me she wanted to be outside playing instead of trapped inside clothes that itched and smelled like a department store. *Sucks to be you*, I would think to myself.

She always came back smiling, though. She showed off the arts and crafts she'd made in Sunday school as if they were threads from God's robe. I thought church looked pretty cool when it looked like rainbows made out of colored macaroni noodles or an ark made out of pretzel sticks. Yet, this father figure bearing the name of God seemed so mysterious. And perplexing. I mean, if my father couldn't figure God out, then maybe He was as hard to understand as astrophysics or people who never smile.

Though I had little training in the religious arts when I was living alone in that big, old house near campus, I instinctively felt like God didn't need my approval in order to exist—He existed with or without me. I suspected that He wasn't sitting around on a cloud somewhere saying, "I could really be amazing if only Helena would add me on Facebook." It seemed to me that my lack of understanding affected me more than it affected Him.

But I wasn't sure about all this Bible stuff. I wasn't even sure where to begin. I knew I believed in God and Jesus, never questioning their existence, because somehow it always felt right. This acceptance without proof is like knowing the sky is endless—you don't feel the need to take a yardstick to it in order to believe.

Actually, I've always felt that the argument against God's existence makes no sense at all. Even though I didn't know much about God back then, I could tell He was a math guy. There's such order to the movement of the earth, the cycle of life, the seasons, the cosmos, the tides, the pull of gravity, the ways of planting and harvest, and the predictability of the animal kingdom—we can literally set our watches by it.

To me, the idea that such perfection could come from a mindless explosion of pixie dust is ridiculous and a major insult to the nature of shit happens: Shit happens, but it never happens all on its own—something has to move the shit one direction or the other. So I couldn't help but wonder if The Big Bang was the result of an even bigger God.

But then comes the question, If there really is a God, then why do bad things happen? I don't suppose any of us can answer this question with certainty. But, my mind has settled on the idea that most of the problems plaguing our world are man's own do-it-yourself projects.

I don't believe hate, bigotry, apathy, and destruction are the work of heaven. I think we create darkness in our own minds and carry it out with our own hands. It doesn't surprise me that everyone's looking for a fall guy to explain our own madness. Humans tend to throw fire, then sit back and wonder why the forest burned down.

I find it curious that God gave us free will—the right to choose for ourselves—but we've suffered under the weight of our own freedom for eons. Yet, within the natural world, everything goes according to God's plan and every creature is at peace with itself. It doesn't take an Einstein to theorize that we've turned our greatest blessing into our own curse—I guess even free will casts its own light and shadows.

Perhaps the simplest explanation for why bad things happen isn't because God doesn't exist, but because unhappy people can suck the joy out of life. And they suck because God gave them the right to choose their own path, and apparently, sucking is all they could come up with.

A lot of people need more proof before they're willing to accept God because the questioning is part of their journey. We're empirical thinkers by nature, so we like flow charts, graphs, and scientific studies. Usually this is a good thing, but even logic casts shadows. Just because we can't explain something doesn't mean it isn't true—a blind man can't see the ocean, but that doesn't mean the ocean isn't there.

I look at it like this: I can't fully prove love exists either. Yet, the joy and healing that come from love is so self-evident that I've never spent a minute wondering if love is real.

These were the notions I was entertaining some thirty years ago when my mind first began wandering up the path of spiritual enlightenment. It seemed like everyone I asked had their own take on God. I wasn't inclined to embrace, or dismiss, others' interpretations because the God experience is so personal. I innately believe God is loving. I believe God is involved. I don't believe God is an egomaniac or a scientist watching us through a sterile looking glass, removed from the outcomes of His creation. I believe God smiles. I believe He sheds tears, too.

I'd read a lot of books in my life, but curiously, the one I'd never considered reading was the Bible. The Bible scared me. I had the sensation that reading it was some kind of lifetime commitment with a verbal contract expected at the end. I couldn't shake the feeling that reading the Bible might be an experience that forever changed me.

I wanted a deeper understanding of all things spiritual, but I wasn't sure I wanted to be transformed on such a wide scale. I knew I didn't want to go around quoting Scripture—people who do often hurl the words like stones. I also knew I didn't want to stop listening to AC/DC or Janis Joplin. And I certainly didn't want to feel like I had to change my circle of friends or stop believing that everyone is beautiful in God's eyes no matter how they worship or who they love. Or even what they call Him, for that matter, since I'm pretty sure all prayers land on the same desk anyway.

Perhaps because of these hesitations, I'd never owned a copy of the Bible. Your grandparents had a very old one handed down from generation to generation, but it was frail and tired, more like a museum artifact than something you could fall asleep reading while snacking on corn chips.

I didn't wake up one morning and say to myself, *time to read the Bible*. If I'm being honest, I suppose most mornings I woke up and thought, *time to read anything but the Bible*. So I came across my introduction to it through the back door. It wasn't a conscious decision by any means, but a twist of curious fate instead.

January decided to brew a tremendous snowstorm while I was living on my own in that big, old house. I'd experienced many snowstorms before, so I knew I needed to take precautions, but there was nothing overly threatening about this particular storm. Northerners view winter storms like Southerners view summer hurricanes—it's important to be prepared, but in the end, it's just an inconvenience you have to step around from time to time.

I threw an extra comforter on my bed, pulled out my thermal long underwear, and stuffed towels and newspaper around my windows and doors to help keep out the bitter wind. I was prepared to shelter in place for however long the storm decided to throw its wrath across Columbus. Shortly before the storm was predicted to hit, I realized I didn't have a book to carry me through my downtime. Hoping I could make it to the closest second-hand bookstore before the wind turned to freezing rain, I bundled up in my oversized parka with fake fur around the hood, threw on my hiking books, and headed out the door with my hands stuffed inside my pockets and my mind stuffed inside the need of a good book.

The bookstore up the road was one of my favorite places to visit. It was an imposing Victorian home that still held the romance of its era. Painted rose and teal, it had a spectacular stained glass window looking down from its widow's walk. The wrought iron fence bordering the yard made the house appear confident, maybe even a little arrogant. Bookshelves lined the large wraparound porch, overflowing with books collapsing from mildew, leading me to believe that the proprietor thought a moldy book wrapped in cobwebs was better than no book at all.

The energy inside the house always made me feel like a very large family of books inhabited it, not a bibliophile peddling his second-hand wares. Lamps with Tiffany shades sat on thoughtful wooden tables next to crystal candy dishes filled with potpourri and cubes of scented soaps. A gray tabby cat weaved its way through the aisles. Dust covered everything, but quaint did too, so the vibe felt peculiar but inviting.

I stepped inside the door on that stormy January day, setting off a tinkling of bells attached to the brass door handle. "Hello?" I said to no one in attendance, seeing my breath before me as I unwrapped my scarf.

No greeting was returned. I assumed the owner was upstairs, where he lived. He was a dowdy old man who always wore cable knit sweaters and a fiddler cap. I often saw him shuffling along carrying a stack of books, mumbling to himself. Even though I'd never seen the upstairs, I couldn't envision his private space as anything grander than his love affair with old books. I could picture him sitting in a threadbare wingback chair with his feet resting on a forgotten oriental rug, huddled over a cup of chamomile tea, lost in the works of Dickens or one of the Brontës.

Unzipping my parka, I walked into the parlor, which served as the nonfiction room, and began searching through the dense forest of books, hoping to find one on animals of North America, specifically bald eagle, wolves, and grizzly bears. I suspected that tales of the wild would keep me interested through the storm.

I was running my hands along the rows, letting my fingertips lightly caress each spine, when one book in particular caught my attention. It was tall and thick, with a faint odor of patchouli and peppermint. It was bound in cracking leather and I could tell it was either very old or had spent a fair amount of time on the front porch. I was instantly intrigued.

My initial hunch was it was an old copy of *On the Origin of Species* by Charles Darwin. I'd tried reading it once before, but found it surprisingly dull, even though once upon a time its subject matter was considered riveting. To me, books with an emphasis on science often come off sounding like car manuals, as if science and creative writing don't waltz together very well.

I pulled the book from the shelf—it felt heavy in my hands. I was surprised to see the words, *The Bible,* staring back at me. Beneath the title stamped in gold leaf, it read, *King James Version.* I was dumbfounded and asked myself, *What is a copy of the Bible doing next to a book on elephants?*

A book out of place was certainly nothing unusual in that riddle of a bookstore. Actually, I had the impression that most of the books living in the house had never even heard of the Dewey Decimal System, so I'm not exactly sure why I was surprised. I can only report that I felt jolted in some way. I stood there holding the Bible as if it were a conundrum in my hands, looking around to see if anyone was watching.

Suddenly, I felt like I was standing at an impasse: I could return the book to its place on the shelf or I could accept this moment as fate. It sure felt like a polite request from heaven—the energy moving inside me felt powerful and strange. And I had to admit the timing was perfect. But I hadn't come to the bookstore in search of a life path, I just needed something to keep my mind busy for a while.

My head told me to put the book back on the shelf and run, run like hell, but my heart simply wouldn't let me. I couldn't shake the feeling that the moment was too genuine, too personal, not to be in perfect order somehow.

I hesitantly opened the cover, not wanting to be pulled inside, and found an inscription written in pencil: "To my darling husband on our anniversary. May our love last for eternity. Your devoted wife, Vivian." The handwriting was faint, as if the pencil had barely touched the page as she wrote, and her words leaned to the right with feminine curlicues, as if she wanted her words to float instead of stand at attention.

It was a love note from a stranger. And I was immediately smitten.

The book itself reminded me of the family Bible I'd seen as a child. There was something fantastically poetic about its antique appearance, its loving inscription—even its scent. I have no doubt that if I'd been holding a shiny new Bible on that cold January morning, one that wasn't familiar or lacked intimate appeal, I would've immediately returned it to the shelf. As I reflect on the moment, I can't help but smile when I realize how wonderfully safe God tried to make me feel when He offered me a Bible for the first time.

There's something truly magical about serendipity—a random moment that fits so perfectly, it feels like it was meant to be. It seemed unlikely that God would take the time to reach out to me personally, but I knew God was kind of peculiar, so regardless of how or why the book fell into my hands, I accepted the challenge and purchased it for $4.25.

The price alone suggested I could get comfortable with the book—I could read it while taking a bath or eating pudding without worrying about drips or smudges. I love a book that likes to be touched. Some books can handle the caress of human hands, willfully absorbing the conditions we bring them, while others seem most at home under fireproof glass or lying so elegantly on a coffee table that you just know they don't want to be bothered.

I wrapped myself up in my winter gear and made my way home with long, confident strides. My determination was impervious to the winter chill around me. When I reached my front porch, I looked up and saw the storm was now on the city's doorstep, it would soon cover our world in confetti of silvery white.

I stepped into my apartment, bolting the door behind me. I drew the heavy curtains and lit a candle in my bedroom. I changed into my favorite pair of sweatpants and green flannel shirt, then slipped into the kitchen to make myself a cup of hot chocolate. Grabbing a package of graham crackers on my way back to my bedroom, I declared myself officially ready to settle in for the day.

As the fierce wind began to rattle my windows and the snow began to fall, I nestled deep inside my comforter and leaned back into my fortress of pillows.

Then, I began to read.

I approached reading the Bible as I would any other book—starting at page one, chapter one. It began well enough. I learned God formed the earth and sky, then created man. I read the stories of Adam and Eve, Cain and Abel, Noah, Abraham and Sarah, and Moses. *So far, so good*, I thought to myself.

But by the time I got to the Book of Leviticus, I was horrified. The tenets in that chapter were nothing like the God I wanted to understand. I reasoned that maybe God wanted to make the idea of earning your way into heaven look like an impossible task so when Plan B came along—Jesus—people would be more open to a less suffocating solution.

It made me remember the time I wanted to buy my first car. Your grandfather told me I had two options: I could get a job and work for the money, but it would probably take a long time and be difficult to manage with my school schedule, or I could simply improve my grades and he would help me.

I think that God offers us the same two options: You can try to do heaven the hard way, or you can do it the more efficient way and He will help you.

As I continued roaming through the books of the Old Testament, I was surprised to discover how often the Bible is misquoted or taken out of context. The words staring at me seemed far different from many of the summaries I'd heard. I realized I'd put far too much faith in others' interpretation of God's word. It became abundantly clear that humans tend to cherry-pick their way through the Bible. And it's curious that those who profess the deepest understanding also happen to carry the most expensive baskets.

Once I made my way to the New Testament, I found a need to dig out a highlighter and begin taking notes. Much of the New Testament is profound, beautiful, and thought provoking. My heart ran toward the apostles. I can't imagine the strength it would've taken to openly proclaim Jesus as the Messiah in a world where such a declaration could bring punishment, imprisonment, or death. Many of the men and women who witnessed the miracles of Jesus spent the rest of their lives talking about them, regardless of the consequences that followed. This just added credibility to their words. Only an idiot is willing to suffer at the hands of another man's lie. Sooner or later, we surrender to reason and let the lie save itself.

It didn't take long before I realized that much of the Bible is left up to interpretation. Don't get me wrong: There are sections that leave little room for doubt regarding what God is trying to say to His people, but there's a whole lot of mist in the Bible, too. God left us with only Ten Commandments, yet the book is roughly 1,200 pages.

His commandments may be one-size-fits-all, but much of His message is delivered through a series of letters, stories, metaphors, and parables, which inspire a more intimate connection with the reader. Maybe God didn't want all of His thoughts to be ingested as though they were proclaimed from a megaphone—maybe He knew his compassion was big enough to allow everyone to find comfort and meaning in a way that speaks directly to them.

The book itself is unlike anything I've ever read before—I think that's the point. It's not an easy read, and it creates as many questions as it answers. I began to wonder what the Bible was like way back in the beginning, back when it was first written. I had no problem believing that the original authors had been inspired by God, but I couldn't help but wonder if subsequent translations reflected a mortal spin.

I'm not suggesting that evil got its hands on the Bible, but we're only human. If you believe in something with all your heart, it's only a small step from there to changing the nature of something so it's more in line with what you believe it should look like anyway. Maybe the guy translating the Bible a thousand years ago didn't think his interpretation was an act of selfishness. Maybe he saw it as an act of love.

I can offer only one opinion on the subject—regardless of whether or not the Bible as we know it today is the intended word of God, one truth stands highest in my mind: If God didn't like how the Bible portrayed Him, He would have destroyed it. After all, He's God, and the Bible is only made of paper. It's impossible for me to believe He wouldn't have the will, and the ability, to wipe it from the face of the earth if it didn't please him anymore.

So, even though my mind paused for a moment, I kept on reading. I read throughout the long storm, often falling asleep with the book still in my hands. I would sleep for a few hours, then wake, eager to begin reading again. I skimmed some chapters, skipped some chapters entirely, and read some chapters word for word. I quickly realized that deciphering the Bible isn't a weekend project, it's not like building a shed. It's the quiet journey of a lifetime. It's an essence, a feeling, a state of mind.

My first investigation brought a satisfying relief: The Bible isn't an ancient manuscript that tells us all the ways we can really piss God off. I couldn't understand why some people would try to present it that way. For example, if you opened the children's book *Oh, the Places You'll Go!* by Dr. Seuss and only read the page that says, "You'll come down from the Lurch with an unpleasant bump," it would be easy to believe the entire book is pretty shady. You have to read the whole book to understand that one page wasn't meant to stand alone, it's merely a single passage in a book that's overflowing with encouragement and the power of positive thinking.

If you want to sum up the message of the Bible, you would only need two words:

Love matters.

Our city stood still as the storm raged on, but I remained oblivious, burrowed deep inside my thoughts. The storm lasted for days, yet I seldom left my bed. I didn't shower. I didn't change my clothes. I lost all track of time.

I felt a wide range of emotions as I read the Bible—confusion, disbelief, joy, sorrow, and awe. There were moments when I cried. My tears always came as a surprise. My brain absorbed the Bible from a studious perspective, yet my emotional self couldn't be separated from the passion of Christ. Still to this day, I can't make it through the Gospel—Matthew, Mark, Luke, and John—without openly weeping when it comes to the part where they nailed Jesus to the cross, then mocked him as they watched him slowly die.

And still he forgave them.

Compassion had never looked so brave before.

After the storm passed, the sun returned to our city, and our world began to thaw. I opened my heavy curtains for the first time in days. I stretched my arms, releasing the fatigue that had settled into my bones during my spiritual hibernation. I set the Bible on the table next to my bed, its bookmark resting on the last page of Revelations. I held its final verse in my mind for a moment longer, pleased that His last words wished us well.

I went into the bathroom to wash my face, surprised to see myself looking so haggard. My eyes were bloodshot, my skin was pale, and my hair stored more grease than a mechanic's rag—it's funny how focus can look so unappealing sometimes. I leaned into the mirror, looking myself right in the eye. My green eyes stared back at me, and in them I saw a sense of accomplishment. I couldn't help but smile.

I went into the kitchen to gaze out the window, admiring the breathtaking beauty of sparkling sunshine on a blanket of glistening snow. I bundled up in my heavy coat, slipped into my unlaced boots, and stepped outside. The air was clean and crisp, scented with the smell of wood burning in a nearby fireplace. I took deep breaths, filling my lungs, staring into the blue of a fortunate sky.

I felt older. A little wiser. The world seemed to make a little more sense. I didn't feel the need to throw away my Led Zeppelin CDs, or begin shopping for churches. My new relationship with God wasn't the lightning bolt I'd expected. And I'm glad, because no one wants to get struck by lightning. The healthiest relationships take time, patience, and mutual understanding.

As I sit here lost in these memories, I reflect on my younger self during that bitter cold January. I'm thankful the storm provided an opportunity for complete isolation, allowing me to give God my full attention. Maybe He knew that was His best chance of getting through—like I said earlier, He's kind of tricky like that. The experience made me feel like God personally handed me a missing piece of my puzzle. When I hear people say they feel touched by grace, I get it now.

I certainly found myself thinking a lot about God in the months and years that followed, but my fellowship was a quiet, groovy sort of thing, like listening to jazz on a country road on a day bursting with autumn. I was amazed to discover His presence in ways I'd never noticed before, like the timing of love when I needed it most, or when help arrives in ways that can't be easily explained.

Suddenly, it seemed like God was everywhere. How had I not seen this before? I suppose that, until we know who to thank, we tend to thank no one at all. We chalk up our good fortune to luck or coincidence because the suggestion of anything more divine seems kind of spooky somehow.

I don't just love God. I like Him, too—He's a guy I'd want to hang out with. I don't believe He sees us as the manifestation of our worst mistakes, our most horrible thoughts. I think our imperfections give him something to do, an opportunity to experience His own wow factor.

I think it's normal to feel naked when you're with Him. I think it's okay to ask him tough questions—He can handle it. I don't think we should ever feel guilty when we ask Him to bless us with a wonderful life—He wants it for us.

I believe that the only thing that can separate us from His love, His desire to bless beyond all knowing, is our self-created insecurities. God doesn't put labels on us—He doesn't need to. We place those rocks on our own hearts for reasons that never justify the pain.

I don't believe God is a bully. And I don't believe He wants to scare us into submission. Even a fool knows that forcing someone to love you is about as useful as a pack of wet matches. The God I've come to know is the very essence of love, light, goodness, and mercy. You don't need to change everything about yourself so He can like you better, He just wants to be near you, to be invited in, hoping for a little one-on-one time because in his eyes, you're worth it.

Though God is certainly a very important part of my story, He doesn't need me to tell His story. There's already a book for that. So I won't spend any more time turning my letters into a theological symposium taught from my perspective. As you know, I'm deeply spiritual, but I'm not religious at all. It seems to me that organized religion started out with the best of intentions, but then got a little too full of itself. I'm not knocking anyone who finds comfort in organized religion—if a religion is healthy, spiritually sound, and adds to your life and well-being, then it's doing exactly what it's supposed to do.

God's love feels good. It should never feel like a hammer. It shouldn't suck the joy out of life. So listen to your inner voice. If a religion or ideology is worth believing in, then it should always walk the talk of tolerance, truth, sincerity, honesty, peacefulness, healing, openness, compassion, and inclusiveness. If it doesn't, then someone is lying to you. God will never ask you to be an arrogant asshole in His name. He will never ask you to wound someone to get His point across.

Remember, pastors are human, too—they make mistakes. Blind faith should be offered to God alone, not to a person or an institution.

So how do you know if a set of beliefs has God's seal of approval? By letting God marinate within you. This gives heaven the opportunity to speak to you in a language you can best understand. If it's true that it took God six days to create the world and it takes nine months to create human life, then God may need more than an instant to give you the insight and clarity you seek. Trust your heart—that's where God writes his personal messages to you.

I believe each of us is entitled to experience faith in a way that feels right to our soul. As for myself, whenever I want to enrich my connection or even just talk to God for a while, I head toward the water, the woods, a sunrise. It feels the most natural to me.

There's a lovely saying that reads, "Take time for quiet moments because God whispers and the world is loud." Though I find great comfort in His written word, I don't search for God in a shrine, building, or temple. I don't search for Him in the voice of another man's words. I search for God from within. And whenever I go looking for Him in the stillness of my mind, in the openness of my heart, surrounded by the beauty of His kingdom, I'm delighted to find that He's already there.

It's time for bed now. And my favorite pen is out of ink. I'll take this as a not so subtle hint that it's time to end this letter. But I will leave you with one final thought for the day: Even though I love you with the entirety of my being, you can be certain that it was God who loved you first.

Sending positive energy across the miles and holding you close in thought,

Your Loving Mother

Six

Dear Sparrow,

I woke up early and headed to the lake to welcome the sunrise. Now I'm sitting beneath the ancient oak that's become our trusted friend. This mystical tree holds the memories of our picnics, our celebrations, our bottles of wine, and our laughter. The tree has become part of our history just as we've become part of hers.

I look forward to spending the day writing in a place that remembers you so well. I can picture you standing under these massive branches, Spanish moss swaying in the breeze like ghosts at a gathering, as you watched the boats go by or a great blue heron fly gracefully past. I can see you with your hair in a messy bun, looking like a Disney princess in jean shorts and cowboy boots, commenting on the expensive houses across the lake that command the shoreline as if they're announcing that a visit to their side of the lake is by invitation only.

I came here this morning to get lost in myself. The more I share pieces of my journey, the more I capture something whole. I guess reflections can become threads of revelation once we see that scattered strings of happenstance are actually the outer rings of an intricate web.

I knew choosing a good spot would be essential to allow my mind to drift back and recreate a period of my life that holds such meaning for both of us. I feel I express myself best when my surroundings make me feel like I'm nestled inside a Karen Carpenter song. My mind struggles to focus when I'm pressed against the noise of the world.

But a secluded spot that welcomes a woman with only a notepad and a peanut butter and jelly sandwich is harder to find than it should be. It seems like conglomerates have gobbled up every piece of open space, leaving only fields of asphalt and gardens of rusty shopping carts. Orange barrels and do-not-enter signs are the jewelry of progress, I suppose, funneling us into rat mazes that leave no room for a soul to stretch. It does concern me that the future of our natural world rests in the hands of those who seem to care so little about it.

There's a powerful Cree proverb that tells a haunting truth: "Only when the last tree has been cut down, the last fish has been caught, and the last stream poisoned will we realize we cannot eat money." These words speak a prophecy we don't want to hear. It's mind-numbing to consider that we could destroy ourselves pursuing investments that rise and fall like empires, sacrificing the very air we breathe for the financial benefit of only a chosen few.

Thankfully, I believe there's still time for us to make a difference. Hope is still with us because hope knows that tree huggers are a fierce and passionate tribe. Maybe when we look outside our windows and see nothing but dollar stores, strip malls, and car lots, those with a commitment to the bottom line will finally stop to consider the world they want their grandchildren to enjoy.

I chose this peaceful setting for a very important reason: Today I will begin remembering your father. I feel a tug of responsibility to speak of my memories in a way that allows you to step into this season of my life with the most honest image of who your father and I were when we began our walk together.

I see your father differently than you do, and that's okay because he was never my father and he was never your husband. People aren't one-dimensional, anyway—we're as multifaceted as a geode. If I cracked open a stone of agate, one side would show dirt, ugly lumps, deep crevices, and the abuse of the seasons. Yet the other side would sparkle with bands of color and the lace of crystal artwork. How you see the agate depends entirely on your view, so neither observation is incorrect. When descriptions are combined, they help us better understand the unique characteristics of the stone.

I'll begin by saying your father has grown into a capable man and a devoted father. He adores you—he always has. Even when he was at his most reckless, his love for you was the one thing that helped guide him to a better place.

I will admit, my memories of your dad contain as many thorns as fragrant blossoms, but if he were sitting next to me right now (and thank God he isn't) I would imagine he would say I had my very own set of thorns. A few thousand yesterdays ago, I would've refused to believe that I shared any blame in the destruction of our relationship. But, I've grown up since then. And bullshitting myself isn't as much fun as it used to be. Now I can freely admit that I was emotionally unavailable and nursing old wounds when I was with your father.

That's the problem with letting wounds fester—you try to convince yourself that your past doesn't matter, but in reality, your past is holding your future hostage. Feelings of failure, anger, resentment, rejection, and trauma are not solid objects—they have the consistency of motor oil, seeping into the subconscious, coating our feel-good emotions with harmful toxins and fragments of pain. You have to clean house in order to remove the sticky residue, otherwise the next chapter in life will look suspiciously like the last.

I probably should've taken the time to process the rape before I began a life with your father. Back then, I had no idea how to let go of my emotional baggage, so I suppose I just threw it at your dad, hoping he'd know how to dispose of it. I failed to see he had his own pain.

The memories that I will share with you are the highs and lows of a relationship between two people who weren't emotionally ready to turn their past into something that made the whole stronger. We did the best we could, I truly believe that, but neither one of us was a ghost whisperer. And we were naïve enough to believe that love without healing is like a bleach that dissolves unwanted stains.

Your father and I didn't have a lifetime of tomorrows like we thought we did in the beginning. But I found him to be a pretty good life jacket for a while. Through him I learned a lot about myself. And most importantly, he was the path that led me directly to you. Because of this, I feel I have a responsibility to honor the memory of our relationship for the building block that it was, even though when our story ended, it ended badly.

But a crappy ending between lovers doesn't begin to diminish the love a parent has for a child. Nor does it lessen the light of the people those parents will become. Regardless of the bitter ending to our love story, your father never saw you as anything less than perfect. And even though he wasn't my hero, one day he would jump into raging water to save the life of a child he didn't even know. I'm glad your father found his way to his better self. I'm glad the story I will tell doesn't fit him anymore.

Like me, he's learned how to embrace the sparkly side of the geode.

When I fell in love with your father, it was like a whirlwind set to music. Our love came quickly, overtaking us like a tornado overtakes a house. One moment he didn't exist in my life, then suddenly he was my life. Love is like that sometimes—one minute you're busy minding your own business, then bam! Love hits you upside your head like a brick with candy hearts on it. I suppose it's the "I never saw it coming" aspect of love that leaves us feeling so dazed and breathless. And beautifully alive.

As you already know, we met in a bar. Not exactly the most romantic place to begin a love affair, but we could have met in a vacant parking lot and I still would've felt the same whirl of excitement. No matter where we could have met, I would have known the minute I saw him that our destinies were meant to intertwine.

Your father never seemed to hold grudges or wallow in his own pain, even though he'd had a pretty tough childhood. It was one of the qualities that drew me to him. He was always infectiously optimistic about life, and, best of all, I felt like I could be myself around him. It never occurred to him that I was odd, so we laughed a lot, climbed a lot of trees, talked about things more like friends than lovers. He helped me learn how to get out of my head, how to live in the moment, how to appreciate the space between words so thoughts and feelings have a chance to relax.

And the music—always the music. Our relationship centered around music. It was the nectar that brought us together as well as the bitter brew that lead to our downfall. We shared a deep passion for music and spent most of our time talking about it, listening to it, or writing songs that no one but us would ever hear.

He felt the same way that I do about music—it's an intimate form of therapy. Few things can touch us more deeply than a song that sings like our diary. I can look at a painting, read a poem, or watch a movie and not necessarily *feel* them, but I find it impossible to resist feeling music. Music speaks a healing language—it's the tempo of understanding, the strings of connection, the rhythm of all that is. If ever two sides disagree, their greatest hope for a peaceful resolution would come from sharing a good meal while listening to the likes of John Coltrane, Frank Sinatra, or Sarah Brightman playing softly in the background. Music unites us in a way that words don't. The most powerful speeches throughout history—the ones we still quote and remember—weren't speeches at all, but the spoken melody of a universal song.

I've been a music-head as far back as I can remember. Most of my memories from childhood are kissed by the sounds of Simon and Garfunkel, Joni Mitchell, Lena Horne, and Kris Kristofferson. When I was growing up, we carved pumpkins while listening to The Mamas and the Papas, made chocolate-chip cookies to Patsy Cline, and cleaned house with Fleetwood Mac or the Commodores in the background. Music wasn't just around us, it was the tablecloth welcoming the feast.

So it probably came as a surprise to absolutely no one when I fell in love with your father—the lead singer in a local band. We bonded over classic rock, bars with gum stuck under the tables, and late-night breakfasts at Denny's.

Your father's talent was amazing. He was a gifted singer and talented showman. But, although music was his passion, he struggled to turn it into a career. Unfortunately, he lacked the drive to market himself relentlessly or show up for band practice on time.

And the pay was awful. While his singing career would have made a wonderful hobby, it failed to make a comfortable life. But his inability to see life beyond a song had a silver lining: After we moved in together, I was forced to stand taller in the ways of responsibility, budgeting, and planning. I began unfolding layers of myself I'd never tried to before, making me feel like I was successfully adulting. When he asked me to marry him with an Eddie Van Halen twinkle in his eye at a Burger King drive-thru, I said yes without hesitation. When he asked if he could borrow ten bucks to pay for the food, I said yes to that, too.

Your father represents a time when I came to know my own resourcefulness. I fell in love with his lighthearted nature, not his attitude toward hard work and stability. He shrugged off anything that smelled like responsibility and multitasked with the efficiency of a single-celled organism. He wasn't the wisest choice for a husband, but he did offer a lot of icing, even though he was never really willing to help bake the cake.

So I stepped up to the task of mending the seams between his job as a musician and my job as a waitress by pinching pennies, clipping coupons, and learning how to cook. I grew basil, thyme, rosemary, and oregano in small pots on our kitchen windowsill. I studied the ways of lavender, aloe vera, witch hazel, and tea tree oil. I learned how to change the oil in our rusted-out Honda, how to change the filter in our furnace, how to use a drill and a stud finder. I sanded down a wooden rocking chair and repainted it barn-door red. I built a shelving unit from scraps of discarded lumber that collapsed as soon as the cat jumped on it, but hey, at least I tried. Before I moved in with your dad, I'd run from the word *practical*. But afterward, I began to understand that practical can feel pretty rewarding.

In the beginning, we rocked the whole love thing. It was transparent and gratifying, uncomplicated and lively. Even though our relationship wasn't perfect, it was important to both of us. We needed each other. Some people are placed in our lives to help us reach the next level of being—whatever we surrender to them, or whatever we gather from them, allows us to know ourselves a little better. Just as a second floor needs a set of stairs in order to realize its full potential, the soul needs relationships in order to learn and grow.

Then suddenly, without warning or invitation, my maternal clock began ringing. I suppose it was the natural way of things for me to start wanting a baby, but its urgency surprised me. And I didn't want just any baby, I wanted a baby just like you. I wanted a child whose heart beat the prettiest colors I'd ever seen. I wanted to raise a child who would experience life buoyantly and abundantly, a child who liked dirt and glitter, books and frog ponds, tofu and stargazing, and moms who say unlikely things.

I never told you this before, but we suffered several miscarriages and two ectopic pregnancies while trying to conceive you. I secretly worried that the night in the hotel had damaged my body. I worried that maybe I didn't deserve a child like you. I worried that heaven was trying to tell me that I lacked the skills to be a good mother. I worried from every possible angle I could find.

Conceiving a child and carrying it to term is one of the greatest mysteries of a woman's life. Within this mystery lies the greatest joy, and sometimes, the greatest torment a feminine spirit will ever know. Any woman who battles infertility or complications in pregnancy is a woman who needs a strong support system. She hurts inside, yet the ache defies description since it comes from a place words don't visit.

With each failed attempt at pregnancy, and the closer I got to my thirties, the more I began to process what life might look like if I never became a mother. I considered that maybe it wasn't meant to be, maybe I was meant to carry a cause instead of a pacifier. After all, a woman's story is so much bigger than the contributions of her uterus, and destiny has its own ideas about things.

By the time I began to settle into the idea that my future wouldn't know the ways of cribs, diapers, coos, and giggles, I became pregnant with a viable pregnancy. My doctor put me on bed rest at fourteen weeks gestation, which is where I remained until the day you were born.

And that day you came into the world, April was ecstatic. I don't remember a more beautiful April than the one the year you were born. It was as if spring wanted to herald your arrival—daffodils smiled, tulips beamed, and the air was drunk with the scent of honeysuckle and cherry blossom. I can understand why spring was so happy—you were perfect, simply perfect.

I will never forget the first time I held you, lost in your angelic face while the doctors stitched me back together after an unexpected C-section. Your porcelain skin was iridescent, your blue eyes sparkled with wonder. Your hair was the color of mahogany, so silky and thick it looked like someone had stuck a wig on your head. In an instant, I felt fulfilled. Rapture wasn't just a fluffy word poets and preachers used anymore. Instead, it best described what a heart feels like when it experiences a nurturing, protective, all-encompassing kind of love. I may have given you life, but child, you gave me wings. The name Sparrow seemed to fit.

You were a happy baby. I was a happy mommy. We were happiest when we were together. You slept well, ate well, and laughed easily. You grew into a curious toddler, favoring anything sparkly or pink. You weren't much into dirt or anything that made your hands sticky, but you loved books and art and dancing, fairytales and feather boas. You were a "kittens and Indian princesses and heroes in high-heeled shoes" kind of chick from the very beginning.

Before long, your hair came to sweep your shoulders like willow, your delicate nose collected just the right number of freckles, and your stride became thoughtful and confident. Other children loved you, teachers would one day adore you, and puppies followed you home. You're the stuff of excellent dreams.

As you know, I've never been a traditional mother. I have absolutely no idea how to play that role. I am to conventionality what Dick

Cheney is to ethical or what Mr. Rogers is to edgy. It's just not what we do.

I wasn't traditional back then, either. I was careful to provide nutritious meals, dependable bedtimes, and routine doctor visits, but beyond that, I focused more on the philosophical elements of raising a child. I was hyperaware that the wellness of a soul supersedes the benefits of Brussels sprouts and neatly made beds next to toys lined up in a row.

I wasn't a nervous mother, and I'm glad because nervous mothers make me nervous. Instead, I slipped into a calmer shade of me, letting you be free to be yourself, doing my best to keep you safe while encouraging your imagination, knowing it's the tour guide to your future and the spark of a brilliant flame.

Your dad was an involved father. He loved you completely. I still remember how his face lit up every time you said his name. Whenever he walked through the door at the end of a long day, he went searching for you, unable to consider himself home until you were in his arms. As soon as you saw him you would giggle, reaching up your little arms, knowing he was about to swing you around and shower you with kisses.

To his credit, he'd landed a good position in a factory working hard at a mundane job he didn't enjoy. Knowing your father as I do, I realize that his willingness to pack away his dreams of becoming a singer so he could be the father you needed was an amazing act of selflessness on his part.

Life was very good for a while. We were a happy little family wearing happy little smiles. We were far from rich, but it didn't matter. We were walking toward our future feeling loved and holding hands.

I guess this is the perfect stopping point for the day. I want these memories to linger a little longer before I move on, certain that these were some of the most celebrated days of my life.

The time is quickly approaching when you will have your moment in the sun, too, as you experience the joy of having a daughter. I eat this thought like candy, overwhelmed by sheer delight as I think of the warm colors she's about to add to your life. The love you feel right now will soon be eclipsed by a love you can't even imagine. All I can do is give thanks that I get to be a part of this journey. I give thanks that our circle will widen to welcome the next woman of strength, wisdom, and light.

Life blooms.

Sending positive energy across the miles and keeping you close in thought,

Your Loving Mother

SEVEN

Spring 2019

In my room

Dear Sparrow,

I fell asleep last night resting in the softness of my memories. So golden were your tender years, I bet even gold was a little jealous.

Of course, things would change quickly. Nothing perfect lasts forever. Perfect, like happy, is an energy that rests on gossamer wings. Perhaps the lesson about perfect is this: Each of us experiences moments wrapped in a bubble we call perfect, and we should cherish them while they last. Otherwise, after perfect fades—and it will, because we can't evolve if we never step off a cloud—we're left with regret lingering in perfect's afterglow. I'm thankful to report that I fully cherished the time when we found ourselves surrounded by good health, family, and the feeling of something special.

Change happens. The seasons of life move on. For a while, we were three little dreamers growing sweetly in the sun, as if Dolly Parton wrote the soundtrack of our life. But your father and I didn't know how to hold on to it, and time is an impatient friend, never willing to hang around until you figure everything out. So we did the best we could until the day I couldn't do it anymore.

Shortly after your first birthday, your father and I decided to move away from the hustle and pop of the big city. We hadn't enjoyed living so close to downtown Columbus—too much crime and too much noise—but we hadn't been able to muster the energy needed to move. Removing my eyelids with a rusty spatula sounds more inviting than packing up a house, loading everything into a truck, then unpacking it again. However, after you came into the picture, we found our motivation. Wanting to raise you in the slow lane, we boxed up our belongings and headed to the greener side of life.

Once again, I fell in love with a huge, old house with a large, covered front porch that was simply begging for a porch swing and a hanging basket of ferns. I could feel our happiness sitting on the front steps when I drove by it the first time.

Inside, the house had many of the same features as the house I'd loved when I lived near the University—tall ceilings, arched doorways, glass doorknobs, and character galore. It had a beautifully crafted wooden staircase that announced itself in the middle of a quaint foyer. The rooms were spacious and open, and dappled sunlight streamed softly, almost elegantly, through the many windows. We immediately began making plans for all the ways we would fill the house with colorful art made by little hands.

The back of the house had an inviting sunroom that looked out on a lawn dotted with mature shade trees. I envisioned birdhouses, a garden of elephant ears and coral bells, and a baby pool next to a picnic table. It was the ideal setting for playing hide-and-seek or watching the clouds roll by.

I don't suppose anyone else driving by would have been impressed with the exhausted age of the house—it needed a fresh coat of paint and a healthy dose of vision, but it had lots of curious potential. I felt certain that a little elbow grease, a few home-cooked meals, a little amethyst and candlelight, and the house would release its sleeping energy and smile like new again.

Your bedroom sat next to ours at the end of a long hallway. It had pale-green curtains covered in orange and purple polka dots with embroidered monkeys and elephants dancing along the hem. Your bedspread was pink gingham. We bought a large canvas and let you paint your first masterpiece, smearing and splattering handprints and footprints in shades of fuchsia, goldenrod, and cherry. We hung the painting between two large windows that overlooked the front yard. A red-winged blackbird visited your window often. We named him Bop-Bop. I can't remember why.

A bookshelf overflowing with books sat next to your little play kitchen, and a child-sized table with red and blue chairs hosted your magical kingdom—complete with fairies and a horse-drawn carriage. You loved your bedroom. Always an independent child, you valued your alone time in a room filled with endless possibilities. We named your bedroom Bliss.

Your father quickly made friends with a group of musicians in town who were looking for a lead singer. I guess he felt like he needed the release of music in his life again now that his world was full of the demands of parenthood. Practicing with his new friends became a healthy escape for him for a while. Every Sunday after dinner they would get together in a rickety, old shed made into a makeshift studio. To me, the room smelled like mold and forgotten trash, but the band seemed to think it smelled like rock and roll.

Before long, your father and his friends expanded their practice schedule to every Tuesday, Wednesday, and Sunday evening. By the time you were two, they were playing gigs at neighborhood bars and parties. I usually didn't attend the shows because they lasted well into the night, and I was less interested in his musical aspirations now that I was a mom.

Your father, on the other hand, went full throttle into his new "career" and began missing a lot of work at his day job. He also began to smoke pot daily. It didn't take long before bills were piling up and I was asking your grandparents for loans. I was terribly embarrassed—the asking felt like failure. I began to carry resentment toward your father, feeling like he was no longer holding up his end of our cozy, little life.

What started out as a healthy release for busy dads soon occupied all their thoughts and free time. Lawns weren't getting mowed, family functions were being neglected, and any loose change was being spent on amps, cordless microphones, and flashy clothes that looked good on stage. Perhaps the band saw itself as an up-and-coming Aerosmith, but I began to see it as a problem.

I've come to understand that the art of life is knowing when to say when. It's knowing when to try your hardest and when to conserve energy, knowing when to make a move and when to hold your position. It's knowing when to see the writing on the wall and when to look the other way, when to offer advice and when to keep your mouth shut. I'm still learning this art. I'm better at it than I used to be, but even now, I sometimes fail to see the forest through the trees before the trees become a forest. I guess we all do. Life happens fast.

In hindsight, I probably should've expressed my concerns sooner regarding your father's moodiness and his time away from home, before the situation took on a life of its own. I guess I let it get ahead of itself because I was content living in that big, old house with you as my constant companion.

Let's face it, men have a natural ability to really screw up a good time—apparently, having a penis means they're predisposed to making fools of themselves.

So even though our marriage was showing signs of stress, I was happy when you and I were free to do our own thing, spending time together making a village out of popsicle sticks and snowflakes out of construction paper. We even rolled pinecones in peanut butter and bird seed, then made up stories about the birds that came to visit. Your father once enjoyed these things, too, but after he joined the band, he was never in the mood.

Whenever he was home, he was often sulking on the couch like a teenager who wasn't allowed to go to the mall with his friends. With glassy eyes and the temperament of a spoiled dachshund, his presence ruined our feng shui and fizzled our creative energy. And you know what? That shit can get really irritating after a while. It didn't take long before you stopped noticing his absence and I began to welcome it.

You completed us, but we no longer completed each other. I would've wanted us to stay together forever if we'd thrived when he was around, but I didn't see that happening anytime soon. I felt like your father had returned to his child state, and he probably felt like I'd swallowed a big glass of nagging and lost my zest for life. Our Dolly Parton song had ended, replaced by some Muddy Waters.

When one piece of a circle longs to be a rock star, the remaining pieces must learn that sometimes letting go is the healthiest way to hold on. I knew we couldn't sacrifice our happiness for a person who wasn't happy, and we couldn't sacrifice our stability for a person who wasn't stable. You and I would remain a dynamic duo. As for your father, he needed to be free to chase his own dreams—along with however many different women joined him for the wild ride.

Eventually, I asked him to move out. I simply couldn't spend one more evening walking on eggshells. Pretending takes a lot of energy—

too much energy. And it's a piss-poor way to model the importance of harmony in your home. I became a better person the day I met your father, and I became a better person again the day he packed up his studded leather pants, carefully ripped t-shirts, and notebook filled with lyrics, and moved in with someone else.

You and I continued our sweet journey together. The house seemed to breathe a sigh of relief once he was gone, as if a musical yet dark cloud had lifted. We became the team we were destined to be. Many afternoons saw us taking long walks, you nestled inside your little red wagon, heading to the town square to enjoy window-shopping and people-watching. A parade of two, we wove in and out of the quaint little shops, buying antique toys or second-hand costume jewelry to wear that night at dinner. We always stopped for ice cream, followed by a visit to the playground just down the street from our house. With the play structures as our props, we pretended we were the first women to walk on the moon or pirates in search of buried treasure. We attended the big family dinner at your grandmother's house each Sunday. You loved children's hour at the library. We listened to free concerts on the town green. And we cut pictures out of catalogs and stuck them to a poster board we called Our Wish List.

We smiled.

We giggled.

Together was enough.

It was the March just before you turned two. I remember it well. It had been a beautiful spring day. I'd opened the windows to welcome the warm breeze, letting it fill the house with the fresh scent of lilac and sunshine. After putting you to bed later that evening, I lay on the couch reading until sleep lowered my eyes, dropping my book on the floor.

I hadn't seen your father in a while. His visits with you had become sporadic and every phone call turned into a heated argument. He was growing increasingly angry with me. I was aware of the rumors speeding through town that Neil, the lead guitarist in your father's band, had developed a crush on me, but little towns often make up their own drama because little towns yawn a lot. I knew the rumors were untrue, so I gave them no consideration.

Neil and his wife Cindy were good friends to you and me. After your father and I separated, they'd stepped in to help with things like childcare and car repairs. They lived one street over and Cindy was a stay-at-home mom with five young children. And Neil had one thing your father never did: a toolbox. I appreciated their willingness to help because I was a single parent living on a tight budget. So friends and family were a much-needed support system.

I think Neil and Cindy could see that you and I were happier living on our own. Perhaps Neil felt the need to pitch in out of a sense of duty or obligation because it was no secret that the band had contributed to the downfall of our marriage. Regardless of why they were so kind to us, I dismissed the rumors about Neil's crush as ridiculous. I relegated them to the simple noise of busybodies who longed for a Jerry Springer moment in their "by-golly" world.

I realized too late that I should've given the juicy gossip more of my attention, because how I felt about it wasn't the problem. But how your father felt about it most certainly was. He hadn't dismissed the rumors like I had. Instead, he'd grown more and more uncomfortable with Cindy babysitting while I was at work and with Neil spending time in our driveway fixing my car's worn-out alternator. Your father began to resent their presence in our lives.

The negative energy brewing inside him grew darker once he began using heavier drugs—something I didn't know about at the time. If I'd known he believed the rumors and was using powerful drugs, maybe I would've tackled the gossip head on. But I didn't. I went about my life, never once considering how the rumors could affect me until that March night when I lay on the couch sleeping and your father stood outside the living-room window feeling vengeful and holding a grudge.

I don't know how long your dad stood there, but while he did, rage began to consume him. Fueled by jealousy, alcohol, and mind-altering chemicals, he quietly removed the screen from the window and slipped inside the house.

I was awakened by the cement-hard slam of a fist to my temple as someone yanked my head off the pillow by my hair. I felt repeated blows to my face and neck. Caught so off guard, I struggled to stand against the force of the brutality.

I didn't know at first that the person attacking me was your father. I remember seeing the window screen lying next to the couch, I remember smelling spring in the air, I remember feeling panic and confusion. Blood from a gash above my right eyebrow was rushing into my eyes and blurring my vision. I tried to wipe the blood away, but another punch to my face sent me reeling backward into a recliner. The recliner tipped, me with it, smashed an end table and sent a lamp crashing to the floor.

My body was pummeled by fists and kicks and slaps, blood began draining into my mouth, its warm stickiness dripping from my chin. From the corner of my eye, I could see a splatter of blood speckling the wall. I felt a piece of tooth lodged in the back of my throat. Everything seemed to be happening at once. I was falling, bending, and thrashing. I was gagging, bleeding, and blind.

Suspended in disbelief, I seemed to be viewing the unfolding scene from somewhere outside myself, as if I were watching the abuse from another realm. This feeling of physical detachment was the closest thing to an out-of-body experience I've ever known. Time went by in slow motion as I watched my body being tossed like a rag doll, but I never felt any pain.

Finally, I noticed my attacker's shoes—your father's signature black boots with three silver buckles. For the first time, I stared into his face. I hardly recognized him. His face was distorted with pulsating muscles, a clenched jaw, and wild eyes. Sweat dripped from his brow, gluing his long hair to the side of his head. He looked crazed. A shudder of fear ran through me, electrifying my spine.

For just a moment, after I looked him in the eye, he softened his hold on me. I broke free from his grasp and ran to the window, screaming out into the night, "Help me!"

He grabbed me by my ankle, pulling my feet off the floor, and began dragging me into the dining room. I reached for the coffee table leg, hoping to use it as leverage, but it toppled over, sending all if its contents rolling across the floor. Your father had become a tornado of fury, and the house bore witness to the rage he contained.

Then I heard you crying.

The sound of your voice was faint and afraid, drifting down the staircase into the dining room. Still to this day I can't explain what awoke inside me the moment I heard your frightened voice. In less time than it takes to think a thought, I was pulling myself off the floor with a warrior screaming inside me. My eyesight began to clear as if the blood had turned to fire. I could feel the shift of energy in the room. My mind became singularly focused: I had to get to you. And no one was going to stop me.

There's a wise saying that warns, "The most dangerous place in the world you will ever find yourself is the space between a mother and her child." I know this to be true. Your plea for help changed the course of that night in an instant. The victim in me fled as the fighter began to rise.

And. She. Was. Pissed.

I grabbed hold of the brass lamp that had fallen to the floor, and in one smooth motion I ripped off its mangled shade, gripping its base tightly. Your father ran toward me. With a strength more powerful than I'd ever known, I swung the lamp like a bat, leveling it perfectly against the side of his head.

"Take that, you son of a bitch!" I heard myself shriek in a voice stinging with venom. Your father dropped to the floor instantly. With one perfectly aimed blow, I'd knocked him out cold.

For a split second, I wondered if I'd killed him. But I didn't stop to check. I jumped over his limp body and ran up the stairs into your room, forgetting about the blood on my face. Your eyes were wide as I rushed to your bed, scooping you into my arms. I ran to the bathroom, grabbed a washrag, then descended the stairs two by two. You held on for dear life, your tiny hands white as pumpkin seeds as you clung to my shirt. I grabbed my purse and keys and ran to the door in a panic to get you far away from the house as quickly as possible. I figured that if I hadn't killed your father, he'd be waking up soon.

Before I knew it, we were pulling into the parking lot of the police station. You were very quiet. Strangely, neither one of us was crying. During the drive there, your eyes searched mine each time I looked in the car's rearview mirror to check on you. I will never forget your searching eyes that seemed to need to know that I was okay.

"Mommy is fine," I said in a gentle voice. "The police will help us." You seemed relieved.

All that remained of that night was the business of making a police report, your father being escorted to jail, and me being photographed naked under the glare of a single bulb hanging from the ceiling in a room that felt like defeat. I felt humiliated as the female officer instructed me to "turn to the right, now turn to the left, now lift your arms, now look toward the ceiling."

Each click of the camera felt more painful than the physical damage it was trying to capture. It shamed me to be photographed naked in order to prove that I'd been abused. I never saw the developed pictures. I never asked to.

Your father pleaded guilty to domestic violence. He had no choice. I refused to agree to a lesser charge of disorderly conduct. He and his attorney had felt certain I would agree to the lesser charge in order to avoid a trial that would force me to relive the events of that night.

They were wrong.

To consider what happened on that March night as merely disorderly was a gross understatement. Pissing on your neighbor's trash can is disorderly. Being drunk in public is disorderly. Breaking into a house and beating the mother of your child while your child sleeps upstairs is domestic violence.

I refused to allow the pain you and I had experienced to be diminished by the clever rephrasing of a legal definition. The pictures taken of me at the police station must have spoken volumes to your father's defense attorney, because before long, your father agreed to plead guilty to domestic violence.

Throughout this ordeal, I felt a tremendous sense of responsibility to fight for our truth. I knew one day you would learn of this night, and I wanted to show you—not just tell you—that if a man ever puts his hands on you in anger, no matter who it is, you fight back, get away, and stand tall. You hold him accountable for the choices he made.

And you *never* blame yourself. Equally important, you never permit yourself to let the memory of the event disappear into *but he loves me*, or *he didn't mean to do it*, or *he said he was sorry*.

Let's get one thing straight, child: If a man ever takes his hands to you, please know he damn well meant to do it. You don't beat someone by accident. *Never* allow anyone to take away your right to feel safe in your own home or in your own skin. If love hurts or leaves bruises, then it isn't love at all. It's called control. And control can be deadly.

I carefully weighed my decision to discuss this event in my letters. I've known that one day we would need to talk about it, the night that forever severed your parents' friendship and dramatically changed your father's presence in your life.

I felt maybe it was time you knew the truth, because without it the aftermath makes less sense. But we're not going to linger on yesterday's pain, we're going to focus on the growth.

In the years following this incident, two remarkable things happened: Your father became a better man, and I learned how to forgive him. We would never be together as a couple again, but as a family, we began to heal.

Now that you're a young woman making your way in this world, and soon to be the mother of a female child, I decided to mention this experience so I could better illustrate that my advice comes from one who walked through the fire and made it out alive. Not every woman is so fortunate. Many women stay stuck in a toxic situation because they feel they have no options. Others choose to pretend it will never happen again, some dying at the hands of their abuser, never having believed the next blow would be the last thing they would ever feel.

Many years ago, I ran across this saying: "If a man has to use his fists to win an argument, it's a sure sign his brain couldn't handle the challenge." Please keep this in your arsenal of truths so if you ever run across a person who is prone to violence, you can see them through wiser eyes.

Your father had never been violent with me before, but he did brag about the many fights he'd been in. I dismissed his boasting as boys being boys, but upon reflection, I probably should've taken his tendency to throw punches instead of arguing skillfully as a warning sign.

Though that night with your father felt devastating, once again, I denied the need for a grieving process. Just like after the rape, I stuffed the experience so I could hold myself together. In my mind, I had to do that for your sake. Thankfully, a busy life creates movement, so I just kept on living. It took many years before I arrived at the formula needed to finally forgive your father, but I did and I'm glad.

Forgiveness, however, doesn't silence truth. Actually, it makes it more potent. I learned a very powerful lesson that night, one I will never forget: Weakness comes in many forms, but none are so destructive as the crushing blow of fist to skull from one who says he loves you.

My heart is with you as you read this letter. I wish I could take white-out to that fateful night, but I can't. It was certainly the end of something, but chapters in our books don't always become the entire story of our lives—one night doesn't have to define a lifetime if you don't want it to. So let it soothe your soul to know that quicker than an angel can blow a trumpet or Athena can raise a fist, heaven was ready to smile on us again.

A weary moment in March gave birth to something new.

Sending positive energy across the miles and holding you close in thought,

Your Loving Mother

EIGHT

Dear Sparrow,

I like to begin my letters on a lighter note since much of what I write is often, well, thick. Reading the story of my life probably feels like doing shots of molasses. But, I'm eager to pick up right where I left off.

After I ended my last letter, I sat quietly for a while with my pen still in my hand, thinking I might go back and cross out much of it, wondering if I'd said too much. Knowing that truth is an organizing medicine, I set down my pen and prayed instead. I gave thanks for the remarkable resiliency of the human spirit. Even though life can be big and scary sometimes, we are never fated to the shadows of our past, the soul naturally seeks a better way to experience the decadence of who we are.

Following the night with your father, years would pass during which you and I felt young, healthy, vibrant, and blessed. Wild winds were certainly on the horizon, but the bubble called "perfect" returned to us, forming the cocoon that swaddles the butterfly.

Your father moved on.

His sister, Mindy, bought him a one-way plane ticket to the Gulf Coast of Mississippi with an invitation to live with her after he was released from jail. He boarded the jet with only the clothes on his back, disappearing from our lives for the next six years.

In the days and months that followed that night, you asked about him less and less. I did my best to explain the situation in the simplest terms: "Daddy wasn't allowed to be mean. He had to talk to the police. He needs to get some rest. Daddy loves you very much. He misses you. It's okay to think about Daddy. You can see Daddy as soon as he's feeling better."

These explanations seemed to satisfy you.

After your father's departure, you and I became even closer. Something shifted in the atmosphere once we became a duet. We read each other's mind fluently, sensing each other's moods as if our thoughts were written on a chalkboard. We formed a tight, loving bond that still, to this day, no man or any other external force has found a way to untie.

The seasons marched on.

We filled our world with simple joys. We baked homemade cookies, danced ballet in the pool, and used British accents at the grocery store. We took long walks in the woods, admiring the shapes of trees and the sound of the wind when it tickled the leaves. We busied ourselves with art museums, history exhibits, and trips to the lake so we could build sand castles. We planted daisies and gladioli, carved pumpkins, picked apples, and built a snowwoman in the front yard, giving her a pink tiara and a nice set of pearls. We set up a tent in the middle of the dining room, and read *The Velveteen Rabbit* and *Harold and the Purple Crayon* by flashlight. We wore bright red shoes and feathers in our hair, we collected rocks and interesting sticks, we kept rainwater in a jar, adding a dash of purple glitter and a few drops of blue food coloring so our imaginary mermaid felt more at home. Wrapped in the colors of family, faith, and love, we stood brave against the world.

Understandably, after the night with your father combined with the night in the hotel, my sense of safety was shaken. I had no idea how to navigate life safely with a small child now that my rose-colored glasses had been shattered. I still believed people were good, but I'd learned the hard way that it's difficult to get a good night's sleep when you don't feel safe inside, and it's remarkably easy to stuff memories until your mind feels more rested.

Right around this same time, your grandparents got divorced. Like so many marriages that span decades, they simply fell out of like with each other. Their love would remain timeless, but their mutual interests headed in separate directions once their grown children stepped into lives of their own. So they shook hands, pledged to remain friends, and went about chasing their own dreams on their own terms.

Your grandfather bought a condo in an affluent neighborhood. It offered a community pool and clubhouse, an imaginatively designed playground, well-tended lawns and gardens, state-of-the-art security systems, access to a high-performing schools, and neighbors who were fortunate to experience the prosperous side of the American dream. Your grandfather was kind enough to offer his extra bedrooms as our safe haven so you could have a male role model and I could spend more time focusing on our future. I eagerly accepted his offer.

We didn't mosey toward this opportunity, we ran.

I know how much you adore your grandfather. I do, too. He's one of the most capable men I've ever met. He's a jack of all trades—knowing the ways of carpentry, electricity, building and design, math and science, patience, and love. Sensible and well educated, he is of the earth. It's easy to feel safe when you're with him. But it's easy to feel challenged, too, since he isn't one for excuses or a person falling apart when they should be rising.

After we moved in with him, the heavens seemed to open up. I was less financially strapped and slept more soundly. You blossomed in the light of so much attention and plenty. You loved school, had countless friends, and wore happiness like a person who whistles while they walk, waving at geese and squirrels and tender things as if "Hakuna Matata" was your theme song.

I landed a good job in a nearby school system as an instructional assistant tutoring children in reading. I loved everything about my new job. I loved the principal, I loved the staff, I loved the children, and I loved knowing my work was meaningful. I had to get my GED in order to apply for the position. Finally having a high school diploma after all those years of drifting in a sea of dead-end jobs catapulted my confidence into the stratosphere. I began to feel better and look better, too.

Life was back to good again, as if James Taylor and Neil Diamond collaborated on a song and named it after us.

Ocean Springs, Mississippi, is a sleepy little Southern town galvanized by the fusion of opposites. Lying next to the Gulf of Mexico, it's home to some of the most spectacular live oak trees I've ever seen. It's progressive and artistic against a backdrop of tradition and Southern charm. It's sweet tea on the veranda and a drum circle under the full moon. Ocean Springs seems indifferent to the status quo of the outside world, yet it's the pride of all its residents.

After your father headed south, he fell in love with a captain in the United States Air Force stationed at Kessler Air Force base in Biloxi, Mississippi. He quickly moved into her home in Ocean Springs, beginning a new life and trying to piece together the brokenness he felt inside. His girlfriend, Astrid, was a wonderful catharsis for your father. Just as heaven was busy smiling on us, it was busy smiling on him, too.

Just like military service can sculpt a respectable life, Astrid helped sculpt your father into someone more centered and responsible. The caveat to her love, we would learn, was he had to form a healthier relationship with you and begin paying child support. (Shout out to Astrid!)

Unfortunately, the plan they set in motion to achieve this goal involved showing up at our front door unannounced and uninvited. I know you remember meeting your father the summer you were eight. I call it a *meeting* instead of a *reunion* because by then you had no memories of him, so it was like meeting him for the first time. Thankfully, your Uncle Vince opened the door that day and broke the news to us that your father was back in town as gently as he could.

Initially, I was completely unprepared for your dad's ambush style of attack, showing up unexpectedly, hoping to throw me off balance. It took some time before I could see his strategy differently, admitting to myself that if they had called to make plans for a visit, I probably would've spirited you away to a safe house and changed my number.

Your grandfather once told me that things usually work out the way they're supposed to: It's not often you get the best of all possible worlds, it's not often you get the worst. I thought a lot about this pearl of wisdom as I processed whether or not to let you see your father. I knew I didn't want him in my life, but I knew you needed him in yours.

It took an enormous leap of faith to let you spend time with your dad, knowing in my heart that this opportunity was your best shot at finding a comfortable groove with the missing piece in your life.

And then came the week you spent camping with your father and his extended family. Joy happened as you hiked, canoed, and s'mored yourself into an even lighter shade of being. You met family you'd never known, gathering memories like wildflowers as the story of you came to life. You came to know the ways of a family that had never forgotten you, always considering you an important part of their tribe. The night you came home, you fell asleep with a smile on your face—the smile of a child who feels remarkably loved, included, smitten with all things Daddy.

And so it was that our future moved forward with a better version of your father in your life. He continued to grow in his commitment toward you, calling often, sending pictures, cards, and presents, making sure you knew you were a special part of his world.

I came to believe that Astrid was the best thing that ever happened to him.

Never underestimate what a strong woman can do for a man who stumbles. Women have been mighty since the moon first met the night.

A few summers later, your father invited you to come visit them in Ocean Springs, enticing you with a trip to Disney World. You probably don't remember, but you began packing your bags immediately, reducing me to the unimportance of old newspaper. The summer plans we'd made were thrown out the window, unable to compete with a ride through the Haunted Mansion, a Mickey Mouse hat, and a fistful of funnel cake. I was happy for you, but I knew my separation anxiety would be fierce.

You boarded an airplane, and into the heart of Dixie you flew. After I got over the initial shock of having you so far away, I kind of enjoyed having some time to myself. I'd spent the past six years trying to manage the demands of being an only parent—I wasn't used to having weeks stretch before me with nothing on the agenda. I read a lot, I ate ice cream for dinner, I lounged at the pool. I visited family less and friends more often. But it didn't take long before I wandered around the summer feeling like the best part of me was somewhere I wasn't invited.

And then it happened.

The storm.

I know we've talked about Hurricane Katrina many times, but I'd like to share this moment in time from my perspective. I've never offered my reflections before, not wanting you to know how deeply the storm affected me. This letter will be the first time I ask myself to relive this experience, so forgive me if I tell you things you already know, but recreating the events may help explain my reaction.

Hurricane Katrina changed the lives of many people, and one of them was mine.

I will take us back to late August 2005. Summer break had already ended in the school district where I worked, and although I was aware of Katrina's presence in the Gulf, she was projected to make landfall west of New Orleans—so for the most part, I was focused on the start of a new school year. I'd called your father to discuss the situation. He reassured me that at most, Mississippi would receive some rain and wind, but nothing about Katrina was cause for alarm.

Unbeknownst to either of us, Katrina suddenly changed course and began heading due north, positioning herself for a direct impact with the Mississippi coastline. She'd strengthened into a Category 5 hurricane. Her size was immense—spanning the distance of over four hundred miles. And her power was well organized and voracious.

When I turned on the news that morning and heard the updated report, a deep sense of dread spread through me. I knew I didn't have time to get to you before the storm hit. Ocean Springs was over a thousand miles away from where I was, and Katrina was closing in fast—it wasn't a matter of days until she made landfall, it was a matter of hours.

I immediately called your father. He informed me they couldn't evacuate due to Astrid's responsibilities at the base. All hands were on deck in preparation for the storm. So he and Astrid had decided they would ride out the hurricane twenty miles inland at your Aunt Mindy's house.

I thought it sounded like an insufficient plan, and it did little to soothe my apprehensions. Your father reassured me that Katrina wouldn't be a major event like my gut kept telling me it would be. I don't think he was trying to be dismissive—he was probably telling me what he himself wanted to believe. I asked him to keep in touch and he promised he would. After we got off the phone, I dropped to my knees and prayed. The air in my lungs felt like pin pricks.

Then, time stood perfectly still.

America was held spellbound as it watched Hurricane Katrina make landfall, then return to the sea to gather strength and make landfall again as she decimated her way east. Her fourth and final landfall was on the Louisiana/Mississippi border, only twenty-five miles west from where you were. Her landfall meant Mindy's house was on the "dirty" side of the storm. Fear spread through me like cancer, eating its way through tissue and brain matter, threatening my sanity and the very oxygen in my blood.

All of America, and the world, knows of Katrina's cataclysmic impact—she was one for the record books. With a sustained wind strength of 140 mph and gusts reaching 175 mph, her storm surge created a twenty-eight-foot wall of water that slammed into the Mississippi Gulf Coast, leveling ninety percent of its coastline. Structures made of concrete and steel crumbled as if they were made of graham crackers. Trees fell like dominos. Bridges buckled, disappearing into the blackened water. The skies gave birth to deadly tornadoes. Homes fell like Legos.

Lake Pontchartrain breached her levies, sending an ocean of water rushing into the lower quadrants of New Orleans. Eighty percent of the city was submerged. Although New Orleans received much of the media attention due to its massive flooding and the disaster that unfolded at the Superdome, the Mississippi coastline experienced the most damage from a direct hit by Mother Nature.

Katrina created over $108 billion in damage. She claimed the lives of 1,833 people. Thousands were left homeless, wading in floodwaters polluted by raw sewage, alligators, and floating bodies. The scale of devastation was apocalyptic.

The aftermath of the storm was horrific. From Louisiana to the Florida Panhandle, people were left without food, water, shelter, medicine, diapers, electricity, communications, dry clothing, usable vehicles, gasoline, and access to money. Everything was simply gone. Trees stacked like pick-up sticks created an impenetrable wooden wall, encasing the hurricane-torn region in its own suffering. Mangled power lines looked like balls of yarn dangling from the ancient oaks.

FEMA took days to establish realistic operations in the region. Our government clearly lacked a sound plan of action, displaying a frightening ignorance as to the magnitude of the situation. Even though the storm itself was catastrophic, the most devastating impact came from the chaos that ensued as everyone slipped into survival mode. The utter desperation escalated with each passing day—news reports told of brother turning against brother over a bag of ice or a warm package of bologna.

Martial law was imposed. Strict curfews were set to prevent further looting and mayhem. Police were overwhelmed and outnumbered. The National Guard arrived to help restore order, but among fear, madness, and faces of death, there is no order.

And you were right in the middle of it.

My life stopped.

I simply could not grasp my reality, it all seemed too impossible to believe. Stuck inside a nightmare unfolding a thousand miles away was my only child. And I couldn't get to you. I have never felt more powerless. Helpless. I was desperate for any word about your safety, but for three endless days no word came.

For three days I didn't know if you had made it through the storm alive. Still to this day, this thought impales me. For three days I didn't eat, sleep, or allow myself to feel anything. I was utterly frozen and entirely numb. I dared to be too hopeful. I dared to fear the worst.

The brain can only process so much before there's a system overload, shutting down vital components in order to protect itself from permanent damage. We're designed to short-circuit before we self-destruct. I went through the motions of living, but inside I felt a certain kind of dead. The only thing I lived for was waiting for the call that you were okay.

I tried repeatedly to reach your father or Astrid on their cell phones. The news continued to report that power lines and cell towers were down. I had no choice but to wait for someone to contact me. The wait felt endless and agonizing.

The call I'd been praying for came in the middle of the night on the third day after Katrina struck. The connection lasted only a few seconds, but it was long enough to hear your father say, "Sparrow is okay." Then the line went dead.

I immediately tried to call him back and got only a fast busy signal. I held the phone in stunned silence. It felt amazing to know that God had somehow made a way for your father to break through the gnarled rubble and release me from my torment. The relief echoed through my entire body, it came quick and powerfully. I dropped to my knees and wept. My tears came from a place I didn't know existed, its origins felt primal. I purged the haunting thoughts of losing you and the images I'd seen on TV. I let go of the fear. I allowed myself to breathe.

After the phone call, our family kicked into high gear, making plans for a trip into the hurricane zone to bring you home. We had no idea how much damage Mindy's house had sustained or how much food and water was available to you. I had no idea what you'd seen or lived through, but I knew you needed me.

And it would've taken a force greater than Katrina to keep me from you.

Many people tried to talk me out of going down South so soon after the storm, citing the risk of danger, the likelihood of a failed mission, and the probability of the National Guard turning me away. But I knew I had to try. Thankfully, your grandfather offered to make the trip with me. So while the government was busy trying to get its head out of its ass, one mother, one family, and one mighty big gun were busy making plans for a journey into no man's land, headed straight for the belly of hell.

I can't do justice to the outpouring of love and support I received from family and friends as we planned our trip. Whenever I hear people speak of the coldness inside the human heart, I quickly float back to this place in time. I'm reminded that although we may have a lot to learn about compassion, humanity's heart is still beating. I've seen for myself that people with nothing to gain will rise to the occasion in times of crisis, stepping inside the circle of light because at our core, we know the circle of light matters most in this world.

When word spread that I was heading into the hurricane zone, people began offering items your father and his family would need in order to begin rebuilding their lives. Perfect strangers and loved ones alike offered prayers or gave donations of clothing, food, money, batteries, toilet paper, paper towels, socks, underwear, and t-shirts. They donated trash bags, bleach, cleaning supplies, latex gloves, diapers, blankets, flashlights, and cases of bottled water.

Their giving was bigger than you and me—people wanted to send hope to any life they could touch. It was going to be a wonderful accomplishment to bring you back home, but I knew it would elevate wonderful to new levels of human decency if my journey could help others, too. So people gave and gave and gave until not another Gatorade or protein bar could fit into my car.

Our family became a finely tuned machine. All emotions were put on hold as we began plotting and planning the trip. Your grandparents, aunts, and uncle did an amazing job anticipating hurdles we might encounter, staying abreast of news reports that contained useful information. They expertly judged time and distance, assessed availability of food and gasoline on our route, monitored road closures and openings.

They determined that if your grandfather and I left on Friday, we should arrive in Gulfport, Mississippi, just as the roads were beginning to open.

Timing was critical. To avoid being stranded, we didn't want to arrive before roads opened. But to avoid being turned away, we wanted to arrive before checkpoints were set up. The evening news kept reminding us that due to the lack of gasoline and the sheer size of the devastation, no one was getting out of the disaster zone—and no one was getting in.

Your maternal great-grandmother used to say that all you need is a prayer and a plan. I've come to realize that's very sage advice. We did our very best to plan for our trip, and I prayed heaven would step in and do the rest.

On Friday morning, we loaded up the car, I slipped behind the wheel, and we began our journey south.

Once we passed Meridian, Mississippi, on Interstate 59, we saw no other vehicles heading south. Not one. I don't suppose you can begin to understand how eerie it feels to be so alone on a normally busy freeway.

We turned off the radio and readjusted ourselves in our seats, the severity of the situation now resting on the front porch of our minds. Our car had an out-of-state license plate—anyone who saw us would know we had a working car, gasoline, and resources. The risk of being carjacked, or worse, became very real as we kept heading south on a road overcome by deathly silence.

The closer we got to the Gulf, the more we began seeing abandoned cars lining the road and people standing in the sweltering sun waiting for help to arrive. I wanted to stop, at least offer them a bottle of water, but stopping would've been a tactical error we might not recover from. At one point, we came across a group of perhaps six or seven people standing next to a minivan with all its doors open. From a distance, we could see the group staring at us. They began to form a human barricade stretching across the road, trying to force us to pull over.

Your grandfather grabbed his gun from under the seat and calmly said, "Don't stop" as he rolled down the passenger window.

He stuck his arm out the window, pointing the .357 Magnum in their direction. As we drew closer, I kept hoping the line of people would move. They didn't. The closer we got, the more I realized they saw us as their only chance at escape, our car and their barricade playing a deadly game of chicken.

For a moment, fear stung me like a red-hot poker drawn fresh from fire, but self-preservation cooled the pressure, forming a snarl across my lips. I put the pedal to the floor, slipping the engine into overdrive. The sound of the motor revving into high gear clearly stated that I had no plans on stopping, but still the people didn't move. I watched as they held hands tighter, bracing themselves for impact.

When the moment of choice was at hand, I gripped the wheel tightly, staring straight ahead. Only then did the line of people notice your grandfather pointing his gun directly at them. Finally, they scattered, diving into the tall grass on the side of the road. With the pedal still to the floor, we rushed by them as if we were Calamity Jane and Dirty Harry bound for glory.

All they could do was stare.

There's no doubt that had it not been for my father's calm, immediate reaction, our journey, and most likely our lives, would've ended on that desolate stretch of road. Reality descended upon me like a vice grip. But there was no turning back.

I suppose I could write a book about all the strange coincidences, near misses, and instances of perfect timing that befell us on that trip. But suffice it to say, God was ever present in our mission.

Our family had thought of everything—except for the fact that the closer we got to the Gulf, the more road signs had disappeared, making it difficult to navigate a region we'd never been to before. Thankfully, your grandfather has a keen sense of direction and a knack for storing data, allowing us to make it safely to Mindy's house. That's a story in and of itself—remind me to tell you about it someday.

When I finally saw you, I hugged you like I'd won the lotto. I was relieved to see that Mindy's house had escaped the worst of the storm. A tornado had blown the chimney off and debris was everywhere, but the house itself was in good order.

Your father, Astrid, your Aunt Mindy and your Uncle Rock had done a wonderful job of shielding you from the unfolding drama— you seemed unfazed by the chaos surrounding you. Mindy reported that the only time you'd cried was when you ran out of clean clothes and had to wear a shirt that didn't match your shorts. I guess waves may crash, tornadoes may bellow, and buildings can disappear into the sea, but being forced to wear mismatched clothing is more than any self-respecting princess can handle.

We quickly said our hellos, dropped off the mass of goods, gathered up your things, and headed back north toward Ohio. Our goal was to make it out of the storm zone before darkness fell.

Near Tuscaloosa, Alabama, with you sleeping comfortably in the backseat, we came across a sight that made our jaws drop. In the distance—and as far as the eye could see—was a large military convoy heading south into the war zone of Katrina. Camouflaged trucks carried huge generators, dozens of port-o-johns, tankers of gasoline, and thousands of boxes of desperately needed supplies. We saw ambulances, all-terrain military vehicles filled with proud and ready soldiers, and American flags waving in the wind. The convoy went on for miles, like a serpentine of angels commanding the highway.

I felt a swell of pride as I watched the parade of soldiers roll by. And I silently offered up thanks that help was finally on its way. Then a sobering thought occurred to me: We'd managed to amass a collection of sensible resources, plot a sound course of action, make it to the Gulf, deliver supplies, collect a precious child, and head back out of town before the United States government ever set foot on Ground Zero.

I pray there's never another disaster of such epic scale on our shining shores or on the vast wealth of land that lies in between. But if there is, I hope the agencies we have entrusted—and funded—to respond quickly and efficiently to tragedy are able to move with as much focus and determination as a mom, her faith, and her family.

And shame on them if they can't.

We returned to Ohio without a hiccup, deeply indebted to those who contributed to the overwhelming success of our journey. You were welcomed home as a hero, a survivor. And you basked in the attention even if you didn't understand what all the fuss was about. You displayed no signs of aftershock. Instead, you threw open the door to your bedroom and stepped back into your whimsical childhood.

I wish I could tell you that our lives returned to normal, that we picked up right where we'd left off, but we didn't. Well, more accurately, I didn't. The numbness that had seized me when I first learned you were in the path of the storm wouldn't go away. I felt a strange kind of nothing inside. I watched myself going through the motions of day-to-day life trapped in the mother lode of melancholy. I couldn't focus. I had trouble sleeping. I startled easily. I felt lost in plain sight.

Little did I know as I moved through life feeling detached from everything around me that soon I would need my strength and sanity more than I ever had before. I now know the importance of providing steadfast nourishment to your mental health, because you never know what's waiting for you just around the bend. You may not have time to heal before the next crisis is upon you.

I tripped when I told myself the numbness would fade without help. I tripped when I kept my feelings hidden as if they were a secret. I was so busy tripping that my next challenge easily brought me to my knees—because by the time it hit, I was already halfway down. Everything that was behind me would come to feel like the stuff of dime store novels.

The greatest battle of my life was about to begin.

I will close this letter. I'm not eager to remember the next chapter of our lives. Even though I'm stronger now, I don't revisit it easily. I hate to think of the woman I lost. I would never know her again.

The next decade of our lives would be the battleground that decorates the soldier, allowing us to become the women we are today. We are no longer victims of anything. We are survivors, masters in the art of bamboo.

Sending positive energy across the miles and holding you close in thought,

Your Loving Mother

NINE

Summer 2019

At the beach

Dear Sparrow,

I'm sitting at the beach with my feet dangling in the water. The waves rush toward the shore as if they're eager to greet me, the moon quietly rests on a blanket of silver clouds, and the stars twinkle like fireflies dancing in a celestial jar. It feels pretty good to be me right now.

I'm waiting for the sunrise to welcome the first day of summer. This will be the season of babies and granddaughters, wrapped in the golden glow of sunshine and sweet corn, iris and sunflowers, popsicles and fireworks, and the celebration of all things water. It's delightful to know that we will celebrate her birthday each year when the earth is full of laughter, when the days of summer stretch before us like the lighthearted path of a hot air balloon.

I'm in a contemplative mood this morning. I came to the beach believing I could center myself poetically by leaning into a pillow made of sky. I feel the need to get cosmically comfortable because today I begin the task of untangling the next season of our lives.

Ugh.

Putting my head into this mess seems like a thankless task. I almost prefer the idea of tattooing my esophagus or dragging a Waffle House around the front yard.

Of course, the season I'm referring to wasn't just a season, was it? Seasons yield, spinning beauty and bounty, reminders of the earth's sovereignty, before ending their cycle in a predictable fashion. So it wouldn't be fair to categorize the next chapter in our lives as a season. Instead, I should refer to it as an ordeal. Ordeals can last a very long time, writing chapters that require a lot of thought, use a lot of words, take up a lot of energy. If you aren't careful, an ordeal can rewrite the story of your life.

I suppose you've always wondered how all the madness began—I've often wondered the very same thing. It would seem reasonable for you to question what marked the beginning of an event that would grow so big and weird, spanning more than a decade of our lives. I wish I could tell you as I write this letter that I'm certain of a whole lot of things, but I'm not. I am certain, however, that it started out innocently—most things wicked usually do. If evil were more obvious, it would gather unwanted attention; evil moves slowly so busy people can stay focused on other things.

They say things happen for a reason. I firmly believe this is true. Some people think destiny and free will are concepts at war with each other, but I think they hold hands. I believe it's our destiny to complete a mission designed just for us—we are hardwired to love, give, do good works. And whenever our free will blows us off course, it's our destiny to find our way back. Staying on track is a matter of choice. It's a choice to overcome hurdles, bypass negativity, empower ourselves with self-love and self-confidence—it's a choice to stick our heads into the positivity of life. We may take different routes and learn different lessons, but free will doesn't cancel destiny.

Our destiny is always waiting for us because it's ours alone to claim.

But destiny can be interrupted. Destiny can be put on the back burner by the impetuous hands of fate.

Fate happens. It's the culmination of choice, circumstance, the eagerness of the world to alter a soul's direction, and the unchosen path we're forced to endure when the outside world comes tumbling in. Fate is a fickle friend and a bipolar lover—sometimes it's the best thing that ever happened to us, sometimes it's the fission of particles that leads to our own atomic bomb.

It's no one's destiny to die in a dark alley with a needle stuck in their arm, and it's no one's destiny to die on the battlefield. Fate intervened, destiny suffered, free will got lost in the din. It wasn't supposed to be that way, but when life gets heavy, the stuff of dreams and light and missions can seem so far away.

I suppose it was fate that led to me to our next ordeal, combined with a series of poor choices and ignored signs, but thankfully, it was always our destiny to reclaim our lives. It took a lot of guts to get here, and it wasn't an easy path, but the courage we displayed and the life we fought for have allowed us to know ourselves so much better. The battle offered a context that a life of leisure never could, connecting us to something richer, more fragrant, evergreen and everlasting.

Meaning becomes a potent gift to the eye that viewed the storm.

There's a synchronicity to life, I'm sure of it. I used to believe in coincidence, but I don't have much faith in the concept anymore. Coincidence pals around with chaos theory, but even in chaos theory, patterns begin to emerge—chaos struggles to find meaning, too. I believe life flows intentionally, like notes on a sheet of music. The notes at the beginning may think they have little to do with the notes in the middle or the notes at the end, but as each note is brought to life, blending seamlessly with the next, it becomes obvious that each individual note is part of a bigger plan. The concept of coincidence shatters at the hands of deeper things; the music of life quiets the dissonance of chance.

Of course, things do happen that aren't washed in the river of life. I'm not suggesting that biting into an apple and finding a worm means you're destined to become a worm farmer or getting a parking ticket means you shouldn't have gone to work that day. But when a random event alters the course of your thoughts, your thoughts can reshape your day, and sometimes even your life.

Before things turn to shit or sugar, there are signs pointing in its direction. Signs are the deliberate language of the universe, affirming our path, foreshadowing our future, reassuring us that we're not alone and heaven is always aware. The universe is well versed in the gift of precognition—it doesn't write our stories, but it already knows the stories we will write ourselves. It tries to warn us of the roadblocks ahead, but all too often, hitting our mental snooze button feels safer. Less troublesome. Less weird. And signs are subtle—those who don't look, don't see. We should consider it a blessing that heaven insists on doing what heavens do—organizing fate into teachable moments so we can better understand the core of our inner self by experiencing the many layers of meaning.

For a very long time, I haven't wanted to talk about my stalking ordeal. I was still too raw. And I didn't know how to make sense of it. I guess I still don't, but the miles I've put under me have broadened my horizons, allowing me to see yesterday through a cleaner lens. Once I stopped standing still inside my pain, I came to realize the path I've walked is a tremendously beneficial one.

Make no mistake about it, I didn't ask to be stalked. And I did nothing to deserve it—that card was dealt by a lunatic whose free will invaded my personal space and changed the course of my life. Our life. But it was never my destiny to crumble at the hands of a deviant, so the experience became a roadmap leading to the empowerment of me.

Before we dive into all the ugliness, before I lay myself utterly bare, I want to begin by saying thank you. Thank you for allowing me the time I needed to heal. Thank you for allowing me to get my head on straight before you asked a lot of questions. Thank you for being wise enough, compassionate enough, to understand that the woman writing this letter is very different from the one who lived the story. Your patience has allowed my story to tell itself from a much healthier place.

In this letter and the ones that follow, I hope to answer many of your questions. But the one I won't be able to answer with any certainty is *why*. I have no idea why he did what he did. The closest I've come to understanding his wicked motivation is what I found in the parable of "The Turtle and the Scorpion." I stumbled across this simple, little story in the pages of a weathered book I found lying on the front porch of an abandoned house. One might say finding the discarded book was a coincidence, but there's nothing random about its message. Or the answer it provided to my sad and tortured mind.

The Turtle and the Scorpion

Once upon a time, a lazy turtle was sitting next to a riverbank when a scorpion came to ask him a favor.

"May I climb upon your back so you can take me to the other side of the river?" the scorpion politely asked.

The turtle, knowing that scorpions are dangerous, quickly replied, "No! If I let you climb upon my back, you will sting me and I will die."

The scorpion laughed. "Silly turtle, if I sting you then I would die, too!"

The turtle thought for a moment, then allowed the scorpion to climb upon his back, and they set course for the other side of the river.

Just as they were nearing the shore, the turtle felt a horrible pain on the side of his neck. He knew he had been stung. Before the turtle took his last breath, he looked up at the scorpion and asked, "But why?"

Before the scorpion took his last breath, he narrowed his blackened eyes and hissed, "Because it is my nature."

And so there it was, nestled inside the yellowed pages of a strange, little book, waiting for me to find it—the only explanation that has ever made any sense. People can't help but show their true colors, even when it's no benefit to them at all. They just fly their flag of hate as a symbol of how empty they've let themselves become. It's the very nature of darkness to want to proclaim itself, risking everything for the chance to experience the stench of its own vomit and the feel of its own knife.

Though the story "The Turtle and the Scorpion" answered the question *why*, I've never been able to understand how such sickness became a part of his nature in the first place.

For years, I wondered, *How does a soul get this bent?* In my feeble attempt to make sense of it all, I lost plenty of sleep, shed an ocean of tears, and fell into my darkest despair—until the day I gave myself permission to stop wondering anymore, no longer certain that the answer would make any difference anyway. Knowing why or how doesn't fade scars or erase pain. And there isn't a pen big enough to write him a reasonable excuse for his unreasonable behavior.

So I can't speak about what creates a stalker, but I can certainly tell you what creates a frightened victim, and then a warrior. And I can describe the arch of enlightenment bridging the two.

I would imagine that you will be shocked by many of the things I'm about to say, so maybe I should begin with a little disclaimer. Please understand that at the beginning of my stalking ordeal, you were the tender age of ten. You had just lived through Hurricane Katrina. I did everything I could—lie, deny, pretend—to prove that I was okay and our life was fine. Through it all, the one I worked hardest to protect was you. And I must say I did a fairly good job because for years you were innocently unaware, and you turned out beautifully.

But you're a woman now, so it's time you learned why I changed so much, why we had to move, why I didn't seem like myself for so many years. When the madness first began, I was a woman doing her best to deny the existence of my Pandora's box. I had so much pain stuffed inside my hidden chamber, I was tripping over my own two feet. It became remarkably easy to trip my way into being a victim, then trip my way through the whole damn experience. But I'm not tripping anymore.

And I'm finally ready to talk about it.

So I return to that night—the night that spawned the need for intimate letters some fourteen years later. This would be the night that began the evolution of me, even though I didn't know it at the time.

Some evenings are just moon and stars and quiet dreams, some evenings are more sinister. Some nights flutter, some nights burn. It seems to me that evening in late October 2005 was supposed to be a very ordinary night—nothing about it seemed important at all. It was only much later that I would realize that that evening wasn't like any night that had come before it.

For this would be the night the madman cometh.

And so it was that exactly two months after Hurricane Katrina struck, I sat at my antique vanity, lost in my own world. I don't remember all the details of that night because its significance wouldn't be revealed for a long time, but I do remember the general mood. I remember the feelings inside me, the desire for a night out with my best girlfriend, and the signs foreshadowing a night of fate and free will.

My favorite jeans and black leather boots, the ones with heels too high to run in but perfect for dancing, were probably laid out on my bed, waiting for me to slip into them. My vanity, most likely littered with make-up, jewelry, homemade scented lotions, and pictures of you, would've felt like my personal throne. I'm certain my room was cast in a soft glow of candlelight, creating a relaxing ambiance complemented by the serenade of Spanish guitars. I'm sure I spent the better part of an hour curling my boring brown hair, recently streaked with blonde, into wide ringlets like colorful ribbons winding around a maypole. Section by section, I would've done my best to create the carefree, tousled look that I'd admired in fashion magazines and spent years trying to perfect.

Most likely, I was enjoying the evening from somewhere inside myself, free from the hustle and bustle of a busy week. Getting dressed up felt like a rite of passage almost, shedding my outer layers of motherhood and responsibility, trying to connect to the feminine energy within.

A night out with Tandy was always a welcome pause from the demands of being a single mom. Since Tandy was a single mom, too, we seemed to gravitate toward one another, thoroughly enjoying each other's company. She had a way of making me laugh at a time in my life when laughter called for a lighter spirit than I could manage on my own.

So soon after Katrina, I was still struggling to get past the gray and numbness that seemed to distort everything. I watched my hands cook dinner, check your homework, fold laundry, pack your lunch, and fulfill the requirements of my job, but I felt entirely detached from the process.

Hurricane Katrina had triggered something inside me, and suddenly, my junk drawer of stuffed pain was hell-bent on prying itself open.

During the days, I had recurring thoughts about the rape, the abuse, and the fear of losing you. I couldn't seem to stop the images from playing over and over in my mind, marching through my head like soldiers in a North Korean parade. I blamed myself relentlessly for letting you go to Mississippi in the first place. And each night, I had vivid nightmares of being chased through a dark forest. I often awoke in a panic. I did my best to pretend I was fine, hiding behind a mask, mimicking the ways of happy while secretly feeling tremendously alone and strange. *Surely this can't last*, I told myself more than once.

Back on that October evening, as I sat curling my hair and adding a few more strokes of mascara to my lashes, I'm sure I wasn't thinking about Pandora or storms. I was looking forward to a mindless evening, an opportunity to escape my reality for a while. I probably felt like I could use a night out since music and dancing made me feel alive again—it made me feel free.

As you read these words, you probably envision in your mind's eye a woman more likely to be wearing sandals and carrying a hammer or a paintbrush than a woman in heels swaying on a dance floor. But this is the story of my younger self, the woman looking for a temporary escape from everything dying inside her.

Looking back, I know one thing for certain: If my head had been in a better place, I never would've gone out that evening. There were too many signs advising me to stay home. I didn't place much importance on signs back then, so it wasn't too hard to dismiss their annoying persistence. I dismissed the floor lamp in the corner of my bedroom that kept turning itself on and off, thinking it had to be a faulty switch or a light bulb that needed changing. I'm not suggesting that an invisible hand was manipulating the lamp, but the fact that the problem with the lamp presented itself on that night of all nights certainly seems curious to me knowing what I know now.

I also paid no attention to the numerous times the evening almost cancelled itself: a babysitter backing out at the last minute, Tandy and me getting into a slight tiff over who would drive, the threat of a strong thunderstorm, and a paycheck smaller than I'd expected. And lastly, I ignored the balsamic moon hanging low in the sky—the phase of the lunar cycle meant for rest and introspection.

But I didn't notice the moon. Preoccupied and human, I ignored all the signs as I reapplied my lipstick, ran my fingers through my hair one last time, grabbed my keys, and headed out into the night, blindly driving into a future that never would've happened if I'd let the universe choose my evening for me.

As I drove across town toward Tandy's apartment, I was completely oblivious that everything I was and everything I believed in were enjoying their last ride as my reality. Soon I would stand beneath the electronic clatter of a cheesy, one-star nightclub washed in neon lights and pulsating music. I would be blissfully unaware that a predator stood in the shadows cast by the dance floor lights, quietly watching me, somehow sensing my vulnerability as if it were the sweet perfume of one who falls easily.

Numbed by alcohol and a reckless disregard for safety, I would soon stare into the face of a madman. He approached me with chiseled features, a worldly stature, an air of smugness, and a peculiar twinkle in his eye, introducing himself as Cain Cook. We talked for a while, but by then I was drunk. I hold no memory of our conversation. I only remember I was intrigued. He was tall, fit, well dressed, and handsome. He spoke in a calm, smooth voice. With my beer goggles on, I immediately began tripping, seeing things that weren't really there.

I tripped when I interpreted his arrogance as confidence. I tripped when I let his polished words convince me he was harmless and intelligent. I tripped when I didn't notice the maniac lurking behind his mysterious, black eyes.

His eyes revealed nothing, like black holes in space. I remember thinking his eyes felt strange, but I explained the feeling away by telling myself that I was being overly sensitive. As the music played on, I continued to fill my cup with drinks and laughter. The madman retreated into the shadows, but I never noticed.

The evening seemed to go off without any fireworks. After enjoying ourselves for a few hours, Tandy and I left the club and stopped for a bite to eat. I dropped her off at her apartment and made my way home. Only a few hours had passed since I'd left the quiet of my bedroom, and I returned feeling fuzzy-headed and lighthearted. As I kicked off my heels and rubbed my aching feet, I gave no more thought to the man named Cain I'd met at the bar.

I'd foolishly given him my number and casually said, "Call me sometime." I didn't really expect him to call—what happens in a bar is fantasy, washed away by the morning light. So even though Cain seemed interesting in the context of a nightclub, my late-night burrito from Taco Bell made more of a lasting impression on me than he had.

There were no indications as I prepared for bed that fate was already at our door. Under a pitch-black sky with only storm clouds bearing witness, Cain had secretly followed me home, meticulously searching through my car for personal information. Within a matter of days, he would research me and our family in an effort to learn everything about us. He would soon know our schedules and habits with devastating accuracy, dissecting our strengths and weaknesses as if they were potential strategies in a game of chess.

What began as a casual, flirty conversation in a forgettable bar on a forgettable night would prove to be the beginning of something wicked. With the precision of a switchblade and the determination of barbed wire, Cain Cook began his tragic mission—a mission born inside a decaying mind, seen through the vacant eyes of a monster.

One day I would learn the indecency of his demand: Love me or I will destroy you. And destroy he did. Before the warrior within in me would rise again, I would come to know the desperation of brokenness, the feel of homelessness, the taste of hunger, and the sickness of a mind skillfully wrong. I would experience a loneliness so profound I thought death was my only escape. You and I would suffer in my struggle against the inhumanity of a man who felt it was his right to punish me for not wanting him. I would learn that pride can be vicious. I would learn that apathy and denial can be vicious, too.

Exactly two months after Hurricane Katrina struck, darkness came into my life like a purring kitten hiding a psychopath in full-blown rage. Of course, I knew none of this as I turned off my light and settled into bed. As the quiet sang its peaceful lullaby, I was completely unaware that I had just met the essence of evil disguised as an ordinary guy in an ordinary bar on an ordinary night.

But it wasn't an ordinary night, was it? This was the night weakness found its obsession, when destiny held its breath under the weight of all things wrong.

I must admit that, as I write this letter, one hand holds a pen while the other forms a fist. My heart weeps for the woman I was back then. She was so unprepared for the challenges she'd be forced to endure.

But mostly, I weep for you. You lost so much in the battle. You were handed a fate you did nothing to deserve.

Before I lose myself in the poisonous ink of my memories, I will look toward the light. I must remind myself that one day we would link arms and tie the hands of fate.

But thirteen years is a long time to live without a sense of freedom, privacy, and safety.

Thirteen years is a very long time, indeed.

The battle we fought was awful, but I wouldn't change much if it meant we would have to give up everything that defines us now. Because when fate finally surrendered to destiny, the light gleamed so fantastic.

Sending positive energy across the miles and holding you close in thought,

Your Loving Mother

TEN

Dear Sparrow,

I'm relaxing on the deck at our favorite coffee house. There's something so inviting about lounging on a comfortable couch that faces the Gulf, like a picturesque wall in a breezy house with carpet made of sand. No need for a remote control—the scenery changes all on its own. I'm admiring the view while I sip my chai latte, gathering my thoughts, hesitant to recreate all that I've tried hard to dismantle, these memories now banished to the island of *His Sins Became Her Salvation*.

I guess I'll begin this letter by discussing the relevance of habits in our lives. It probably seems like a silly thing to talk about, but it lays the groundwork for everything after.

Our habits are the product of repeated patterns of behavior. We create habits because they make life easier—patronizing the same gas station, bank, and places of business gives us a sense of familiarity, allowing us to perform daily tasks without having to put too much thought into it. It's been said that human beings are creatures of habit, and I've come to understand that our habits reveal far more about us than we would probably like to believe.

Normal people don't look for the blind spots in someone else's routines. But not everyone is normal. Some people, as bizarre as it may seem, actually study the nuances of another person's habits, hoping to capitalize on their steadfast predictability.

Suppose, for instance, it's part of your morning routine to stop at Starbucks for coffee. It can easily become part of someone else's morning routine to watch you stop at Starbucks. Normal people would find this code of conduct a huge waste of time, but a mentally unstable person can find it rather intriguing. The voyeur has the clear advantage because it would never occur to you that someone might enjoy watching you tend to the insignificant details of your life.

Take this analogy one step further and suppose the mentally unstable person gets bored watching you buy coffee. The rush is gone. So he begins following you to work. Then he begins to follow you home, too. Soon, Mr. Creepy is parking across the street from your bank because he's learned that it's your habit to stop at the bank on your way home from work each Friday, just as it's your habit to go to the library on Wednesday evening. He's also discovered that you eat dinner at your mother's house every Sunday.

It doesn't take long before Mr. Creepy begins incorporating all of your routines into his own. To you, he's invisible. To him, he's brilliant. He considers you a fool because you've never noticed him before. The stalking comes so easy, it's mere child's play. In the blink of an eye, he changes where he lives and works so he can be closer to you. Meanwhile, you have no idea that someone is going to great lengths to monitor all of your movements.

You keep on living. He keeps on watching.

Stalking is never stagnant. Like a disease, it changes and grows, feeding off the healthy tissue of an unsuspecting mind. The more a stalker stalks, the more voracious his appetite becomes, creating a world in his head that is completely separate from his victim's reality. The stalker reassures himself that his victim needs his protection. He tells himself that who he is in the dark is no one's business but his own, and if people weren't so stupid he wouldn't be so effective.

A stalker's mind is riddled with lies—the ones they tell themselves and the ones they tell others. Usually intelligent, they're adept at making reasonable excuses for missing chunks of time away from work and home. The stalker's co-workers and loved ones willingly believe the well-crafted lies, never suspecting someone so close to them could be leading a double life. A stalker is equally versed in explaining away missing sums of money secretly spent on gadgets to monitor their victim. Technology is a stalker's closest friend—it keeps all his secrets while exposing all of hers.

There are well-defined rules to the mind-numbing game of stalking: See without being seen, leave no evidence behind, never blow your cover, and most importantly, never admit to stalking or allow anyone to believe anything is amiss in your life.

A stalker's motto: Lie well and lie often. For the truth could end the game.

Stalking is a crime that falls below anyone's natural radar. We've become comfortable with our apex predator status, no longer hunted by monsters bigger than ourselves. Our instincts have become dulled, our zone of awareness reduced to the three-foot world around us. It's from this place of assurance and narrowed vision that a stalker finds his footing, and someone unaware can go months—sometimes even years—having no idea that a weirdo has infiltrated their safe zone like a virus of the mind.

The longer his secret remains hidden, the more his delusions multiply.

Your habits become his habits. His habits become an obsession.

You were too young to know this, but several years after my stalking ordeal began, I took my case to the Columbus City Prosecutor's Office in an attempt to file charges against Cain Cook. From there, I was referred to the Stalking Unit within the Columbus Police Department.

During my initial meeting with a detective, I received a pamphlet entitled "The Seven Stages of a Stalking Victim." The detective informed me that most stalkers follow a textbook style of stalking, and as a result, most victims have textbook responses, living through the experience in seven predictable stages.

I was mortified to discover the brochure read like my personal diary. I was further mortified when I realized I still had many stages to get through—and the worst were yet to come.

Stage One is denial. This stage usually lasts the longest since a woman is none too eager to admit she has a problem. Instead, she tries to rationalize the stalker's behavior as merely a misunderstanding or considers it a coincidence that he keeps showing up wherever she is.

Stage One is of particular importance to the shelf life of her stalking experience because the longer the victim remains in denial, the less likely she is to put proper defenses in place to ward off the stalker's advances. While the victim is busy denying, the stalker's obsession is steadily growing—unchecked and unobserved. As his feelings of invincibility escalate, he begins to take greater risks. Her oblivion is an enticing invitation to test the limits of his Machiavellian desires.

Before a victim finally realizes she has a full-blown stalking situation on her hands, the stalker already knows everything about her. He knows the names and addresses of her family and friends. He's learned where she works and what routes she drives each day. He knows who she visits and where she shops. He knows where her children go to school. The stalker has carefully studied what matters to her and what doesn't. He comes to believe he knows her better than she knows herself.

The information the stalker craves becomes the trident of his existence, fueling his need to booby-trap her life so even when he isn't with her, he is always with her. Given the advances in technology, this is an easy task to accomplish. A GPS on her car, hidden cameras and listening devices in prime locations, spyware embedded in her phone and personal computer—and suddenly a person with a dark heart can have complete access to her private world. Before the victim realizes she's being targeted, the stalker already has her surrounded.

The stalker has successfully played a wickedly clever game. No longer a loser at life, he's now the puppeteer pulling the strings, a man rejuvenated by his own resourcefulness.

His obsession offers a sense of power he's never known before.

The call came at 10:04 precisely, just like all the calls before it. I sat waiting for the phone to ring, knowing the call would come—it always came. For weeks, I'd been receiving a litany of calls marked Private or Unknown Caller on my caller ID. They came every morning and every evening at exactly 10:04. I'd long since stopped answering these calls because the person on the other end of the line never said anything, only listening as I said *hello* over and over until I finally hung up.

The calls began shortly after I met Cain, but I didn't make that connection at the time. I didn't give much thought to the calls at first, but I began to notice a pattern. Hoping to confirm a hunch, I scrolled through my caller ID and discovered the calls always came at exactly 10:04. Something about it made me uncomfortable—automated calls aren't so precise. I wanted the calls to stop.

One afternoon, while searching through your grandfather's garage looking for an empty box, I stumbled across an air horn. An idea formed immediately, a Cheshire cat grin spread across my face. I grabbed the air horn, marched into the house, and set it next to the phone in my bedroom. The next time I received one of my mystery calls, I would be ready.

Later that evening, I sat on my bed with the air horn in my hand. For the first time, I actually looked forward to my nightly nuisance call. When the phone rang at exactly 10:04, I picked up the receiver and said, "Hello?" The person on the other end of the line clearly didn't expect me to answer, because for the first time I heard a male voice make an audible gasp. I blew the air horn directly into the phone. It screamed an obnoxious wail until the person finally hung up.

And that was the end of my calls at 10:04.

Enter the theme song from *Rocky*.

Running concurrently with this time in my life, I'd begun a very casual friendship with Cain. It surprised me when he contacted me so soon after the night we met. Even though I didn't remember much about him, it was unusual for me to give out my number so I reasoned he must have been somewhat impressive, never once considering that I was drunk when I met him. Our first date was forgettable, our phone conversations were dull and unimaginative. Thankfully, due to my responsibilities at home and work, our newly formed friendship was largely sporadic, and Cain never pushed for anything more.

I'll make this clear from the onset so you don't have to wonder: I never saw my friendship with Cain as a relationship in any way. To me, a relationship is the pursuit of something deeper than just drinks at a bar or casual sex. Relationships require certain protocol: Both parties stay in touch regularly, both parties open up their lives, and both parties agree the situation feels nice and has potential for growth and future commitment. Then lives begin overlapping, holidays are shared, and family and friends begin to meet.

The above scenario never described my interactions with Cain. From our first date, I knew he would never be my boyfriend, we would never spend holidays together, and our families would never meet. He remained compartmentalized in the most private part of my life, seldom rising above the occasional fling category I'd intentionally placed him in.

I wasn't opposed to spending time with someone, but I didn't want the term *boyfriend* to enter into the equation. To me, having a boyfriend seemed about as inviting as drinking a warm cup of fire ants. Perhaps it was Cain's overall lackluster personality that kept me interested, knowing he would never inspire me to grow more interested. He was convenient. And at that time in my life, convenient was sexy.

In the beginning, Cain's approach toward our friendship fit me pretty well. I rarely heard from him, so it was a hassle-free experience. It wasn't unusual for us to go a month or two without speaking, and whenever we did make time for each other, I must be honest by telling you that our connection centered around sex more than anything else. It's not that he was good at sex, he wasn't, but he was very good at fading into the background until I was ready to see him again. The time we did spend together was cordial and meaningless, polite chitchat vs. "I'm trying to get to know you" conversations.

I can't begin to say how many times I may have seen Cain in the months following the night we met because none of those evenings stands out in my mind. He continued to occupy the space in my brain that a playground would—when I wasn't with him, I rarely thought of him. When I did make time for him, I was well aware the clock was ticking and I had to get back to my real life soon.

Then came early summer of 2006. You and I had already begun our daily trips to our community's private pool. As you already know, the pool was the hot spot of our neighborhood and we spent much of our time there. You were an amazing swimmer, the place was overrun with kids, and I enjoyed socializing with other moms, grilling a lunch of shish kabob's on the community grill, or lounging under a shade tree with a book in my hands.

One lazy summer afternoon, I happened to notice a beat-up-looking car parked just outside the pool's fence with a man slouched down in the driver's seat. The car stood out painfully in a parking lot filled with expensive cars and it struck me as odd that the man in the car was trying so hard to appear inconspicuous.

I couldn't see the driver well since he'd disguised himself with a ball cap pulled down to his eyebrows, and mirrored sunglasses covered his eyes. Based only on the size of his upper body, he appeared to be a rather large man. It struck me how uncomfortable his position must have been for a person of large stature, folded up like an accordion in order to fit as much of his body into the floor space as possible. *That's weird*, I'm sure I said to myself.

A little while later, I got up to take a quick dip in the pool. I was surprised to find the man was still sitting in his car in the same uncomfortable position. I swam for a few minutes, keeping my eyes on him. Each time I glanced his way, he appeared to be staring straight at me, which struck me as peculiar since our community pool was filled with what one would consider "the beautiful people." I began to feel uncomfortable, almost vulnerable somehow. I returned to my chair with the intention of writing down the car's license plate, just in case. I sat digging in my purse for a moment, but when I turned around, the car was gone.

Meanwhile, during the summer of 2006, you were blossoming into a social butterfly. You kept a busy summer schedule with birthday parties, sleepovers, and church camp. I had more free time on my hands, so my friendship with Cain began picking up a little steam. I wouldn't say I saw him often, but I would say I saw him more frequently than I had before. I was beginning to develop stronger feelings for him, but the more I got to know him, the more erratic his behavior became. Sometimes he was fantastically warm and attentive, and then suddenly, he could turn cold as ice. He was becoming increasingly moody and unpredictable. He complained about his job and his family more often and began discussing money woes. He was drinking more heavily, too—even in the middle of the day.

Cain had always projected an image of a confident man of the world, so I felt his sudden change in temperature indicated he was going through a rough patch. Since his demeanor and poor-me monologues made for horrible foreplay, we often wouldn't have sex when we were together. I would listen to him complain for a while then make an excuse as to why I had to leave. Within a day or two, Cain would always call, offering an apology for his behavior.

The next time we would get together, he'd be the polar opposite from the time before. He would act spellbound by my every word, laughing in all the right places—one would have thought I pooped glitter and wore a halo of diamonds and footballs for all the fuss he made over me. During these better moments, we began having deep discussions about life and philosophy. I was surprised to learn we were both reading the same book, *Their Eyes Were Watching God*, by Zora Neale Hurston. I came to like the philosophical side of Cain.

For every step we took forward, however, we took two steps back. His bouts of moodiness followed by overkill kindness followed by long stretches of silence came to feel like a challenge I didn't have the energy, or the desire, to endure. I walked away from the whole situation.

By then, there were enough flags on the field, but I didn't pay much attention to any of them, never considering that the little box I'd built for him could never house the bulk of his insanity.

Weeks passed and I met someone new. Even though I was still opposed to having a boyfriend, Emory-James was a breath of fresh air. He seemed to fit my life better than I thought a man could. As a single father with full custody of his two children, Emory-James understood the demands of being on only parent, and we clicked on many levels.

I know your memories of Emory-James are rather vague, you once telling me you only remember his perfect, white teeth and his infectious smile. I remember his smile, too, since it decorated most of his face. Looking at him certainly wasn't a painful experience, with his caramel-colored skin, his smoldering eyes the color of topaz beneath a hedge of camel-length lashes. His easygoing nature made his companionship feel safe and sweet. By then I'd purchased my first cell phone, and Emory-James and I kept in touch daily. I wasn't ready to introduce him to you since I felt that was a really big step, but I was beginning to open my mind to the possibility.

Meanwhile, the mysterious man wearing the hat and dark glasses kept making an appearance at our pool. The car he drove was often different, but his overall mode of operation remained the same. He parked in different locations, but always in direct proximity to the pool.

I notified the manager of the pool, but he brushed off my concerns, reassuring me that the man must be a visitor of a fellow resident. I wanted to believe him, so I did.

Since the man in the car had never approached me in any way, I convinced myself I was making something out of nothing. Yet, I couldn't sweep away the feeling that he always seemed to be staring at me. And he sat motionless in a car far longer than a less suspicious person would.

I tried to get a better view of the driver many times but had little success since the car windows were always tinted and the steering wheel often obscured his head. But I instinctively knew he was staring at me—I could literally feel the weight of his gaze. It felt menacing somehow.

As fate would have it, late one afternoon as the sun was beginning to set, the mystery man reappeared, making his first mistake. This time, he didn't wear a hat and wasn't slouched down in his seat. The car he was driving had deeply tinted windows, so dark they were almost opaque, so he probably thought the windows successfully shielded his identity. He didn't seem to realize the sun was shining directly through his back window, illuminating his silhouette.

My heart stopped.

I knew immediately the man in the car was Cain.

I'm sure you don't remember since you only met him once, but Cain Cook has an oddly shaped bald head, cresting to a prominent point at the top of his skull. I would recognize it anywhere, so his sharp silhouette through the windshield was equal to his wearing a nametag. I rose from my chair, staring at him in utter disbelief. *What in the hell is he doing here?* I wondered, completely flabbergasted that the mystery man in the car had been Cain all along.

Something stopped me from confronting him face to face—the whole situation felt too uncomfortable. Wanting to keep a safe distance, I dug my phone out of our pool bag and texted him immediately.

"Are you sitting outside my pool?!?!!!" I asked, using plenty of question marks and exclamation points to convey my astonishment.

No response.

Cain continued to sit in the car as if he were invisible. I gathered up our things, made an excuse as to why we needed to leave, hurried us home, and locked the door behind us. I can't say I was frightened, but I was certainly baffled.

By bedtime, I was already doubting my observations, inventing reasons why it couldn't have been Cain. Surely he had better things to do with his time than watch me at a pool, and I'd never once told him where I lived. I reasoned that Cain wasn't the only man I'd ever seen with an unusually shaped head, and I never saw the driver's face, only the outline of his body starkly illuminated by the setting sun. I shook off the incident as a case of mistaken identity. I began to feel embarrassed I'd accused him so impulsively.

Late that same evening, I receive a text from Cain saying, "You are a crazy bitch."

His insult shocked me. Though I was eager to convince myself that Cain wasn't guilty as charged, I was surprised by his harsh comment. Something didn't feel right. I ignored his text and deleted his number.

As I sit here writing these memories, I believe I knew in my heart it was him at our pool. I also believe I would have done anything to convince myself that it wasn't. There was something too unsettling about the idea of Cain knowing where we lived, too disturbing that he chose to spend his time sitting in a car watching me.

As I mentioned earlier, a stalking victim's first reaction is denial. I would like to think that with all of my life experiences, I would've stepped out of denial and into reality much more quickly. But I didn't. It's from the deepest shade of blue that I must admit I was in denial for far too long—even when things got stranger.

I've thought about this paradox for years, beating myself up, wondering how I could have been so stupid and naïve even though life had already taught me much about the importance of trusting my instincts.

The simplest answer is this: I didn't want to know the truth. Still trying to recover from the numbness, maybe my subconscious willingly concealed the truth, knowing that one more brick in the wall would've sent me spiraling backwards—denial is always the easiest way to keep things humming along.

So there I was, pretending everything was fine and Cain was normal. After he was exposed at the pool, I stopped hearing from him. But the stalking didn't stop, and the more he watched and followed me, the stronger my feelings grew that something wasn't right. There would come a time when my reality could no longer deny itself, but regrettably, I held it off as long as possible. Unfortunately, while I was busy living, Cain seized the opportunity to perfect his crazy and cunning into a sickness that ravaged my life.

I will close for the day. I'm a little weary. I think I'll order a virgin piña colada and take a walk along the beach, clear my head, feel the scenery, get lost in the waves for a little while.

I'm extremely grateful that I can slip to the water whenever I feel the need. I look forward to visiting the Gulf with my granddaughter one day. We'll watch the sun set over the horizon, and I'll sing the song, "Got an Angel on My Shoulder"—the song I always sang to you, the song your grandmother sang to me.

It's always good to keep a song in your pocket.

Sometimes it soothes a child, sometimes it soothes a soul.

Sending love across the miles and holding you close in thought,

Your Loving Mother

ELEVEN

Dear Sparrow,

I'm sitting among the ancient oaks and gravestones that have a spectacular view of the ocean. I suppose anyone else reading these words would find it difficult to believe that I would choose to be sitting in a cemetery writing a letter. You understand though, don't you, child? We've often discussed how peaceful a cemetery can be. If a person is looking for a quiet place where they won't be bothered, a cemetery is an excellent choice—it's like a library without walls. And books. But it has that whole, "hush I'm trying to think" vibe down pat.

Now that I'm comfortable, the stillness stirs my memory. I will begin this letter with an overview of the expanding mystery that consumed the year 2006. Since I came home with the intention of telling my story, I've spent some time trying to figure out where my head was when my life first began to fall apart.

Of course, back then, I didn't realize it was starting to fall apart, I only knew that the feeling of being watched was growing ever stronger. I often felt a strange sense of anxiety, as if I were wrapped in cobwebs, but I wasn't ready to admit that my inner radar might be telling me the truth. It seemed like I kept running into the same strangers while shopping or out in public, but I wasn't ready to play connect the dots.

In the beginning, the randomness of puzzling events failed to paint a big picture, as if each incident stood by itself, unconnected to a whole. But it wasn't long before I was receiving strange phone calls that seemed unusually personal, like the time an unfamiliar voice called to inform me that Foot Locker was having a shoe sale on the very morning we'd planned to go shopping for sneakers. Another time, immediately following a conversation in which you asked for a new Bratz doll, I received a call from an unknown female telling me that K-Mart was having a sale on Bratz dolls. The person on the other end of the line never gave me a chance to speak before hanging up. I tried to re-dial the number, but a recording always announced that I'd reached a non-working number.

Now I know that someone was using a payphone or a calling card to place these calls, but back then, I just stood staring at the phone with an uneasy feeling resting in the pit of my stomach. The more the frequency of these calls increased, the more I did my best to convince myself that the calls were odd, but nothing more.

Stage One, the denial phase, becomes a poorly fitted coat trying to shield you from the draft of a chilling truth. Pretending makes more sense than a phantom you never see.

When a good investigator is trying to crack open a case, they set out to answer six main questions: who, what, when, where, why, and how. Answering each of these questions is essential to understanding the complexities of any given situation. Typically, when a stalking victim begins to notice that something isn't right, she becomes too focused on the *why* factor.

To the victim, *who, when, where*, and *how* are of lesser importance because she can't begin to fathom why anyone would be targeting her in the first place. Of course, rational thinking is the first mistake a victim makes, trying to view the bizarre through a logical lens. As a result, the denial phase becomes a breeding ground where insanity is free to thrive.

As the victim struggles to understand why, she remains in a state of denial because she doesn't have all the facts. She doesn't know that over 2.5 million people in America are stalked every year. She doesn't know that stalking is often referred to as "America's dirty little secret" by members of law enforcement who specialize in stalking cases. And she is certainly unprepared to accept the fact that most stalkers stalk their victim for an average of five years before moving on to their next victim or becoming incarcerated for reasons that have nothing to do with stalking. A stalker usually lacks the financial means to successfully stalk their victim. Therefore, they often resort to criminal activity in order to fund their increasingly expensive operation.

The victim is unaware of other things, too. She doesn't know that according to the FBI Center for Crime Analysis, all stalkers have personality disorders. Stalkers are described as being emotionally immature and socially maladjusted; they suffer from feelings of powerlessness and low self-esteem; they feel as though society's rules don't apply to them. Compounding the situation, stalkers feel no remorse or embarrassment while they stalk their victim because they never see their actions as a problem.

While the victim is temporarily disabled, grappling with the *why*, the stalker is methodically plotting his *how, when, where*, and *who*. One day the victim will realize that the answer to her most pondered question lies in the very fibers of his being. How it got there is a mystery science still struggles to understand. Is it nature or nurture? Whether it's genetics or upbringing that creates a predator, the debate weaves a meaningless dialogue that fails to defend against the matrix of madness. Knowing why he does what he does doesn't begin to lessen the victim's experience or stop the slow creep of insanity gathering in the stalker's brain.

I can't say for certain when I first knew I was being followed. It seems to me that I began having a sense of being followed fairly soon after meeting Cain, but I continued to go through the denial phase quite convincingly. Once it became a more regular occurrence, I'm certain I expressed to family and friends that I felt like I was often being followed whenever I left our house.

Of course, the mere suggestion that someone would want to follow my dumb ass around while I shopped for bananas or picked up dry cleaning was so utterly absurd, it was difficult for even me to believe—I can understand how friends and family might have found my declaration completely unlikely. Wanting to adopt the beliefs of those around me, who, like me, lived inside a three-foot world, I decided that I probably just needed more vitamins and better sleep.

As frustrating as it was to try to explain why someone would be targeting me, understanding *how* they were doing it was beyond my comprehension. Nowadays, we are so familiar with technology that we don't bat an eye when we hear of tracking devices, drones, or surveillance equipment. But not so long ago, this type of technology was unheard of. Gathering intelligence through subversive means was the stuff of spy thrillers and hostile foreign governments, not yet mainstream reality.

The world has changed a lot since my stalking ordeal began. Until the internet matured and began expanding our awareness, apple-pie America was oblivious to the new frontier gigabyting its way toward us. Back in the early 2000s, your average person would've had no experience with high-tech gadgets and spyware. Landlines were more popular than cell phones, and cell phones were still push button, without any of the features we rely on today. Since the general public still believed that futuristic gadgets only existed in Hollywood movies, we were completely unprepared for the dark side of technology, unable to foresee its impact on an ordinary life. This era of innocence was a tantalizing time for anyone with a devilish curiosity and a weak mind—super-sleuth technology, readily available if you knew where to look, became the best-kept secret of the morally challenged.

I can tell you with a great deal of certainty that at the beginning of my stalking ordeal, my instincts were telling me that something dark was moving about, yet I was completely ignorant as to how one would go about eavesdropping on my private conversations or obtaining accurate information regarding my whereabouts. My lack of understanding had a significant impact on my ability to gauge my situation. Had I known Cain was utilizing technology to gather real-time information about me, perhaps I could've reacted differently.

In the beginning, I think Cain was quite pleased with my utter refusal to accept the fact that he had become such a problem in my life. My disbelief worked to his advantage, so he did nothing to garner any unwanted attention.

Then he got bored.

After Cain amassed a team and an arsenal, he wanted me to know my life was under attack—apparently, incognito isn't any fun. My hunch that I was being followed was confirmed when I began finding notes tucked under the wiper blade on the windshield of my car.

These notes, which seemed innocent in nature but intentionally personal, would read, *You look good in pink* on a day I was wearing pink, or *Why didn't you go to the library today? You always go to the library on Wednesday,* or *Don't forget to brush your teeth.* The notes became a regular occurrence whenever I was out in public. Even though they seemed harmless, I felt strangely violated. I began to dread walking to my car.

Once the notes appeared but didn't elicit the desired response (I read them with a poker face before tossing them on the ground and continuing on with my day; after a while, I stopped reading them at all), Cain turned up the heat a little bit. I became aware I was being followed more often, more blatantly, as we moved through the routines of our day-to-day life, and I began recognizing cars I'd seen in my vicinity too many times to be considered a coincidence.

The drivers were often different, usually wearing a ball cap and dark glasses, but the handful of cars were always the same. I came to know the distinguishing features of each vehicle—a dent, a gash, an off-colored panel, a white Hawaiian lei hanging from the rearview mirror. It didn't take long before I could easily identify these vehicles from a distance as they sat in the back of a parking lot whenever we emerged from the movie theatre, a restaurant, or retail shops. As soon as I would see one, a feeling of nausea would spread through me. I began to dread going places with large parking lots.

I started hiding my eyes behind dark sunglasses so I could get a description of the drivers, pretending to be unaware of the tail in hopes of drawing them closer—I needed license plate information. My strategy worked, allowing me to record plate numbers, descriptions of the drivers, dates, and times, but these multiplying scraps of paper gathered in my glove box without any clear destination since I didn't know anyone who was able to run car tags.

Collecting these useless tidbits of useful information made me feel stupid somehow, like I was holding pieces of a puzzle no one but me was trying to solve. I began to see myself as incompetent—surely a smarter person would have made sense of it all by now.

I'd called the police several times to report a suspicious vehicle following me, but each time I was told that if the person hadn't approached or threatened me, then there was nothing the police could do.

"It's not against the law to be near you in traffic, lady," I was reminded as though I were an imbecile.

I hung up feeling rejected, knowing I sounded like a person who swears Martians are controlling their brain. With each of these police interactions, I began to feel more and more powerless. As I sit writing this, I am well aware that by then, Cain already had my phone bugged. So he would have been privy to the fact that the police were turning me away—no doubt my inability to acquire help added to his delight and his feelings of invincibility.

I mentioned to Emory-James that I felt like I was being followed and that I was receiving a barrage of strange notes and calls, but I think he was no more prepared than I to believe that an average woman of unimpressive means was being stalked like a movie star.

Of course, neither of us knew that over eighty-five percent of all reported stalking victims are ordinary people leading ordinary lives. Your average stalker isn't a delusional fan seeking the attention of someone famous—it's most often a former intimate partner who can't let go. I also reported that I felt Cain was the instigator—it was the only option that made sense—but Emory-James didn't believe Cain would do such a thing, even though he'd never met Cain and had no reason to doubt my suspicions.

Denial is like the common cold—it spreads easily.

I kept mentioning the growing situation to Tandy as well, but it almost became a running joke between us. I told her I thought Cain was behind all of my strange experiences. I can't say for certain whether she believed me or not, but she did her best to dismantle my fears by making light of the situation. After a while, I stopped telling her how uncomfortable I truly felt because I feared it would make me look foolish in her eyes.

Typically, whenever I spoke to anyone regarding my situation, the number-one response I received was "Ignore him." I do believe this advice came from the best part of their sensibilities, because even if what I was suggesting was true, surely Cain—or whoever—was bound to move on if I didn't engage in any way.

I suppose we all failed to realize the level of mental instability needed in order to become a stalker in the first place. And ignoring mental illness never makes it go away.

The more I realized I had a problem, the more I tried to deny it. Sadly, the menacing situation only escalated the more I gave myself permission to do absolutely nothing.

Then came the tails on foot. I began to notice someone following close behind me whenever I was in public for an extended length of time, especially at the library and the grocery store—places where I was most likely to be preoccupied.

The person following me always did a miserable job of trying to blend in. I would offer that even Helen Keller could have spotted them—Waldo, they were not. They always fit the same general description: young men in their late teens or early twenties, wearing blue jeans and a plain white t-shirt, and boasting a stupid grin. The look in their eyes told me they had no more idea why they were following me than I did, giving me the impression they were just happy to be included in some secret club or make a little extra cash.

If I stared at them, indicating their cover was blown, they would immediately busy themselves with whatever item sat closest to them on a nearby shelf, engrossed in the list of ingredients on a box of tampons or laundry detergent. If I directly confronted them, they would laugh with impish delight and casually walk away.

I would feel stupid. You would get embarrassed when you were with me. I began to dread being in public for any length of time.

It was around this time that my relationship with Emory-James began to deteriorate. The stalking incidents were becoming a bombardment, collapsing on top of each other like a pile of fall leaves, forcing me to step out of the denial phase. I was still mystified as to why someone would spend so much time and energy targeting me, but my inability to justify the behavior no longer lessened my fear or the feel of its ever-tightening grip on my life.

I had yet to positively identify the source of my predicament, wondering if Emory-James was actually the culprit. I wasn't yet convinced of Cain's guilt—I suspected it but couldn't prove it. Without proof, I felt I had to consider everyone in my world as a possible suspect. I feared that a rush to judgment could lead me looking in the wrong direction, ignoring clues that shouldn't be ignored. I knew I needed to stay calm and keep an open mind; if I didn't, I would only be creating more ghosts than one mind could handle.

It did strike me as odd that as soon as I accused Cain of sitting outside our pool, the mysterious man vanished, never to be seen again. But you and I had began spending far less time at the pool, so maybe I just hadn't seen him.

Also, I hadn't connected the calls at 10:04 as being a part of my unfolding situation. Had I done so, I would have realized that I hadn't known Emory-James during that period in my life. It wouldn't be until much later that I would remember those series of calls, which began right after I met Cain. One day I would learn Cain's birthday: October 4. When translated to the hours on a clock, his birthday becomes 10:04.

Cain had created his own little DaVinci code, laying out clues as to who was behind the madness, but I failed to see his psychological mindfuck as anything but annoying and meaningless.

By fall 2006, I was suspicious of co-workers, neighbors, friends, and acquaintances. Suddenly, every person in my life was on my radar, and I was analyzing everyone's personality for any signs of defect. Growing more distant and distrustful with each passing day, I began to dread seeing people I knew.

Though none of Cain's tactics seemed overly threatening—and sometimes were even ridiculous—they always carried a feeling of mean-spiritedness, with an ominous undertone as to their true intent. Forever in the back of my mind were the questions: *Where do we go from here? What's the point of all this? What's the end game?*

I couldn't see how things could get much worse because I never once considered that Cain would grow bored with existing only on the outer edges of my life and would soon begin moving inward.

By the beginning of 2007, Tandy and I had decided to move into together. It seemed like the right choice at the time. I'd made it through the holidays without so much as a note, call, or the feeling of being followed. Soon, the whole situation seemed like a bad case of misreading tea leaves. As a result, I was beginning to regain my equilibrium. I reasoned that family and friends had been correct when they said, "Ignore the situation and it will go away."

By now, Emory-James had taken his sweet smile and trotted off into the distance, hurt that I'd accused him of acts of mania. I did find it strange that right after Emory-James and I broke up, the stalking stopped.

It was during this interlude—this time when Emory-James was gone, the stalking was over, and I was feeling more confident—that Cain began texting me again. He reappeared in my life after a long absence with the excuse that he'd been busy at work, and a family emergency had run its course. At this point, I was enthralled with the prospect of you and me moving into our own place. My internal grayness was beginning to dissipate and life was starting to feel yellow again.

It certainly helped that when Cain resurfaced, he seemed much more stable than he had before. He wasn't asking to be lovers, he was hoping we could at least be friends, claiming he missed my humor and my unique way of seeing the world. I suppose with this new version of Cain, I allowed his harsh text after I'd accused him of sitting outside our pool to fade into the fog of yesterday's misunderstandings.

I realize, of course, that only a complete idiot would have begun communicating with Cain again—even a dead baboon would've known better. The only piss-poor excuse I can offer is that I must've been living in the furthest reaches of stupidity at that time in my life. At best, I can say I was so eager to put the whole situation behind me that perhaps I wanted to believe it had been a stranger who had been targeting me rather than someone I knew. At worst, I can say that your mother is dumber than a dead baboon.

I know you have fond memories of the time when we lived in that cute little split-level with Tandy and her two boys. For a while, the situation worked pretty well. I think everyone was happy in our cozy, little house, nestled together like a cut-and-paste family. I remember laughing a lot in that house. I remember feeling alive. I loved my job, you were thriving, and Tandy and I shared babysitting responsibilities and bills. It was a great way for me to step back into life again, and the stalking saga fell further and further from my mind.

Upon reflection, I now realize that my stalking ordeal actually began to get worse once we moved out on our own. I'd never considered that the sudden relief from my strange experiences was due to Cain's secret agenda: He had to regain my trust in order to gain access to the inside of our house.

I suppose our new freedom was exactly the opportunity Cain had been waiting for—two women living alone with no gun, no dog, and no security system must've seemed like Christmas morning to a festering deviant.

Cain and I stayed in touch more regularly than we had before. It became his habit to text me first thing in the morning with a cheerful greeting such as *Good Morning, Sunshine*, or *Go get 'em, Tiger*. Each time I received one of his encouraging messages, I felt a hint of remorse that I'd ever suspected him of such egregious acts against me.

Before long, I felt comfortable enough to begin inviting Cain over to our new place when you were spending the night with family or friends. He rarely stayed the night, only when he was too drunk to drive, and he often preferred to sleep on the couch. We had begun having sex again, but I was no closer to considering him a boyfriend. I'd made it very clear that I didn't have time for a commitment. Even though the new version of Cain was a lot more likeable, he still didn't strike me as The One—only a 'Til Something Better Comes Along.

Months bounced by and Cain and I saw each other occasionally, but we continued the dance of one step forward, two steps back. His biting sarcasm often pissed me off. I was never sure if my "bitchiness" warranted such a remark like he claimed it did, so I would ignore him for long stretches at a time.

Then came early spring, and Emory-James resurfaced in my life. I was ecstatic. I'd felt miserable that our friendship had ended on such a sour note due to the stress in my life. I was excited to know he'd been thinking about me, because I'd been thinking about him, too.

By then, my head felt clearer, I was less distracted, and you were busy with school and friends, so it seemed like the perfect opportunity to reconnect with Emory-James. Adding to my delight, he promised to take me horseback riding, even though he'd never been on a horse in his life. I'd once told him that my idea of a perfect date would be horseback riding followed by a picnic under a tree. His face had fallen when I said this—clearly, my idea of a perfect date was his idea of suffering. His willingness to indulge my wish felt like the equivalent of a hug and a kiss and a Hallmark card.

And so it was that with one phone call from Emory-James, followed by one Saturday afternoon spent on the back of two appaloosas, followed by a deep conversation about God (not under a tree, but close enough—there was a tree outside the restaurant), Cain was reduced to nothing more than a thorn bush in the back of my mind. I wished him well. Then, I deleted his number once again.

Emory-James and I began spending more time together, deepening our connection, making our friendship seem more real. His smile felt safe, his hands were tender, and our conversations were steady and interesting.

Life had returned to groovy. And groovy had returned to life.

I suppose I'll shut down my thoughts for the day. I would love to tell you that Cain respected my right to move on, but of course, we both know that he didn't. And unfortunately, by the time I severed my friendship with Cain in order to rekindle my relationship with Emory-James, Cain's listening devices and hidden cameras were already installed and steadily taking notes. His Olympic mind games were ready to begin.

I'm disgusted with myself for being so careless with our safety. My willingness to believe that Cain wasn't a problem was devastatingly irresponsible. Regret sucks. But regret is merely the stopping point for an experience that doesn't incite meaningful change. As I sit writing these memories, I'm well aware that you and I both learned much in the years that followed. It's a sweet reward, indeed, when you can look back and say that who you were when tragedy struck was only a piece of who you would become.

And the woman you became, you like a whole lot better.

Sending positive energy across the miles and holding you close in thought,

Your Loving Mother

TWELVE

Dear Sparrow,

Another day of scorching heat. The air outside is too oppressive to work in the garden or finish fixing the fence. It feels like Mother Nature knitted a humidity sweater and draped it across the shoulders of the South. It's hard to get motivated to do much of anything when you're sweating in the sauna of a Southern heat wave—it creates a perfect day for writing, though.

I'm sitting in my room with my ceiling fan on high and my A/C set low. I've pulled my hair into a bun, changed into a loose-fitting sundress, and fixed myself a glass of ice-cold water with sprigs of rosemary, lemon balm, and chunks of cucumber and ginger floating at the bottom. I'm caressing a laborite stone in one hand, and my crystals are busy sending a cleansing energy into the air. I feel languid and reposed, ready to dig deeper into my journey.

My memories take me back to early 2007, before things took a darker turn, before I came to experience the scarier side of strange. During that time, spring was blissful and romantic. Even Mondays felt lovely. As you know, spring has always been my favorite time of the year. I find endless delight in the sweetness of the air, the laughter of trees, and the frolicking sensation of well-rested sunshine catching a ride on the wind.

During the season of rebirth, Mother Nature shakes off her winter blahs and dresses in her Sunday finest. I suppose the earth is willing to suffer the indignities of winter, knowing that when springtime comes, the color and scent of her cheerful wardrobe will inspire us once again.

For me, a Saturday in springtime spent baking or painting, or with my hands working the soil, with windows open, sheets on the clothesline, and a simple dinner of grilled vegetables and homemade bread is an extravagance more inviting than eating tiramisu from a Ming Dynasty teacup. It is the essence of internal well-being that all other experiences are measured against—the mulberry silk balancing out the wool of life.

I can almost reach out and touch the feeling of satisfaction I remember from that long-ago spring when I was feeling more complete than I had in years. I can still hear the sounds of The Wallflowers, Van Morrison, and Melissa Etheridge filling the house with music, adding the secret ingredient to my zucchini muffins and lightness to my step.

I remember that spring as being a time of transformation. Not only was I feeling better, but I looked better than I had in years. My skin was finally beginning to clear, my body was fit and toned from regular exercise, and I'd amassed a wardrobe that would make any fashionista feel as though we were kindred spirits. I still didn't see myself as beautiful, but I often liked the reflection I saw in the mirror. This feeling of acceptance regarding my appearance was the boost I needed to usher in a greater sense of self-confidence. I seemed to stand a little taller, breathe a little easier, and find more satisfaction in the shape of our future.

During this time, I began to take my relationship with Emory-James more seriously. By then, I'd met his two young children, and I'd finally allowed him to meet you. Bringing Emory-James into our orbit was a big moment because he was the first man I'd ever officially dated since leaving your father. I'd always imagined that introducing you to an important man in my life would feel like Beethoven's Piano Concerto No. 5—intense, powerful, with carefully orchestrated crescendos.

But it wasn't. Emory-James walked through the door with an expectant smile, hoping to engage you in some gentle conversation. You waved a bored hello as if he were nothing more than a frog on a fence post, passed by him like he was contagious, then headed out the door on your way to something more interesting.

So much for a scrapbook-worthy kind of moment.

After you left, I apologized to him. "I'm sorry you're so dull and unimpressive, E.J. You really need to work on that."

I can't say whether or not Emory-James saw our relationship as the start of something big because we never felt the need to clearly state our objectives. Perhaps he sensed that I was still hesitant to embrace the word *boyfriend*. Lord, how I hate that word—it's so dumb. I enjoyed spending time with Emory-James label-free. He seemed to feel the same.

But falling in love makes you do weird shit, like cleaning out your car even though you've never been one to keep a clean car before. One Saturday afternoon, I decided to spend the day whipping our car back into shape. I began sorting through all the jackets, socks, homework with shoeprints on it, and fast-food wrappers that were gathering in the backseat as if our car were a rolling junk drawer.

While vacuuming in between the seat cushions, I sucked up a piece of paper that then lodged itself in the hose. It was an old receipt from a bank deposit. There wasn't a name on the receipt, but I knew it wasn't mine due to the sizeable balance printed at the bottom. Then I remembered the time I'd given a teacher at my school a ride to the bank when her car was in the shop. Apparently, she'd accidently left her receipt behind, and since I never cleaned my car, I'd never noticed it before. So there it had sat among the discarded debris for almost two years.

I was surprised to see she had well over $40,000 in her account—not bad for an elementary school teacher. I stuffed the receipt in my purse and returned it to her the next time I saw her.

My co-worker's bank receipt was meaningless to me, but it would prove to have been very meaningful to Cain. One day I would learn that the night I'd met Cain and he'd secretly followed me home, he'd found the discarded bank receipt when he'd searched my car for information, and he assumed it was mine—the dumbass thought I had money.

I can't begin to say how much the prospect that I had $40,000 lying around motivated Cain's interest in me, but let's go a little crazy and assume it was a helluva lot. Of course, at the time I had no reason to believe Cain's secret fascination was due, in large part, to the idea that he thought he'd found a cash cow. The nice condo we lived in probably confirmed his assumption, especially since I'd never told him we lived with your grandfather.

The deposit receipt helped answer the *why* question, but it failed to answer why Cain kept on pursuing me even after he discovered that I often raided our coin jar just to buy gas.

My season of transformation didn't last. Before school let out for the summer, the weirdness had started again. I began sensing a follow and started receiving disturbing phone calls. These calls were considerably darker than they had been before. A stranger would ask if I'd douched that day or if I was on my period, then they'd burst out laughing. Sometimes the person on the other end of the phone was obviously masturbating. I would quickly hang up, feeling grossed out inside.

I changed my number. When the calls started up again, I changed my number again.

Just like before, these random incidents were troublesome but didn't fall into the category of threatening in my mind. I did my best to ignore the situation, pretending it wasn't a problem. Denial phase: take two. Unfortunately, my attempt to pretend nothing was wrong only encouraged Cain to become more obnoxious without ever quite crossing the line between weird and criminal.

One evening, after a night out with Tandy, I stepped out back to enjoy the quiet and sit among the stars. If you remember correctly, the back patio was my happy place, trimmed in flowers and tall grasses in colorful pots making the outdoor space seem more like a spot for a tropical siesta than just a slab of concrete under a weather-beaten awning. Since Tandy and her sons hated bugs and flies and you weren't much into space designed for quiet relaxation, the back patio had become my little nest in a house of constant noise.

When I stepped outside that evening, I was surprised to discover that all of the flower pots had been rearranged. Though the sight was certainly baffling, I figured it must've been the work of an adolescent prankster in our neighborhood looking for an innocent thrill. I returned all the pots to their proper place, letting the event slip from my mind.

One evening shortly afterward, I came home to find a Heineken beer bottle sitting on our picnic table. The beer was almost gone, and when I picked it up to throw it away, I realized the bottle was still cold. This alarmed me—whoever had sat on our back patio drinking a beer had only recently left. Our house was empty that night, so there was no reasonable excuse for the still-cold beer bottle to be on the patio table. A chill ran through me. Even though the presence of the bottle unnerved me, it was the sensation that someone was nearby watching that made me feel uneasy—the hair on the back of my neck felt charged. I did my best to reassure myself that I was overreacting, yet I hurried up my pace into the house, locking the deadbolt behind me.

It came to be a regular occurrence that items on our back patio were moved around, or partially eaten food was left on the table as if an uninvited guest had sat enjoying a midnight snack. I mentioned the incidents to Tandy; she claimed to have no knowledge and seemed to think the whole situation was kind of humorous, unconcerned at the prospect of a nightly visitor so close to our back door. It became my habit to survey the patio each morning. I stopped seeing it as my private retreat, no longer feeling like it was my safe zone.

As I think back, I realize my happy, little world was beginning to disintegrate. Notes on my car now read, *Do something about that zit on your chin. You're disgusting,* or *No make-up isn't a good look for you.* The volume of strange calls, the sense of being monitored, and the nightly visitor to our back porch were beginning to take its toll on me. I was doing my best to deny that I had a problem, but the effects of Cain's campaign began to manifest themselves in ways I seemed powerless to control.

I was becoming nervous. I began to have difficulty sleeping, I had trouble concentrating and staying on task, and I became uncomfortable whenever a stranger looked at me for longer than just a quick glance.

Understandably, my relationship with Tandy began to sour. I had to consider the possibility that she was somehow involved. Once again, I began to analyze everyone in my life for any sign of moral bankruptcy. I began to crave solitude like never before, which made our living arrangements feel like a pillow over my face.

I guess because of all these factors, I began doing what over-whelmed people often do: I began drinking too much. I was having a glass of wine or two almost every evening when I came home from work. My inability to cope with the expanding stress often left me feeling irritated and moody, so I reached for calm in a bottle. When I wanted more calm, I opened another bottle.

Finally, Tandy decided to move out. I was relieved. I think you were, too—the vibe in the house had become strained. I knew I couldn't afford the bills on my own, but for the time being, her absence opened up some space, leaving us more room to breathe.

I suppose I would've always wished Tandy well if it hadn't been for a late-night text from Cain. One evening shortly after Tandy had moved out, Cain texted me unexpectedly. I hadn't heard from him in several months and had no idea how he'd gotten my new number. His text read, "LOL. When I was fucking Tandy, she said no one likes you at work anymore. You lose."

I stared at my phone in amazement—there were so many layers of juvenile weirdness in his words, I didn't know which to address first. *Cain is sleeping with Tandy? They discuss me while they're having sex? She gave him my number?*

The comment "You lose" was lost in the overall ickiness of his message. I failed to realize that those two words were an important glimpse into Cain's internal world, revealing that his one-sided game of war centered around the concept of winning vs. losing.

I would later learn that after I had begun dating Emory-James, Tandy had begun a secret relationship with Cain. It turns out that the easiest way to gain access into a person's private space doesn't require gadgets or brilliance. All you have to do is sleep with someone's room-mate—it's such a shame that unevolved people do this so naturally.

I never felt the need to confront Tandy. This might be difficult for you to believe, but I actually felt sorry for her—she had carelessly stepped into a dragon's lair. Even though I wasn't certain that Cain was the source of my troubles, I instinctively felt that he was using her for his own benefit. His text alone told me that he wanted to incite jealousy rather than protect their secret. I felt like no amount of hostility I could throw at Tandy would ever be more damaging than the weight of her own foolishness.

I would later learn that not only had Tandy kept Cain updated as to my personal business and my new phone numbers, but she also had given him a key to our house.

Karma wasn't impressed. Soon, Tandy began reporting to co-workers that she suspected she had a stalker, even alleging that someone had broken into her apartment and stolen money and valuables. The sad lesson here is this: When Tandy gave away the privacy and safety of our home, she compromised her own.

A betrayal given is always a betrayal suffered.

Let's talk about betrayal. Betrayal isn't a pain you ever need to handle on your own—let the universe do it for you. It will, because one of the Universal Truths is that whatever we send out, comes back to us. I encourage you to keep your hands clean and your conscience clear, otherwise you will be wallowing in the same mud puddle as the one who straddles knives—their fate will become your own. If you make the conscious choice to rise above the hurt and anger, you will discover that those who made the choice to betray you, in reality, only betrayed themselves.

By summer 2007, my world began to change drastically. The stalking experience was beginning to take center stage in my life and I was mentally collapsing from the constant pressure.

The feeling of being followed had started out as a sometimes on the weekends, then moved to an often throughout the week, but by now, it was the anvil of always. I vacillated between thinking I was overly paranoid to being extremely confident that someone had made it their mission to deny me any freedom or privacy. I often prayed I was just being paranoid—crazy felt safer than the unknown. I did my best to communicate to loved ones what was going on in my life, but I never seemed to be able to articulate my concerns convincingly enough, rattling on about cars, notes, and half-eaten sandwiches. I knew I sounded absurd and delusional.

Normal people can't wrap their head around the tales of the bizarre. That's the beauty of normal people—they can't think like monsters because they aren't monsters. Since I couldn't wrap my head around any of it either, I'm certain I did a pathetic job of trying to make mentally stable people understand that what was happening to me was real. I knew a person would have to live through the ordeal on a daily basis in order to understand how debilitating the bombardment really was.

Understanding requires connective tissue, a similar experience that allows someone to relate to our problems. I've heard stalking compared to a prolonged rape—I've never heard a better way to describe its effects on the mind. But such a grave experience is hard to describe and even harder to understand.

Unfortunately, whether people believed me or not, the stalking continued.

The impression made quite an impression—things that speak of boogeymen usually do.

The morning I found a man's face print left behind on the glass on the kitchen door was unsettling to say the least. I stared at it like it was an unexpected plot twist in a B-rated horror film.

The image perfectly captured the outline of the side of a man's head, especially the ear, clearly pressed firmly against the glass.

I could tell two things from the impression: The person was tall, and, judging by the oil swirls on the lower part of the print, he wore facial hair.

I backed away from the door, unable to take my eyes off the window, wanting to place a safe distance between myself and the startling image. The truth was staring me right in the face—someone had stood outside our kitchen door eavesdropping in the dark. My list of potential suspects was pretty short, including no one but Cain. It was either Cain or someone I didn't know. Emory-James was excluded because, due to his job, he never wore facial hair.

Regardless of who left the impression, the image had a profound effect on me. A wave of nausea spread through me as all of my unwanted suspicions came tumbling forward in my mind—the sense of being followed, the creepy calls, the flower pots, the beer bottle, the food and pocketknife left on the back porch, the face print of someone listening at our door.

This deluge of information was the first time that the sequence of events happening in my life came together to form a more cohesive shape. I swallowed hard. My senses felt battered. I knew this wasn't just childish pranks at an arm's reach anymore, this wasn't just random acts of weirdness—this was something wicked standing right outside our door.

Weird is easy to dismiss when it happens on the outer edges of your life. A strange note or call, a person trailing you in traffic or sitting at the back of a parking lot is certainly odd, but it hasn't invaded your safe zone, so it's easy to pretend it can't hurt you.

The nightly visitor to our back porch was a sign the situation had moved closer to the interior spaces of our life, but a beer bottle, scraps of food, a cheap pocketknife, or a toothpick don't foreshadow acts of violence. They're weird, but they don't scream like a threatening crime.

However, when someone else's crazy listens at your door in the dark, their behavior doesn't seem so harmless anymore. The image on the kitchen door was the first time I forced myself to confront my sickening reality—our little piece of the world was under attack by a loon-tard who chose to remain anonymous.

After the initial shock wore off, I called the police. An officer arrived, dusted for prints, and made a report. He was steadied by the fact that the person didn't attempt to gain entry.

"Probably a nosey neighbor," he announced, packing up his feather duster, roll of tape, and container of black dust.

I was relieved to hear his assessment, wanting nothing more than to be lulled back into the denial phase, but I couldn't escape the uneasy feeling that all of my strange experiences led me to one sickening conclusion: Whoever was targeting me was getting ever closer to inside our house.

After I made my first official report with the police, the stalking escalated significantly. I began calling the police each time weird made another appearance in our lives.

I called the time I found an unknown car parked in our driveway in the middle of the night, when Emory-James had his tires slashed, each time I found fresh footprints in the dirt just outside my bedroom window. I called when I found the lock on our shed had been cut and when someone had rummaged through my car overnight. I called when, for several nights running, someone would park on the street in front of our house blaring the song, "You Got it Bad," by Usher.

I called and called and called. No matter how trivial or insignificant the event appeared to be, I called, hoping the volume of incidents would be proof of a wider scheme.

My plan didn't work because it was never the same officer responding to my complaint. This made each incident look innocent, unrelated, a waste of everyone's time. I began to feel as though law enforcement viewed me as fragile or a conspiracy theorist with too much time on my hands. I began to realize that making endless police reports wasn't getting me anywhere.

Emory-James slowly drifted from my life. I was becoming increasingly withdrawn and apprehensive, making up lame excuses as to why I couldn't make time for him. I couldn't rule out the possibility that he was involved because I still hadn't proven that Cain was the undisputed source of my anguish. Many nights I lay in bed thinking it had to be Emory-James, or someone Tandy knew, or a neighbor or co-worker I would never suspect. Cain had certainly shown his ass, but that wasn't proof he was targeting me. Maybe I was just an asshole magnet—it happens.

I was still hesitant to use the word *stalking* to describe my problem because it conjured up frightening images and made-for-TV endings. I wasn't eager to view my circumstances in that light, convinced there had to be a more reasonable explanation for everything happening around me.

As I look back on this time in our lives, I realize this phase marks the beginning of when Cain began using the tactic known as *gaslight manipulation* to confuse me. I'd never heard this term before, so I was unaware that Cain's approach to mind control fell into a specific genre.

Gaslight manipulation is a sophisticated form of psychological terrorism. It earns its name from the 1940s movie, *Gaslight*, in which a husband slightly dims the gaslights in their home each day, persuading his wife to believe the growing darkness is only in her imagination. Gaslight manipulation is an extremely effective form of control over a targeted individual—its sustained application is so subtle that it forces a victim to question their own sanity. The victim begins to erase memories, altering their perceptions because their reality feels distorted and they're no longer able to trust their own judgment.

Gaslight manipulation is often called the con game of sociopaths.

I must admit—though it pisses me off to do so—Cain could evil remarkably well. I had no idea I was being groomed to go crazy, but it didn't take long before I began to delegitimize my experiences, especially since the police seemed unconvinced that my experiences spoke of a covert plot against me.

Gaslight manipulation is effective on two fronts: Not only does it impact the targeted individual, it impacts the individual's support system as well because crazy people make shitty advocates. It's easy to dismiss the gibberish of someone who appears off their rocker or just craving attention. Complete isolation is always the predator's goal, so a little bit of crazy goes a long way.

Quiet chaos is a powerful sedative. And obsession can seem harmless to those who know the nature of obsession only through a deep appreciation for chocolate, sports, shoes, or pumpkin spice lattes. But true obsession is spun at the gates of places most of us have never been before.

Distress is the only door open to the one who walks the path alone.

Distress is viewed as a job well done to the one who is obsessed.

This is the point in my story where I tend to say "if only" a lot.

If only I'd listened to my instincts.

If only I'd cared less about the *why* and more about the *how*.

If only I'd had the foresight to demand help no matter how many chains I had to rattle.

It's amazing how quickly a problem can spin out of control. Regret becomes a chokehold when you realize that all is not well and the time of effective resistance has passed.

The land of If Only is such a depressing place that I do my best to never visit it. Though it's true that darkness was gathering steam and assholes were feeling scrumptious, I'm reminded that light was never unaware—even though light appeared so indifferent at the time.

But karma kept a watchful eye, ensuring that the putrid potion Cain served to me, he would one day drink himself.

Sending positive energy across the miles and holding you close in thought,

Your Loving Mother

THIRTEEN

Dear Sparrow,

I'm stuck inside again today. Another perfect day for writing. I'm admiring the bowl of watermelon slices sitting on the table next to me, encouraging me to enjoy a slice.

After I finished my last letter, I set down my pen and leaned back into my chair. I let the emotions come. I always thought when I got to this point my story I would stew or suffer, remembering these haunting pieces of my past. But that's not how I felt at all.

I felt relieved.

It's funny how some memories can feel heavier than debt sometimes.

I sat for a while, holding the stone of tourmaline between my hands, staring at the cross on my wall. I waited for tears or screams or curse words thrown into the air like confetti shot from a cannon.

When the anger didn't come, I went into the kitchen and fixed myself an ice cream sundae for dinner. I slept very well.

Before I step deeper into my story, before the darkness turns black, I'd like to take this opportunity to shed some more light on the nature of stalking in general. A platform of understanding helps dispel myths, stereotypes, and preconceived notions about the nature of hunting humans.

During the beginning phases of my stalking experience, there was little to no information available—no roadmaps to follow, no established protocol, no laws with any bite, and virtually no resources to help a victim better understand the complexities of their situation. In the years since, more information has become available, more cases have made headlines, and women of strength have stepped out of the shadows, sharing their stories of madness and fear, illuminating the tenacious will of the survivor.

As they say, knowledge is powerful. Being able to dissect the mind of a stalker and hear the voices of those who've walked through the gallows allowed me to better understand that my experiences were normal compared to the experiences of other stalking victims. When you've been through hell, knowing your feelings are normal is like getting a gold star from heaven—it's not a star you want to earn, but need to earn if you hope to overcome the shame every stalking victim feels.

A textbook stalker usually begins with harmless pranks before changing his tactics for the sole purpose of inducing fear—because a person is easier to control when they're afraid. This change in behavior moves the stalker from the realm of lovesick and curious into a full-blown nut case. The transition usually takes place once the stalker feels rejected. I will quote directly from the FBI Center for Crime Analysis website, which states: "The reason stalkers are so dangerous is because they stalk out of anger, hurt, and revenge."

The stalking behavior intensifies after the victim begins dating someone else. In the stalker's mind, he feels as though his victim has left him in the dust on her merry road of life. He becomes more aggressive in an attempt to reinstate his level of control. During this phase, property is often damaged, pets may be killed, and the stalker usually begins a smear campaign. All too often, the stalker begins targeting the victim's support system as well—his contempt for his victim carries over into every aspect of her life. Everyone she spends time with is now considered the enemy.

Stalking is big-game hunting, requiring rigorous attention to detail. If the victim closes down avenues of contact, the stalker spends an exorbitant amount of time and money devising new schemes to re-establish access to his victim.

His sole focus is to win back her attention. He believes his unrequited love is merely an obstacle he must overcome, often viewing her as his one, true soul mate. The victim has become the nucleus of his identity—all thoughts he has for the future center around her. He slips further and further into a state of delusional fantasy.

His mind is lost in a world where only his victim exists.

By summer 2007, I was fairly certain that someone was entering our house while we were gone. As usual, it began as just an uneasy feeling, a tingling sensation when I first walked through the door, warning me that someone had recently left. The secret visitor unknowingly left their energy behind—it felt stormy. Violent. It didn't take long before I hated leaving the house almost as much as I hated coming home. Nothing was ever missing, yet the inkling that someone had access to our home was never far from my mind. I couldn't explain it, but I couldn't escape it, either.

My hunches tend to attract confirmation like ephedrine attracts meth heads—it didn't take long before my suspicions were confirmed. One day I returned home to find all the fruit in our fruit basket neatly lined up in a row like an edible choo choo train sitting on our kitchen island.

I knew you hadn't done it—you were at school and couldn't drive. I stared at the fruit in disbelief, a chill running through me. The air in my lungs escaped in a long, deep sigh.

I don't know how long I stood staring at the fruit, but as I did so, I felt a growing sense of despair. The image was so innocent, yet so overwhelming. Ever since my stalking experience began, I suppose I kept telling myself that as long as the inside of our home was safe, I could somehow manage whatever nonsense came at me in the outside world. To see the fruit lined up on the counter like a weirdo's calling card was a heart-stopping bending of my reality. I felt tremendously powerless.

One day I would learn that this subtle mind trick came straight from the playbook of gaslight manipulation. It's typical for a stalker to leave clues that quietly scream, "I was here." But I didn't know this information back then. I only knew that someone was doing their best to frighten me very, very strangely.

Even though the fruit made a statement, I suspected it would mean nothing to the police. I called them anyway. I didn't mention the fruit, only that I felt someone was entering our home, but since no valuables were missing, they wouldn't even take a report. Instead, they offered to have a cruiser drive around the area and to increase patrol on our street. It didn't feel much like the kind of help I really needed, but it was better than nothing.

Coming home to find items rearranged inside our house became my new norm: a candle from the living room sitting on top of our refrigerator, a box of tampons next to the cat's water bowl, a jar of mustard sitting on the shelf on the back of the toilet. Each time I walked through the door, I searched the house for any signs of an intruder as if I were on a demented Easter egg hunt. On the days I didn't find anything amiss, I tried to pretend the crisis had passed.

Sleep became impossible. I was waking up many times throughout the night, rechecking windows and doors in order to reassure myself they were locked. I began taking a mental inventory of everything, counting things incessantly so I would know if something had been moved: one pear, four apples, and three bananas in the fruit bowl; five magazines on the coffee table; seven rolls of toilet paper under the sink. Each time I awoke to patrol the house, I counted these items again.

The numbness returned. I stopped feeling anything. I let my emotions take a sabbatical to the back of my mind in an attempt to stay calm, to remain anchored to something more than fear, trying to maintain my composure so you wouldn't notice the cracks in my façade. This strategy worked until it didn't, but while it worked, it allowed me to better communicate to family and friends that something was very wrong in my life.

Your grandparents tried their best to help, even though I'm not sure they believed me—I think they would've done anything to give me some peace of mind. Your grandfather paid to have the locks on our doors changed and installed those bright spotlights that lit up our house like Caesars Palace in Las Vegas. This added measure of security definitely helped me get more sleep, but I was unaware of how expensive it is to run four spotlights all night long. My next electric bill was so high I couldn't afford to pay it. Yet, I simply couldn't bear the thought of having our house lit by a meager 100-watt bulb.

I realized that my decision to continue using the spotlights was an error in judgment when I couldn't keep to my payment arrangements and our electricity was shut off. Late that very evening, under the darkness of a new moon, there came a loud knocking at the front door and the kitchen door at the very same time, creating a tsunami of startling noise. Springing up from bed, I wasn't sure where to focus my attention. I was frightened. I grabbed a flashlight, reassured you that the banging was just neighborhood teenagers and sent you back to bed. Then I grabbed a butcher knife and called the police.

They came, took a look around, but didn't find anything. As soon as they left, the knocking started again. I didn't sleep a wink that night. I sat on the stairs with the knife in my hands guarding your bedroom like a soldier guarding a flag.

Your grandmother graciously paid our electric bill and offered to help further by purchasing two devices that addressed my two main areas of concern:

1. How is someone privy to so much private information?

2. How do they always know where I am?

We did some online research, quickly discovering that at that time in the internet's history, there were many websites showcasing the newest devices available for the purpose of covert spying, but very few websites offered real solutions for combatting these devices. We were out of our element navigating this new frontier of spyware and electronic surveillance—it was a crash course in creepy. We did our best to select two devices we hoped would put an end to my nightmare: one designed to detect hidden listening devices, and one designed to scramble a GPS signal.

The gadgets arrived in a plain, brown envelope a few weeks later, housed inside a simple, black box with no instructions. I stared at the two contraptions as if they were orbs from space—this was about as high-tech as my family had ever been. I remember feeling empowered, only one click away from freedom and a good night's sleep.

My sense of relief was short lived because neither contraption worked. The device designed to detect a bug beeped incessantly no matter where I was. I didn't interpret this to mean that we had dozens of listening devices in our home, car, and my private office at work. Instead, I suspected the chronic chirping was a sure sign I didn't know how to operate the silly thing.

I know now that I should have unplugged all electrical devices before scanning for a listening device, but I didn't know that then and I didn't know anyone I could ask. Before long, the little device the size of a cigarette lighter was more maddening than it was helpful. I remember the dumb thing going berserk one time while I was using the bathroom at McDonald's. I removed the batteries, shoved the gadget in my make-up case, and ordered a large fry and a Coke like a woman who was trying her best not to lose her mind.

The device designed to jam a tracking device didn't go as planned either. I would soon learn from a detective at the Columbus Police Department that there were two ways of tracking someone: The more sophisticated, expensive option relied on satellite technology and gave real-time information; the less expensive option allowed you to track the exact movements of a vehicle *after* you downloaded the information onto your computer. Using the cheaper tracking device, you could tell everywhere a person went in a day, but it was always past-tense information.

We had unknowingly purchased a device designed to scramble a signal emitted from the less sophisticated form of tracking device. Apparently, Cain had taken the plunge and invested in the more expensive form of GPS, making the simple contraption plugged into our car's cigarette lighter about as useful as a one-legged donkey.

Suffice it to say, we tried. And the feeling of trying helped restore a sense of hope within me. In the end, our attempts to combat Cain's disturbing use of technology was akin to the Brady Bunch trying to match wits with James Bond.

And sadly, there was nothing I could do about it.

Then came the smear campaign. Each time the nature of my experiences escalated, I tried to reassure myself that things couldn't get any worse, failing to realize that things actually could get worse.

And they did.

Cain began spreading rumors to neighbors and co-workers that I was a drunk, a slut, and a liar. He even told people I was suicidal. I wasn't aware he'd begun a smear campaign, but I did notice that people began treating me differently. It seemed like their eyes held either disgust or pity, yet I couldn't figure out why, trying to reassure myself that a lack of sleep makes a person overly sensitive.

Until the day Tuck went missing and I found myself wandering into a neighbor's yard, finding not our cat, but a pathetic truth instead.

While I was searching through a neighbor's bushes, an elderly woman who must've been well into her eighties came out of her house and greeted me like I was an old friend. Her greeting was so warm and sincere, I thought she must've mistaken me for someone else. I apologized for being on her property, explaining that I was only trying to find my missing cat.

"Are you feeling better, dear?" she asked, with a look of genuine concern.

Her question caught me off guard, as did her expression, since I'd never seen her before. "Excuse me, ma'am?" I said, not sure I'd heard her correctly.

"Your ex-husband said you weren't feeling well. He asked if I would mind keeping an eye on you," she said with a look of tenderness in her eyes.

"My ex-husband asked you to keep an eye on me?"

"Yes, he was such a nice man."

I was dumbfounded. *What in the hell is she talking about?*

"Ma'am I think you must be mistaken. I live down the street in the yellow house."

"Yes, I know, dear. You drive the silver car. Your daughter gets off the bus at 3:45," she correctly informed me.

Baffled and unsure what to say, I asked her to describe my ex-husband. She proceeded to describe Cain right down to the make and model of his car.

"I'm feeling fine, ma'am. That man shouldn't have troubled you. He isn't my ex-husband," I replied, trying to hide my disgust for Cain.

A look of confusion spread across her face. She paused for a moment, looking bewildered and embarrassed. "Oh," she said quietly, then she walked back into her house and closed the door.

This incident was the first time anyone had ever positively identified Cain as the instigator of the madness. It also marked the first time I became aware that Cain had thrown a dragnet around the perimeter of my life, gathering information and spreading lies.

I would learn that it wasn't unusual for Cain to pass himself off as my boyfriend, my boss, a neighbor, my pastor, and a bill collector (he actually was a bill collector, but not my bill collector). Sometimes he sweetened the deal by offering cash or favors to elicit information. One co-worker later told me that Cain offered him new rims for his car if he agreed to send pictures of me while I was working. Cain would repeat this practice many times in the years that followed. No matter where I worked or where we lived, Cain would find a way to befriend someone near me, fabricating a story designed to pique their interest, thereby adding another player in his expanding surveillance team.

Knowing what you need to know is cosmically important, but sometimes, knowing can feel pretty heavy. And frustrating. Once I knew for sure that Cain was the madman and his tentacles were every-where, it came to feel like my entire life had been invaded, heightening my distrust of everyone around me.

The confirmation of who was targeting me certainly helped focus my attention, finally putting a face on my phantom. But sadly, knowing the name of your enemy doesn't make them go away. Sometimes, it just makes them scream louder.

Blessings can be such a curious gift. It's the very nature of blessings to show up when you least expect them, but right when you need them the most. It was quite unexpected when your father and Astrid invited you to spend the summer with them in Ocean Springs, Mississippi. The two-year anniversary of Hurricane Katrina was fast approaching and much progress had been made in restoring the Mississippi coast-line to its former state of "y'all come back now, ya hear."

Your father and Astrid had done a fine job rebuilding their home and their lives. They very much wanted you to see their progress, hop-ing to reassure you that Katrina hadn't been the end to anything—it was the perfect opportunity for a new beginning. The entire coastline was revitalized with energy and vision, fellowship had become a living thing. If darkness thought it had won when it leveled the coastal com-munities of the Deep South, then darkness grossly underestimated the sincerity of Southern conviction.

I had mixed feelings about sending you to your father for the summer. A pain seized my chest at the very thought of it—the memories of Katrina were still too fresh in my mind. Yet, I was aware that statistically speaking, the chances of another great hurricane happening right on the heels of the last one were very, very slim. And I liked the idea of you taking part in the healing process.

So you and I talked about it. I carefully explained that you would be trading in a summer of sleepovers and afternoons at the pool for a summer spent painting rooms, scrubbing decks, and replanting gardens. Without hesitation, you wanted to go. I was proud to hear you say you wanted to help. Even at the tender age of twelve, you were already a spirit reaching toward the greater good, not as if it were a burden, but a chance to be involved.

And so it was that once again, you flew into the heart of Dixie. I was anxious, of course. I monitored weather patterns closer than a meteorologist. At the first mention of swirling winds, I was planning to head down to get you.

But in the meantime, your absence gave me a chance to fully concentrate on the task at hand: eradicating the termite doing its best to devour my life. Working full time and being a single parent never allowed me to immerse myself in problem-solving—maybe this was the chance I'd been hoping for.

Shortly after you left, however, things took a darker turn. At the time, I didn't view the increased intensity as a blessing at all, but blessings come in all shapes and sizes. Before you can rid your house of varmints, first you must identify the problem. And until you see the magnitude of a problem, you can't properly assess and prioritize. I had been under the impression that I just needed the whole damn situation to stop. And I did. But first, I needed to see the whole damn situation for the movement it really was.

Emory-James once told me that he was a lone-wolf kind of guy—he had many acquaintances, but few people he considered friends. I could relate. As you already know, I usually have one or two close friends, but I've never run with a clique or gang of friends—it just isn't my style. During our conversation about friendship, Emory-James casually said, "Bitches run in packs."

I didn't place much importance on that comment at the time, but his words would later bear significance, helping explain why I felt like I was being corralled from all sides—Cain's bitches were everywhere. Once our elderly neighbor positively identified Cain, and I was living alone for the summer, Cain's goonies descended on me like a swarm of flies. Cain himself didn't make an appearance anymore, now that he knew I had a tendency to call the police, but he did have the right number of batshit crazy friends who didn't seem to care.

Whenever I was out in public, I would be greeted by a stranger saying, "Good morning, Mrs. Cook," or "You look nice today, Mrs. Cook," or "Can I wash your car, Mrs. Cook?" Gone were the days of fresh-faced teenagers trying to blend into my surroundings. Now the strangers calling me Mrs. Cook were grown men with greasy smiles and jailhouse tattoos. Sometimes, a creepy stranger would walk right up to me and say bizarre things like, "I like women with blonde hair," or "Your feet look good in those shoes."

Their comments were never threatening, never enough to warrant a call for help. I knew I'd sound crazy if I even tried. Who listens to a woman shrieking about a stranger telling her he likes her shoes? Yet, the sheer size and frequency of the movement felt surreal and overwhelming.

It became the summer of Kafkaesque. *Webster's Dictionary* defines Kafkaesque as such: "having a nightmarishly complex, bizarre, or illogical quality." For years, I tried to find a word that best fit my stalking experience, one that summarized it well enough that no other descriptions were needed. When I stumbled upon the word *Kafkaesque*, I knew I'd hit the jackpot.

The notes left on my car now read, "I'm watching you" and "I hate cats." The disturbing calls increased, I was referred to as Mrs. Cook whenever I was in public, familiar cars were often parked on the street just outside our house during the wee hours of the morning, used condoms were left on our back patio, and there was often repeated knocking on our doors throughout the night.

While Kafkaesque was doing its grandest tango, panic began to seize my mind.

I reached out to Emory-James, asking if he would come stay with me for a while. He willingly complied, but suffered in his attempt to restore order. During the week he stayed with me, his tires were slashed (again), sugar was poured in his fuel pump, and one of his passenger windows was smashed. Adding to this, someone had called his job claiming that he was selling drugs at work. Thankfully, anyone who knew Emory-James knew these accusations were false.

His boss issued him a fatherly warning: "Watch out, son. Somebody has it out for you."

Obviously, I felt horrible and tremendously embarrassed. I felt it was irresponsible of me to bring an innocent person into my mess.

This incident marks the beginning of when I started to feel guilty for asking for help from those I loved, fearing the repercussions. I stopped talking about my experiences with friends and family. My world grew more isolated.

The darkness continued to spread.

It was the coffeepot that changed everything.

I once saw a bumper sticker that read: "Beer. Because a good story never begins with a salad." I'd laughed out loud when I read it. I think of this bumper sticker now because I doubt a coffeepot ever marked a turning point in a person's life before, but it certainly did in mine.

One morning I headed into the kitchen to brew a pot of coffee like I'd done a thousand times before. As you know, we coffee drinkers take our morning ritual very seriously. With the mist of sleep still in my eyes, I walked over to my trusty Mr. Coffee machine, but the coffeepot was gone.

I looked around the kitchen—it was nowhere to be found. To make sure I wasn't hallucinating, I opened the curtains in the kitchen to let in more light, then headed into the living room to do the same. That's when I saw the coffeepot sitting in the middle of the couch.

I froze.

Cain had entered our house while I slept. And he wanted me to know it.

I don't know how long I stood staring at the coffeepot. It seemed like a very long time. A thousand different thoughts ran through my head, each of them equaling fear. The coffeepot may have been just a simple appliance, but to me, it felt like a bomb.

I knew calling the police to report a coffeepot on my couch was the call of a crazy cat lady reporting her house slippers had been moved. The seemingly inoffensive placement of a coffeepot on a couch was paralyzingly Kafkaesque, holding no meaning for anyone but me.

In hindsight, I believe something shifted inside my brain as I stood in the middle of our living room, still wrapped in a bathrobe, staring at a coffeepot as if it could hurt me. Fear came to have a place among my thoughts.

I had no idea how long Cain had been entering our house at night undetected, but I seriously doubted he'd left his calling card the first time.

The moment felt delirious, its implications painfully real. *What happens next?* I asked myself. *How much worse can this get? What if Sparrow is home the next time he sneaks in at night?* The blood drained from my head. A fist formed in my stomach. I couldn't take the madness any-more—he was getting ever closer to you.

After the incident with the coffeepot, I began sleeping with Cain again. I didn't know what else to do. I hoped that giving him the atten-tion he craved would de-escalate the situation, letting my life go back to normal. Maybe if Cain got to know me a little better, he would be far less enamored. After all, sometimes the quickest way to fall out of love is to get to know someone really well.

These are the lies a victim tells herself.

To the prey already cornered, giving in is easier than fighting.

I'm writing in the thin light of a setting sun. I have no more words left in me today. I know I lost an important piece of myself when I felt I had to protect us the only way I knew how. I give thanks that I am not that frightened woman anymore. I give thanks that my shame is behind me.

Many years have passed since I first sold my soul to the demon who hunted me. Fear can certainly make us do outrageous things, but handing someone your self-respect is never a path toward freedom, and if a fool is willing to take your self-respect, then they surely don't deserve you. Losing respect for yourself is a quiet kind of dying—it slowly eats away at you.

I've certainly learned the hard way the importance of self-respect. I used to think it was made of nickel, but now I see it wears like platinum—a highly valued precious metal resistant to tarnishing and corrosion, unaffected by common acids, so beautiful and strong that the most famous diamonds in the world are set in platinum.

Which is rather interesting, since the most beautiful women in the world are set on self-respect.

Sending positive energy across the miles and holding you close in thought,

Your Loving Mother

Fourteen

Summer 2019

In the kitchen

Dear Sparrow,

I found it difficult to sleep last night. Sometimes transferring my truth onto paper feels empowering, but sometimes, it just feels sad. After I walked away from my letter last night, I felt restless. I knew I had to change my mood. So, I gathered up the rocks I'd painted—each depicting the image of a lone tree reaching toward the sun—and headed to the park by the beach to hide them in the nooks and crannies of the enormous oak trees.

I remember the first time I ever found a painted rock, at a roadside rest area just outside Butte, Montana. It was sitting on top of a metal frame encasing a state map. On one side, the rock had the image of a single feather painted in peach, pink, and white. On the other, it simply said "wish." I loved it immediately. I still have it.

As a way of saying thank-you to the rock artist I never met, in the years since I've left my fair share of painted rocks hidden in trees, next to streams, under shopping carts. It's a healing kind of magic I can't quite explain.

After I hid the rocks last night, I walked to the beach and sat admiring the moon over the glistening water. Moon glitter has its own kind of magic, like the outstretched arms of an angel. It's mesmerizing, isn't it? Peaceful. Tranquility swaddled in the velvet of a tender night sky is a delicious sort of thing, predictable yet unexpected, never in the forefront of our minds until our eyes remind us it's the most refreshing thing we've seen all day.

I'm now ready to return to the brochure entitled, "The Seven Stages of a Stalking Victim."

Stage Two is called the bargaining stage. This phase marks a period when the victim realizes she has a problem and reacts by trying to bargain with her stalker. She does this for two simple reasons: to help pacify her stalker, and to "earn" her freedom.

In past letters I've described the internal world of the stalker; now let's better understand the psychological topography of the victim.

The victim's reaction, her willingness to bargain, is similar to a woman who has suffered physical abuse at the hands of an intimate partner. Her response to the situation is triggered by a mechanism in her brain. As she slips into survival mode, she utilizes whatever tools she has available to lessen the impact and stop the pain. Those on the outside might view a victim's actions as complacency, but to the victim, *want* isn't a tangible concept anymore; *need* becomes an embolism living deep inside her chest.

Somewhere inside, the victim knows she's lying to herself, betraying her own self-worth. She knows something has to change. She lives the lie by pretending the hearts and flowers the stalker has offered means he won't frighten her anymore. He hands her a bouquet of meaningless promises. She eagerly accepts it.

Stage Two in the life of a stalking victim is often characterized by the victim's futile attempt to let the stalker down easy by showing sensitivity toward his feelings. She mistakenly believes that a kinder approach will deactivate the stalker from continuing his menacing behavior. She often agrees, usually more than once, to meet him one last time in hopes they can come to a mutual agreement that the relationship has ended and it's time to move on. During these meetings, the stalker often becomes agitated. He tells the victim he doesn't want her anymore, he never wants to see her again. She leaves the meeting under the mistaken impression that he finally gets it. But he doesn't get it.

He doesn't get it at all.

The stalker's mental instability won't allow him to let go so easily. He convinces himself that the victim loves him because she was willing to see him one last time. He's set a dangerous precedent—the victim is merely reacting to his behavior, running defense instead of offense, as he trains her to understand that until he says the game is over, he always has complete control of the ball.

The visceral instinct of self-preservation is deeply embedded into every form of life, from human beings to the smallest living creature. Even stars and cells exhibit a primal need to survive. The victim's need to please her stalker is driven by a desire to remain solvent in a situation beyond her control. The victim complies with her stalker's demands because he has shown a cruel and unstable hand, cleverly dismantling her sense of safety one Kafkaesque moment a time.

By mid-summer, apathy and resignation filled my head like puss fills an abscess. I lived an eerie, panicked sort of existence. Entertaining Cain's need for attention worked—all the weirdness stopped, but the self-sacrifice made self-hate easy to find. Adding to my delirium, I'd been so conditioned to expect the unexpected, I was a ball of nerves, doing my best to sink into the background, hoping no one would notice me or stop to say hello.

I grew exasperated trying to come up with ways to dilute Cain's obsession (though I didn't yet know it actually was an obsession); I'd considered cutting my hair, dressing like a nun, changing everything about me so Cain wouldn't want me anymore. But that felt like giving him every piece of me. And if it didn't work, if his feelings went deeper than hair and clothes and the way I talked, then I'd be left completely ravaged by the lunatic in my life.

I wasn't sure why Cain was so enamored with me, but I had a suspicion it had nothing to do with surface paint—I think my weird, my unique, fit his flow. And I had no idea how to change myself all the way down to the molecular level.

After the incident with the coffeepot, I suppose I realized it was an exercise in futility to believe that I alone had the power to change anything at all. Nothing I'd tried was working. Sex helped, but it didn't change anything—it just held the situation at bay. Maybe it even made it worse, I wasn't sure what to think anymore.

I suspected it would take a sustained effort by a team of people to finally eradicate Cain from my life. But, I didn't have a team—I barely had any money. Depression stung me. I began telling myself that women like me don't deserve help. Women like me—the ones who fail high school and get raped, lose babies and take a beating—have to figure things out on our own.

I cringe when I write these words, as if women fall into two neat little categories: those who deserve love and support, and those who don't. There isn't a woman on the face of this earth who hasn't seen her fair share of struggles and doesn't deserves all the kindness she can gather.

My mindset was so damaged by then that the bamboo once taking root inside me began to succumb to the force of brutal winds. Weeds came to take its place. They felt right at home.

Here's a sad truth no mother should ever share with her daughter: Sleeping with someone is easier when you're drunk. I drank a lot that summer. The more Cain asked to see me, the drunker I got. I felt so empty inside, soon the sex, the drinking, and my feelings of self-defecation didn't seem so ugly anymore—the embers of my spirit became saturated in numbness, lies, and wine.

I knew Cain wanted to be absorbed into my world, wanted me to claim him as my boyfriend, painting a pretty picture of how happy we could be. His words were often silky, but his eyes told the story of a suppressed rage. Perhaps he knew that my inability to meet with him unless it was late at night when I was drunk told a truth he didn't want to hear. He did his best to mask his demons and I did my best to pretend he was charming. Secretly, I knew our lie had a shelf life.

I tried hard to ingratiate myself into Cain's favor, even buying him presents I knew I couldn't afford. It pains me to remember how fragile I was back then. It further pains me to remember what I was willing to give up in an effort to keep what little I had.

Internally, I was tormented. I've tossed around other words to describe how I felt inside; *fractured* is a good one, but *tormented* seems to fit better. I began vomiting uncontrollably. I vomited many times throughout the day—even when I wasn't drinking. The vomiting weakened me, and I was unaware that it was my body's way of expelling extreme stress. I began losing a considerable amount of weight. I rarely slept, and when I did, I collapsed in an exhausted heap on the bed only to wake up a few hours later so I could vomit again.

I avoided our family like the plague. I stopped taking calls from friends.

I felt a hollow sense of guilt from living such an outrageous lie. I told myself that my fix to the situation was only temporary. I desperately wanted to believe that after Cain felt satisfied, he would grow bored and move on. I failed to realize that by now, Cain's obsession was clinical, a condition requiring intervention, not just late-night trysts and party favors.

Winston Churchill once said, "An appeaser is one who feeds a crocodile, hoping it will eat him last."

I continued to feed the crocodile.

Privately, I prayed for strength and guidance.

I wasn't sure how long I could manage the pathetic game of "Kiss My Ass Because I'm Crazy," but for a while it brought a needed relief from the calls, notes, foot tails, and car chases. No one called me Mrs. Cook anymore. In an odd sort of way, my life became more normal. I hoped I could maintain the façade until a better solution came along. I tried to convince myself that it was safe for you to come home.

Meanwhile, the vomiting continued.

That summer, the days rolled past like a Metallica song, my head was often pounding and my heart often raced. I continued to pacify Cain's cryptic need for unrestrained access to me. You'd think that bedding a drunk woman would be enough to turn off even the most seasoned sailor after a while, but it didn't. I suppose Cain allowed himself to believe that sooner or later I would find a way to love him.

I never stopped thinking about an effective way to end to my predicament. Actually, I chewed on the idea like a cow chews its cud. I decided to re-enlist the help of law enforcement, but this time my approach was different.

I knew cops who patrol a beat don't have the time or resources to provide long-term assistance, so I decided to take my case to the Columbus Prosecutor's Office. Even though they wouldn't be able to prosecute a case that in their world didn't even exist, in an attempt to appease me they would offer a more realistic option.

My plan worked. The next thing I knew, I was sitting in a detective's office in the stalking division of the Columbus Police Department via a referral from the city's prosecutor's office.

I remember sitting in an uncomfortable chair, mindlessly thumbing through a brochure the detective had handed me. The brochure was filled with strawberry advice and oversimplified explanations—tidy, little summaries geared toward tidy, little solutions.

In the background of my thoughts, I could hear the detective rattling off laws and facts as if I were nothing more than a cardboard cutout. The room, the brochure, and the monologue felt sterile. I disconnected myself from the experience immediately. A stalking victim is usually vacant inside, it takes a helluva lot more than dry toast to convince us you give a shit.

The detective proceeded to describe a typical stalking scenario—his summation was clinical and orderly, leaving no room for the outrageous fears and emotions that seize a victim. He passed me another brochure, something about seven stages, and I nodded my head to reassure him I was paying attention. Within me I knew I was just another case, another sea of paperwork, another unfortunate statistic.

At some point he got around to asking the specifics of my situation. I quickly ran through my experiences, trying to shove as many words into one sentence as I could. The detective concluded that Cain was a "low-lethality" stalker—in his opinion, the chances that Cain would become violent were slim.

I can't write these words without feeling angry. Low lethality— what a load of bullshit. There is no such thing as a "low-lethality" stalker; a stalker is dangerous on every level. To dismiss a victim's experiences as merely the harmless antics of a schoolboy with a bad case of the warm-fuzzies is to take away a victim's right to feel as though her fears and concerns have merit.

Mentally healthy people don't stalk. Suggesting that you can predict what a mentally unstable person might do is like offering a bag of marbles to a barn owl—the gesture means absolutely nothing.

After I stared at him for a few minutes in disbelief, his eyes blinking uncomfortably, I told him that Cain was secretly sneaking into our house. The invasion really, really troubled me. It felt like I was living in a haunted house, every creak and shadow seemed sinister.

The detective casually asked, "Do you keep a diary?"

"Yes, I've kept a diary for years."

"That's why he's breaking in." He announced flatly. "Stalkers have to know everything about their victim. It's not enough to just know where they go and what they do, they have to know what they are thinking, too."

I. Was. Fucking. Flabbergasted. Even my thoughts were no longer safe. It felt as though Cain was clawing at every fiber of my being.

The detective handed me a stack of papers he felt would be informative. He instructed me to begin keeping a detailed journal of any incident in the event my case ever went to trial. He passed me his business card and told me to call him if I needed anything.

The meeting was over. Needless to say, hope didn't hold the door for me as I left the detective's office—hope had probably been wise enough not to show up for the meeting in the first place.

I stopped at the liquor store on my way home and bought a bottle of Jack Daniels, knowing I'd need something stronger than wine if I planned on digesting all the literature on a subject matter so personal and utterly disturbing.

After I returned home, I barricaded myself inside the house and got out a shot glass. I let the first two shots burn all the way to my stomach before I reached for the pamphlet that gave basic information about stalking.

I learned more than I ever wanted to. The sampling of documented stalking cases didn't make me feel like I wasn't alone, they reminded me of how alone I really was.

I read about the young, vibrant woman who was murdered the day before she graduated college because her stalker feared her independence. I read about the middle-aged schoolteacher found bludgeoned to death in her car after her stalker found out she'd obtained a restraining order against him. I read about the young woman who dreamed of being an Olympic swimmer before she was shot to death in the middle of the street. In broad daylight.

Statistically speaking, seventy-six percent of women murdered by an intimate partner were stalked first.

By the time I struggled through all the depressing literature, with frequent bouts of pacing in between, more than half the bottle of liquor was gone. I'd never felt more confused. Or more desperate. Backed against a wall, I allowed myself to cry, but the tears would've come regardless.

Now comes the beginning of what I refer to as the black years. The description fits because immediately following my visit with the detective, my life slipped into a state of darkness that snuffed out any sense of light, hope, or meaning. The literature made a lasting impression on me, highlighting a truth I hated to know: Pissing off a stalker is the quickest way to a violent death.

After I opened a stalking case with the Columbus Police Department, I didn't hear from Cain for several weeks. But before long, his stalking antics began again.

Following the advice of the detective, I recorded all of my stalking encounters in a separate notebook, hid inside a thin space on the back of the dryer between the outer covering and the inner workings of the appliance. Completely hidden from view, it became my secret cubby. In my journal, I recorded people, times, places, descriptions of vehicles, and license plates. I also described how I felt about each incident using a scale of 0 to 10 to summarize its threat level: Someone following me at the grocery store was a 2. A dead bird with its head torn off, tucked under my wiper blade was a 6. Someone entering our house and leaving a porn magazine on the coffee table was an 8.

Hoping to dispel the detective's assumption about my diary, I set Cain up—I had to know the truth. After my visit with the detective, I stopped writing in my diary, but it felt like such a loss, like losing your favorite shirt or your favorite place to sit. One morning, I decided to write in my diary as usual. In between the pages of my last entry, I placed one long strand of my hair, choosing a piece that was the lightest blonde so it wouldn't stand out against the journal paper. If my diary was opened, tilted even the slightest bit, the hair would fall to the floor. Then, I left the house for a few hours. When I came home later, I immediately went to check my diary. The hair was already gone.

I was deeply troubled that Cain had been reading my diary because in it, I'd described him as weak, and as a fuck-up, a loser, a weirdo, a villain, and a psychopath. I'd confessed that sleeping with him made me feel ugly and worthless, which meant he'd known all along that my attempt to appease him was far from sincere. The rage I'd seen in his eyes finally made sense now. I was desperate to retract my words, knowing my private thoughts could be deadly. Somehow, I had to change the narrative.

Then came an idea: Turn his lust for information into an opportunity to use his curiosity against him. If my most honest thoughts were what he wanted, I would color them in lies. I began keeping an alternate journal, one that painted the picture of a woman on the verge of falling in love, regretting calling the police, promising herself that she'd never do it again. I kept the saccharine-coated journal tucked under my mattress as if I were trying to hide it. The hairs continued to disappear.

My plan worked. Before long, Cain called me sounding less angry and less drunk. I invited him over, eager to stabilize the situation, knowing I was only days from your return.

During our conversation that evening, I flat out asked Cain if he was obsessed with me.

He chuckled, then simply said, "Lightweight."

I took his response to mean he knew he was overly infatuated, but he didn't see it as a problem. Then he told me he'd been in love with me for a very long time. I did my best to mask my astonishment. *He thinks this is love?*

Cain proceeded to reassure me that he would never do anything to hurt me, he would do his best to protect me from any harm, that he felt the need to "keep an eye on me" for my own good. He worried about me, he said.

Even though the whole conversation was as improbable as a shark reassuring a seal, I began to think he truly meant what he was saying. I began to wonder if he was just socially awkward, completely unaware of how inappropriate his behavior really was. Maybe Cain wasn't dangerous after all, just unskilled in the ways of human interaction. Suddenly, he seemed like a bird with a clipped wing instead of an arrogant mental case.

I brought up his secret relationship with Tandy. He told me that he'd never had any real feelings for her, he was just trying to make me jealous. He said he'd broken off their relationship because sleeping with her felt like "sleeping with a linebacker," claiming he could never see her as anything more than "Mean Joe Green in a dress."

"It didn't make me jealous. I felt sorry for her," I told him.

"Kinda figured that one out," he replied, staring at his neatly folded hands.

As the evening wore on, I began to doubt my perception of things. I began to wonder if I was the one with mental issues—his version of reality felt safer. I think I needed to believe that he wasn't a crazed stalker like the ones I read about in the brochures. I willingly drank his cup of pretty bullshit—it tasted better than the truth.

So there we were, two idiots doing our best to lie to each other. It would appear that I was a drunk, a slut, and a liar after all.

You returned home like a giggling rainbow, effervescent with delight as you told the tales of an amazing summer spent being a carpenter's helper in the heart of Dixie. I'd never known your father to be much of a carpenter before, but I was glad to see he'd finally acquired some useful skills. And bought a toolbox.

You proudly showed off the pictures of the work you, your father, and Astrid had done to the house. Never had a house, or a child, felt so pampered and adored.

After you got back, I felt more whole inside, yet I can pinpoint this moment as the beginning of when I slipped into a state of extreme hyper vigilance—our safety became my obsession. I skipped a car payment so I could add more locks to the doors and cover the windows with thicker curtains. I regularly changed up our routes and routines. It didn't take long before I realized that living in a state of hyper vigilance requires an enormous amount of energy, adding an unexpected layer of fatigue to my day.

I continued to do my best to pacify Cain, convincing myself the situation had gone from a boil to a slow simmer. After school started, I hardly heard from him, but I often saw him parked in the back of my school's parking lot before or after school. It bothered me, but it was less stressful than dead animals on my car or sleeping with him whenever his little brown crayon got hard.

It was around this time that I began having a nagging suspicion that I was being watched inside our house. I couldn't shake the feeling—which was at its peak whenever I was in my bedroom. I'd searched everywhere looking for a hidden camera; when I didn't find anything, I searched the house again. But I was looking for a camera the size of, well, a camera. Little did I know I should've been looking for a camera the size of a small glass bead.

The feeling of being under surveillance in my bedroom became so strong that I began dressing in the dark. I developed a system for laying out my clothes in a manner that resembled the numbers on a clock, using my recliner as the watch face. I set my bra and panties at 12:00, my shirt at 3:00, my pants or skirt at 6:00, and my belt and socks at 9:00. By following this organized system, I could easily dress with the lights off after showering in the dark. I felt it was a brilliant solution to my unsubstantiated uneasiness.

One morning, while running late for work, I went to the recliner and discovered my bra wasn't at 12:00 where it should've been. In a panic, I began feeling around in the dark and all of my clothes became a jumbled mess. A heightened sense of anxiety rose within me as I frantically searched for my bra and panties. The more I searched, the angrier I became. I began pounding my fists against my forehead and heard myself scream out in exasperation, "You are so fucking stupid! Can't you do anything right?"

With the sound of my own spiteful words echoing back to me in the stillness of my room, I stopped. I stood perfectly still in the darkness. I realized I was punishing myself as if I held no worth because I couldn't successfully dress in absolute darkness. My assault on myself completely ignored the real tragedy at hand: Dressing in the light didn't feel safe anymore.

I suppose out of sheer frustration, I dropped to the floor and began sobbing. I pulled my knees to my chest and began rocking back and forth. Every incident I'd experienced since my nightmare began came firing into my brain like a hailstorm of bullets. My tears flowed like an eruption.

Sometimes one moment changes everything. We tend to think it's the big things in life that have the most significant impact, but I've come to discover that often times, inside the nucleus of a single moment lies a thought that changes the course of things most profoundly.

As I sat there listening to the sound of my own labored breath, I came to understand with unmistakable clarity that Cain Cook wasn't a misunderstood innocent, he wasn't a socially awkward lover, and he most certainly wasn't my friend or my protector—he wasn't any of the roles he'd been trying to play in my life. He was a con man, a predator, a serpent on a mission. I knew I couldn't live the lie one second longer.

Naked and trembling, I sat in the dark for a while on that lonely morning. I cried for a very long time. After the last teardrop fell, I knew one thing for certain: I wasn't sleeping with Cain Cook anymore. And I would somehow find a way to stop the madness stinking like a dead corpse before the vulture circling around my head tried to loosen meat from bone.

I will end this letter here. I wish I could go back in time and give myself a big hug. I'd have so much to say to my younger self. I would comfort her by reassuring her that she was not powerless. And she was not alone.

I was completely unaware that angels gathered near me, quietly absorbing my pain, and that they had a mission, too—to comfort and protect, to win a war using light and dignity, and to guide me toward my own brand of brave.

Angels are like that, sweet child.

They rally well before the battle, and theirs are the last swords to rest.

Sending positive energy across the miles and holding you close in thought,

Your Loving Mother

FIFTEEN

Summer 2019

At the lake

Dear Sparrow,

I'm at the lake this morning. The air feels cool and smells like summer rain. I'm feeling refreshed after spending the weekend with you—New Orleans was just what I needed. I've been so wrapped up in my letters, I'd forgotten that life is waiting for me just outside my front door.

The items you chose for the nursery are perfect. I never knew how much I loved a purple and chartreuse chandelier until I saw one—how could we have gone without one for so long? The animated picture of a brass band weaving its way down Bourbon Street will certainly add an interesting flair to the room since nothing says celebration quite like the French Quarter and the jazz of new life.

I'm ready to return to my letters now that I left remnants of the black years somewhere in Jackson Square. I suppose New Orleans can handle my discarded angst, gobbling it up like beads thrown at Mardi Gras. New Orleans never misses an opportunity to transform ghosts into the Cajun fiddle of zydeco or the hot sauce in a bowl of jambalaya.

I suppose that's why people from all around the world seek the New Orleans state of mind. It welcomes your troubles like an old friend, then lets you forget about yourself for a while. Before you know it, you're buying a bedazzled hat and wearing jangles on your shoes.

I'm staring at the photo I took of you while we were having lunch at The Court of Two Sisters. You look so thoughtful and calm, carrying the essence of a timeless beauty like Venus rising from the foam. Now that I'm feeling refreshed, I suppose this is a good time to talk about the next stage so the memories I will speak about find no place to rest.

As I continued to move through the predictable stages of a stalking victim, I came upon Stage Three quite somberly. Stage Three is the anxiety stage. I can attest that this stage is one of significance because it feels the scariest. By Stage Three a victim realizes that no denial or bargaining can tame the stalker's obsession; it has an unfortunate impact on her ability to cope with the ever-changing situation.

Few people handle anxiety well—especially when it comes from a sustained effort to make a person feel as though their life is under attack. Under such duress, the victim begins to experience a myriad of symptoms that affect the whole body: The mind is unable to concentrate as it races with unwanted thoughts, the physical body feels fatigued and restless, the subconscious suffers from feelings of impending doom, poor sleep quality impacts energy levels and performance, and appetite is suppressed.

The victim is no longer able to live a normal life.

By the time the anxiety phase sets in, the stalker has successfully ensnared her in his trap, enjoying the fruits of his labor, watching as his victim slowly deteriorates. By now, the stalker's entire world rests on his ability to control his victim—losing control is his single greatest fear.

Power is addicting. The power the stalker feels over his victim isn't matched in any other area of his life. Often unsuccessful in personal relationships and the workplace, he craves the attention and control the stalking experience gives him. He's become completely dependent on the victim for his sense of personal identity.

During the anxiety stage, the victim feels imprisoned. The longer the situation continues, the more anxious she becomes. Never knowing what the stalker will do next or where he will turn up, the victim can think of little else. She begins to short-circuit. Nothing feels safe anymore.

All she sees before her is the madman's swinging noose.

I sat on the floor getting real with myself. No more lies, no more whiskey, no more pretending to like a man I couldn't stand. Sitting naked in the stillness on that morning when I couldn't dress in the dark, I gave myself the right to fully declare my feelings, even though my feelings felt tragic and weighted by layers of regret.

I hated Cain. I hated myself, disgusted that I'd allowed such a sick man to touch me, stupid enough to believe that sex equaled freedom. I was repulsed—even my hands looked ugly as I sat staring at them, holding a wad of Kleenex soaked in tears and embarrassment. Those ghastly brochures claimed that bargaining is a victim's normal reaction to an abnormal situation, but in my eyes weakness is weakness—even when it's holding a permission slip from a trained professional.

After picking myself up off the floor, I put on my bathrobe and called in sick to work. I needed a mental health day. Feeling like a frayed nerve in a hollow tunnel, I needed to collect my thoughts and plan a new strategy. I packed your lunch after putting drops of Visine in my eyes, drew hearts on your lunch bag, then sent you off to school with hugs and kisses, slipping a love note in your book bag. Once I saw you board the school bus, I barricaded the front door with the living room couch.

I returned to the quiet of my bedroom, lighting a single white candle as a token of pure energy before assuming the lotus position and bowing my head to pray. I hadn't prayed in weeks—it felt good to reconnect. Even though I often felt like I was losing my mind, it was nice to know I was sane enough to find comfort in my faith. Maybe I was too far gone for heaven to help, but I prayed for courage and clarity just the same.

I pondered my options regarding Cain, which didn't take long since I had precious few. I decided on a strategy I coined "Operation: Fuck You, Buddy" silence—no phone calls, no emails, no texts, no more one-last-time meetings or conversations, and most importantly, no reaction to his behavior.

I decided to stop keeping a fake journal. There wasn't much I could do to keep him from getting in the house since changing locks proved to be an inefficient deterrent. I was suspecting that one of Cain's many deranged talents was lock-picking. I placed a large butcher knife and a three-foot section of metal pipe under my mattress and I prayed I never had to use them. I attached a bundle of jingle bells on the front and back door knobs—a primitive alarm system. I know I told you that I did it so I could train Tuck to let us know when he wanted out. I lied.

I dug out the watch-cat your Aunt Charlotte had given me years before, attaching it to my keychain. In case you don't remember, a watch-cat is a small weapon shaped like the outline of a cat's head. When your fist is closed, the ears become two metal points protruding through your fingers. It's used for self-defense, similar to carrying a vial of pepper spray. Of course, what I really needed was a gun, a vicious dog, and a security system, but all three required money I didn't have.

I made myself an egg salad sandwich and sat on the couch looking around. I felt a little more settled knowing I'd made some simple yet necessary changes, but none of them dispelled the feeling of being watched. It felt claustrophobic. The thicker curtains weren't helping. I decided to cover the windows on the ground floor with heavy construction paper, trying to emulate a stained glass window effect so you wouldn't be alarmed. It did look rather pretty. I hated to shut out the brilliance of sunshine, but I preferred that to the unsettling stares of a peeping Tom.

Cain noticed the change in the windows immediately. I hadn't heard from him since the beginning of the school year, yet within the hour, I received a text saying, "How u doin'?" I didn't respond. Several hours later, he re-sent the same text. I ignored that one, too.

By evening time, my silence was enraging him. "What in the fuck is your problem?" his text demanded shortly before I went to bed. I wanted so badly to verbally slay him, my disgust felt red-hot, yet I said nothing. Then, I turned off my phone for the night.

When I left the house the next morning, I knew I'd have a tail immediately. I took my normal route to work as if I weren't the slightest bit fazed. He parked outside my school all day as if he were a rent-a-cop, watching from his car as I did my recess duty on the playground and bus duty at the end of the day. I pretended not to notice him.

Then, I drove home my predictable route without ever glancing in the rearview mirror. I didn't scurry home like a field mouse, I drove like I was commanding a tank. I deleted each of his texts without reading them, which made me laugh more than I had in months.

I broke the cardinal rule every stalker demands: Never ignore me. Yet, I ignored him all damn day. No doubt I would somehow suffer for my silent resistance, my show of defiance, but for the time being it felt like I had my life back again. It felt pretty powerful.

You and I ate dinner by candlelight that evening. We colored in our coloring books, watching *Kiki's Delivery Service* for the hundredth time. I felt a warm smile come across my face as I tucked you into bed that night. It felt like the smile of a woman who remembered how to live in the moment; it felt like the smile of a woman who remembered the sweetness of her own strength.

Sometimes all you need is a friend. Friends aren't the sprinkles on your ice cream sundae, friends are the bowl—they support you whether you're feeling delicious or you're melting in the sun. Humans tend to casually throw around the word *friend* as if it's as light as a feather, but in truth, it carries with it the weight of the world.

Even in the midst of trying my best to keep myself isolated, I had the good fortune that one friend refused to entertain the sign hanging from my aura that read, *I'm Going Through Some Shit So Please Leave Me Alone*. Of course, I'm speaking of Adia.

Adia was a blessing. She never seemed to tire of listening to me vent or trying to help problem-solve my situation. She never turned her back on me regardless of how strange my experiences became or how long the ordeal lasted.

If I had to pay Adia a nickel for every time she held my heart while I screamed, cried, and denied, I would certainly owe her more than I will ever have in my bank account. She never once doubted that my experiences were real and she never believed I was going crazy.

We were an unlikely duo in many regards—she loved spending a Saturday afternoon watching football and I loved spending a Saturday afternoon not watching football—but her style of friendship fit me perfectly.

Adia's contribution to my life was notable, but her most prolific contributions came in the form of a retired FBI agent named Walter and a pit bull named Quinn. Both appeared in my life right when I needed them most.

Walter was Adia's godfather. She viewed him warmly, holding his character in the highest regard. As Adia and I became closer friends, Cain did his best to scare her off. Adia reported that she now had a prowler coming around her house at night, sending her dogs into a frenzy, and someone had broken into her vehicle while it was sitting in her driveway. One morning, she found the word *lesbian* spelled out on her front porch in little pieces of twig.

Since Adia was extremely private about her sexuality (most people had no idea she was gay because she was recently divorced with a teenage son), she felt that whoever had left the message must know her pretty well, and that the word *lesbian* was a veiled attempt to unnerve her. Of course, we could never prove that Cain was behind any of these incidents at her house, but they followed a predictable pattern of Cain targeting people closest to me whenever I stopped speaking to him for any length of time.

During the black years, it wasn't uncommon to hear reports from people in my inner circle that a pet had disappeared, expensive tools had been stolen, electronics had turned up missing, or a rash of fraudulent charges had appeared on their credit card accounts. I would later learn that Cain had the habit of stealing people's trash as a quick way to learn more about them, and he had the ability to run credit cards at his job.

To the people in my circle, it all appeared unconnected. And maybe it was. But these incidents always came on the heels of Cain not getting a desired response or my spending time with someone else, even if the relationship wasn't sexual. To Cain, it was still a problem.

Adia knew she was being targeted. She had no doubt in her mind it was Cain because the incidents at her house didn't start until we became closer friends. Adia immediately called Walter, filling him in on the growing problem in my life that was now bleeding into hers.

Walter had been retired from the FBI for years, but a good guy never stops being a good guy, so he promised he would look into it. Over the course of the next several weeks, Walter kept his word.

I never met Walter, he never asked to speak to me, but I suppose when you reach that level of law enforcement, you don't waste your time with interviews—you focus on cold, hard facts instead.

I can't begin to tell you what Walter did or what he saw, but after several weeks he issued an unofficial statement regarding my stalking situation. He stated the following:

1. He believed I had a big problem and I didn't know it yet.

2. He believed I was smarter than Cain and Cain didn't know it yet.

3. He predicted my situation would get worse before it got better.

I wasn't given the opportunity to question Walter or ask for advice—Walter didn't step into my problem in the official capacity of an FBI agent, he stepped in as concerned family friend doing a favor for his goddaughter. So I was left with only these few morsels of information, leaving me to wonder how big my situation really was and how much worse it could get.

As much as I appreciated the confirmation from someone highly trained that my experiences were legitimate, it felt almost cruel that he offered no suggestions—it felt like hitting a home run only to have the point show up on the other team's scorecard.

When my stalking began, I'd paid a friend of a friend who declared himself a private investigator $150 to find out anything he could about whoever was targeting me. After a week, he returned with the verdict that I was just imagining things. Though it was frustrating to hear him say this, it helped me rest in the denial phase a little while longer.

Many years later I learned from an associate of Cain's that Cain had simply paid this "friend" twice my measly $150 to get him to lie. But when Walter issued his simple statement, I knew it was the truth. His views were unbiased, impartial, and they felt like a prison sentence. With such little information to go on, I had no ability to predict an outcome or wage a proper war.

After the insight from Walter, my anxiety reached new levels. I continued my silence toward Cain, but it didn't feel quite as liberating as it had in the beginning. The vomiting increased. Cain's weird antics increased as well. Our trash was being stolen—I didn't even need to take it to the curb anymore. Our mail often came up missing too. Cain became a constant presence at my job, and his henchman never seemed to grow tired of following me around and calling me Mrs. Cook as if they were mocking me.

"Mrs. Cook has a fever," one stranger said as he passed by me just as I was leaving a tire store. I cringed inside, but kept on walking.

Perhaps sensing my increasing anxiety, it was around this time that Adia let her beautiful pit bull, Quinn, come stay with us for a while. We weren't really babysitting him like I'd told you—he was a security system that you fed. Quinn and I had a special connection right from the start—he seemed to sense he had a job to do whenever he was with me. Neither Adia nor I could explain how Quinn knew he made me feel safe by just being in my presence, but he took my confidence in him seriously. Even though he was normally a playful dog, he always seemed to be on patrol whenever I was around. It was an act of supreme selflessness when Adia offered to let him stay with us for a while, since to Adia, Quinn was like a second son.

After Quinn arrived, the nightly gifts left on our back porch immediately stopped, as did the footprints outside our windows and the cars parked in front of our house. For a while, the situation was everything I'd been praying for. Cain was hot on my tail the minute I left the house, but at least our home felt protected.

I began sleeping better with Quinn at the foot of my bed. If I felt him get up in the middle of the night, I would follow him. He always headed into your bedroom to make sure you were okay, then took a quick tour of the house. I stopped feeling like I needed to take a constant inventory and I stopped looking for signs that Cain had entered our house because, for the first time in over a year, there weren't any.

I suppose I knew Cain would figure out a way to bypass Quinn. What I didn't expect was that Cain would begin tormenting him. Cain didn't try to get in while Quinn was in the house, but he knew Quinn couldn't get out. I know you remember the period of time when there was always all that banging on our doors and windows, sending Quinn into a complete tizzy. It didn't take long before Quinn couldn't stop pacing, desperate to get out the door and settle the score. As soon as night fell, Quinn would turn into a beast ready to rumble. With each passing day, he grew more and more agitated.

I know you loved Quinn. I did too. But Quinn wasn't the kind of dog you take lightly. And just like people, sometimes dogs make mistakes. It was with a heavy heart that I knew it was best to return Quinn to his peaceful life and his big yard to save you or me from any unintentional damage Quinn might inflict during the moments he was losing his mind.

After Quinn moved out, I began missing a lot of work. I simply hated the idea of leaving our house unattended. I was throwing up more often, knowing I would see Cain camped out in the parking lot as if he were the school's security guard.

I was becoming a real burden at work, dropping the ball with my responsibilities. The students and the staff deserved better. Whenever I was at work, I couldn't sit still, spending most of my time walking around pretending I was in the middle of doing something when all I was really doing was trying my best to not remain stationary—sitting still made me feel like a sitting duck; the need to keep moving felt urgent.

I'd written a letter to the Department of Safety and Security at our school district's headquarters, asking them to ban Cain from school property—normal protocol for such matters. They never responded, but Cain must have been alerted that I'd sent the letter because he soon began parking his car in the grocery store parking lot directly across from the school.

After school resumed, Tandy and I did our best to avoid each other. We never spoke and I couldn't have cared less. To me, Tandy was like a snowfall in Russia—I had no time to think about either of them. So much had happened since we'd been friends, I felt like I didn't know her anymore. I'm sure she felt the same.

One afternoon after school had been dismissed for the day, Tandy and I found ourselves alone in a wide hallway. As I approached her, I began thinking about the way she'd betrayed us. I said something bitchy as I passed her. I would like to tell you exactly what I said, but I truly don't remember. I only know it was quick, cutting, and impulsive—it probably had something to do with linebackers and Mean Joe Green in a dress.

Tandy responded by threatening to kill me. Her reaction surprised me, but I wasn't yet aware of her suspicion that she was being stalked and that someone was breaking into her house, so I can certainly understand why she would've been so easily triggered. After my remark, she followed me into the main office, grabbed a chair, and held it above her head as if she planned to throw it at me, all the while screaming, "I'm gonna kill you, Helena! I'm gonna kill you!"

I walked directly into the principal's office with Tandy following close behind, still holding the chair above her head. I told the principal that Tandy had threatened to kill me and that I was leaving the building for safety reasons.

The principal asked me to stay so we could all sit down and talk, but I felt that was a horrible idea. My workday had ended and I needed to get home—I needed to get far away from the situation as quickly as possible. My mouth was beginning to water—I was only moments away from throwing up. I also knew that the principal was completely unaware of our backstory and I had no intention of bringing my mess to work anymore than it already was. Or throwing up on her shoes. So I left.

The following morning, Tandy and I were sent home without pay pending a review by the district's head honchos. When the day finally came to plead for my job, I was permitted to tell my version of the incident without Tandy present. While I was discussing my reason for leaving the building despite the principal's request that I stay, one of the gentlemen on the review committee noticed the watch-cat on my key chain. He informed me that a watch-cat was considered a weapon.

"Are you carrying a weapon on school property?" he asked, peering over his glasses as if I had a rocket launcher cradled in my arms.

"No, sir, I'm carrying a form of self-defense," I said, suspecting my job was over regardless of my answer.

Several weeks later, I received an official letter in the mail informing me I'd been terminated for possessing a weapon and failing to follow the principal's instructions when she asked me to stay and talk.

Tandy was fired, too. I don't know the exact reason for her termination, but we both fell into the very same pot.

I would like to tell you that I should've kept my mouth shut when I passed Tandy in the hallway. But I can't. I needed to speak my peace—our peace. When Tandy sold me out, she sold you out. I'd refrained from vengeance and payback, but I guess an empty hallway can look a lot like a perfect opportunity to someone terminally on edge.

 I would also like to tell you that I regretted losing my job. But I didn't. Of course, the loss of income royally sucked, but I reassured myself that I could find another job. The pressure of being in that environment had been proving to be too much. It had become more and more difficult to maintain my composure, and teachers have excellent bullshit detectors. To them, I was probably just another low-level aid who didn't share their vision of everyone pulling their own weight.

My level of anxiety had often peaked whenever I was at work—the building had too many windows, too many doors, too many people milling about, too many parking lots, and too many reasons to leave. Between knowing Cain was parked outside and finding out the head custodian was a close friend of Cain's, I no longer felt safe at work.

As you know, the school where I'd worked was inner-city, but what you might not have realized was that it was smack dab in the middle of a community infested with drugs, crime, and gang activity. When I'd noticed a change in the types of people following me—going from fresh-faced kids to older men with haunting eyes and creepy stares—I'd recognized some of them as being part of the tight-knit community where I was working. Some of those men seemed familiar—a father, an uncle, or an older cousin of one of the students at our school. I could never be certain though, because I never had direct interaction with them, they were only faces disappearing in the crowd at dismissal or lost in a sea of adults at an awards assembly.

It's for these reasons that losing my job felt like closing down an avenue, lessening Cain's ability to monitor me throughout the day. I'm sure I should've been more upset that I suddenly had no income and I'd been fired from a really good job, but please understand that at that time in my life, I was in survival mode. When you're operating under the fight-or-flee reflexes in the brain, you're unable to process events in an ordinary way. I saw my job as an area of vulnerability, so it was a huge relief to finally have it over.

It's difficult to babysit your own thoughts when you feel you're under attack, it's difficult to stand when falling to your knees is sometimes the best you can manage. In hindsight, I realize my life truly fell to its knees after I lost my job, and as bad as things were, I would soon be reminded that things can always get worse.

As I lay down my pen for the day, I'm picturing you in the nursery, adding the final touches while rubbing your swollen belly. This image makes me feel warm inside, knowing how happy you are. Tapping into your wonderland of positive energy, I think I'll go shopping for a music box and a collection of Pippi Longstocking books as a welcome-to-the-world gift for my granddaughter.

I will set aside the black years for a while and spend the rest of the day roaming around a toy store, thinking of you and your jubilant smile until my heart feels like champagne.

Sending positive energy across the miles and holding you close in thought,

Your Loving Mother

Sixteen

Summer 2019

Pensacola Beach, Florida

Dear Sparrow,

After our trip to New Orleans, it felt as though I'd cleansed my palate of some of the saltiness that's left behind whenever I write of my journey—the change in scenery did me a world of good. So in the spirit of adventure, I found myself setting out on an unexpected road trip this morning, looking for a new place to write. I drove over bridges and through cities, passing by inviting parks and shady welcome centers. I kept on driving until, once again, I found myself veering toward the companionship of the sea.

I'm now sitting in a funky little vegetarian restaurant enjoying a pineapple smoothie while nibbling on fresh blackberries and a slice of banana bread. The place is deserted since it's past breakfast time, not quite lunchtime, on a rainy Tuesday with no holiday in sight.

I chose a large table in the corner that offers a pier's view of the water; I'm slightly entranced by the monochromatic swirls of silver and pewter as the ocean mirrors the sky. The wind is echoing mischief, making the playful palm trees seem like they're throwing a tantrum.

I've made myself at home, spreading out my notes and pens and blank pages of paper across the table. I look forward to writing this letter in a setting that makes me feel as if a mermaid could glide through the door at any moment to order a lemon tart to go.

I will quickly return to my story.

The voice building inside me is eager to speak its truth.

There was a period of my life so debilitating it seemed as though I were living in a void deficient of air—I simply couldn't breathe. The only way I can describe my black years with any sincerity is to liken them to the feeling of being completely paralyzed—I couldn't move even if I wanted to because my mind and body were no longer on the same page. Every thought and gesture took enormous effort and never seemed to accomplish anything.

After I lost my job, I caved in for a while. I became motionless. I did nothing. I thought nothing. I felt nothing. I was able to collect myself long enough to care for you, but I must tell you that I found myself contemplating suicide almost daily—it seemed like the perfect fix. I knew I couldn't go on much longer living like a frightened child with monsters under the bed.

During my black years, I came to know what it feels like to be a deer pursued by a bloodthirsty hunter. The feeling of being hunted has to be when anxiety is the most crippling. Whether it's a person hunting you, your past, a terminal illness, or an addiction, feeling as though you are only one step away from oblivion is the deepest, darkest hole you will ever try to escape.

Adia must have sensed that I was close to giving up, and I was thankful she had the courage to talk to me about it. I use the word *courage* intentionally because it takes courage to discuss the nature of life and death when someone you know is hurting. It's the most meaningful conversation you will ever have because the fate of a soul rests in the balance.

Many people prefer to look the other way when they sense someone is near the end—not because they don't care, but because helping involves a real conversation that most people don't want to have. Or more accurately, don't know how to have. Let's face it, in a world such as ours, every soul is struggling. It's hard to offer sustenance when you're doing your best to keep your head above water. Looking the other way isn't always a sign of indifference, sometimes looking the other way is a sign that words don't come easily to those lost in their own storm.

Many mornings I woke up confident that today would be the day—the moment of permanent release from my anguish. It wasn't just the stalking either, it was my Pandora's box hitting me like a brick wall, reminding me that my box was full—no more pain need apply. But I couldn't fathom the idea of leaving you motherless, so I bought a locket at a thrift store and put a picture of you in it. Whenever I got to feeling soupy, I'd hold it in my hand. I forced myself to hold on just one more day, desperate to believe that everything would be okay.

Hope is the nourishment of dreams. When a soul dares to hope, it builds a dream worth fighting for.

Even though it felt like the obstacles in my life were insurmountable, my faith encouraged me to hang on. That's when a special song would come on the radio or I'd find a four-leaf clover, or the certainty of *this too shall pass* would seize me and carry me into the next moment.

That's when I would begin feeling a little better, a little stronger, a little more ready to carry on.

I knew I'd feel better if I just started living again, but I didn't know how. I'd reached a point where I rarely left the house, often making excuses as to why I couldn't help with carpooling or attend Sunday dinners at your grandmother's. I didn't want to admit that I was having trouble making it past the front door, knowing I'd sound crazy or weak, so I hid inside myself, hoping my feelings would fade like they always had before.

During the black years, I didn't know how to find my happy place anymore—gazing at the stars, opening the curtains to greet the sunrise, or taking a walk in the woods made me feel exposed and insecure. Even letting my hands make art felt more like a chore than a therapy. I had difficulty keeping my hands from shaking ever so slightly, was unable to empty out my mind long enough to let the creative juices flow. Losing my ability to stay connected to the ethereal realms of art and nature, which had always guided me to a peaceful place, was a devastating loss to my spirit. Without these forms of holistic healing and expression, I simply didn't recognize myself anymore.

I came to see myself as stupid and useless. I fought back against these feelings whenever they threatened to consume me, but for the most part, I sat as still as a dusty piece of luggage whose owner doesn't travel much.

My eyes took in light, but no light was returned.

I've never liked opening the door to an unexpected visitor. I'm not a big fan of surprises, either. I'm sure Freud would psychoanalyze these dislikes as a sure sign that I wish I had a penis, but he would be incorrect—I've never wished I had a penis. I can't think of anything uglier besides a naked mole rat—which looks suspiciously like a penis—or an angler fish—which, strangely enough, seems to have a bioluminescent penis dangling from its forehead.

Anyway.

I can't remember why or when I came to dislike opening the front door to an unexpected visitor, but as you know, it's one of the quirks of my personality. Some people don't like the feel of clothes fresh from the dryer, some don't like food touching on their plate—I guess these are just glitches in our systems meant to keep things interesting.

I never should've opened the door that night, I really don't know why I did. But I did. And in walked Cain.

I hadn't seen him in months. I'd successfully maintained "Operation: Fuck You, Buddy" silence even though the backlash felt enormous—he'd even gone so far as to set a pile of feces in our outdoor dryer vent, creating a revolting stench for days until I finally found the source of the odor. One by one, items were being stolen from our back patio. Once I stopped leaving the house, I received dozens of strange calls a day, as if Cain and his band of rejects had my number on speed dial.

When Cain appeared at our front door, I certainly wasn't expecting him. Ever the bully, he seized an opportunity to show up when I was completely alone. I can't remember exactly how I felt seeing him standing in front of me, I was probably in disbelief. I only remember standing there like an idiot, waiting for him to speak.

He stepped just inside the threshold, his feet straddling the doorplate. He leaned one arm against the doorframe, his body language conveying submission. There was an awkward silence before he forced out the words, "I'm sorry to bother you," which was followed by another round of awkward silence. I stared at him as if he were the devil. He shifted his weight after meeting my gaze. Then he stared at his shoes.

I kept waiting for the words "it's over" to fall from his mouth. I was hoping that, resigned to the fact that I clearly wanted nothing more to do with him, this was the moment he finally let go. Yet nothing but an eerie silence stood between us while he shifted his weight, resting his hands on his hips, now blocking the doorway as if he'd shape-shifted into a police barricade.

I didn't invite him in. I took several steps backward to widen the distance between us, crossing my arms across my chest as if to say, "Will you just get on with it?" After a moment of building up his courage, he got straight to the point: He'd come to ask for money. His breath reeked of alcohol as he explained he needed $40 so he could buy his twins a birthday gift.

I was flabbergasted. *He showed up drunk to beg for money?* I screamed inside my head. I told him I didn't have $40 and began closing the door. He blocked the door from hitting him in the face, took a step inside, and called me a liar.

"See, that's the fucking problem with you. You refuse to work with me," he scolded as if he were an authority figure who had gone out of his way to be patient with a rebellious child.

I could feel the tension escalating in the house. I was infuriated. I demanded that he leave our house immediately. He began laughing—a laugh that made me feel humiliated, naïve, and powerless. I knew I needed help—quick.

"I'm calling the police," I said, passing through the living room, then the kitchen, on my way to my phone lying on a table in the basement. Just as I was beginning to descend the stairs, I felt a blow to the right side of my neck from behind. The force of his fist plunged into to my carotid artery, immediately rendering me unconscious. I blacked out before my body ever hit the floor.

I came back to consciousness in the wee hours of the morning lying in a heap on the stairs. I had no idea how long I'd been there, but thankfully, Cain was gone. My body ached. A sharp pain traveled down my neck, through my shoulder blade, into my right lung. I forced myself to stand, pulling myself up by the railing as if it were the stable arm of God.

I stumbled up the stairs into the kitchen, surveying the open cabinets and drawers—Cain had rummaged through the kitchen while I'd been unconscious. I moved my way into the living room, finding the contents of my purse dumped all over the couch. I knew he hadn't found any money. The front door was completely ajar. When Cain had left, he hadn't bothered to close the door behind him. Actually, it looked like he'd opened it wider.

I felt numb as I closed the door, locking the deadbolt, then relocking it again to convince myself the locks were engaged. I bumbled my way to my bedroom and lay motionless in bed like a zombie waiting for the impending dawn. I knew we'd turned a corner in this insane dual over my right to freedom and privacy. Cain was now physically abusive—so much for low lethality.

For hours I lay in the darkness gnawing on Walter's words like a beaver gnaws on wood. Walter's words forced me to see the dragon living inside Cain. Up to this point, I don't think I'd ever realized the true danger of the situation because no one had ever been hurt. Property had been damaged, items had been stolen, but no one had suffered an injury. A few family pets had come up missing, and of course there were the dead birds left on my windshield, but I'd told myself that Cain had nothing to do with the pets, and he probably found the birds already dead on the side of the road.

This willful softening of my reality allowed me to believe that Cain was a criminal and crazy, but he wasn't physically dangerous. The brochures the detective had given me made an impact, but I'd worked hard to convince myself those women would never be me.

The truth, however, had outlived the lie. I came to see Cain for what he really was—dangerous. Cain was mentally ill. He was unhinged and unpredictable. Walter's forecast that things would get worse before they got better was never meant to be a floatation device, a beacon on the horizon; it was meant to be a warning, the foretelling of a maniac on the loose.

The problem with Walter's warning was it was so ambiguous. Even though I knew things would get worse, I don't think I was ever willing to accept that our physical safety could be in danger. But after that night, I saw for myself that Walter's assessment was correct: Cain was a very big problem, indeed.

As I lay in bed staring at the ceiling, I felt defeated, as if my insides had turned to dust. After the sun began to rise, I felt the need to talk to someone. It was still early on a Sunday morning, so no one answered their phone, but I left a simple voicemail for several of the important people in my life, asking them to call.

I told them that Cain had hit me and I thought I needed some help. Only Adia responded, driving over as soon as she got the message. She expected to see me badly beaten, relieved to discover that Cain had only landed one punch before he scattered into the night like an incubus destined for flight.

Adia insisted I call the police. For reasons I can't explain, I hadn't even considered it.

A fresh-faced police officer arrived with a snarky attitude and prevailing sense of boredom as if I were the only thing standing in the way of a well-deserved breakfast of steak and eggs. I described the events from the night before. I told the officer that I currently had an open case with the Columbus Police Department in case he wanted to fact-check my situation.

He seemed indifferent. He asked if I wanted an ambulance, I declined. He notified me that my detective would get a copy of the police report and I should expect a call within the week.

After the police and Adia left, I sat lifeless on the couch, staring at absolutely nothing. I had no idea what would come next. I felt physically and emotionally depleted. How was I supposed to successfully mother, work, and live a meaningful life with a lunatic who came and went as if it were forever his right to do so?

I felt fear growing inside me like I'd never felt it before. The fear began to tell me a lie that I began to believe: No one was going to save me, no one was going to help change my fate. The lie felt so much like the truth, I didn't have the strength to challenge it.

Cain may not have walked off with any money that night, but he took with him my last vestige of strength. In its place he left a malevolent fear that would follow me like a consuming shadow for the next four years.

The madman had spoken.

The detective never returned my call.

CVS Pharmacy seems like an unlikely place for one to find truth, but of course, truth appears when the timing is right, so I suppose CVS is as good a place as any for a revelation of meaningful consequence.

It wasn't too long after the night Cain hit me that I found myself running a quick errand to our corner CVS Pharmacy. I grabbed a basket as I entered the store and pulled out my shopping list. I don't remember specifically what I was there to buy, I only remember that the list was rather short.

As I weaved my way through the aisles, I saw one of the young men I recognized as having followed me before, back when they looked like choirboys instead of thugs. He looked up for only a split second, noticing that he was no longer alone in the aisle, but he hadn't made the connection that the person heading toward him was me. Then he did a double take, a flash of acknowledgment came alive in his eyes, his face quickly changed expression as if he'd seen a ghost. Our eyes locked. His eyes spoke of embarrassment, my eyes spoke of disdain.

I had no doubt that on the surface of things our meeting was happenstance, but seeing him really pissed me off. I turned away from him, set down my basket, and walked out the door. As I was getting in my car to leave, the man came running from the store.

"Ma'am, can I talk to you for a minute?" he bellowed from across the parking lot.

I ignored him. Just as I was putting my car in reverse, he stood tapping at my window, pleading. "Ma'am, please. I'd really need to talk to you for a minute. Please."

I rolled down my window an inch or two. "I have something I think you should see," he said, pulling his phone out of his pocket.

I stepped from my car and stood next to him as a he rifled through his phone. Then, without saying a single word, he slowly showed me a series of photos. I stared at the photos in complete disbelief. My hand immediately covered my mouth, trying to conceal a silent scream.

There were four, possibly five, photos (after the first three I suppose I stopped counting) of me lying on my bed partially naked. Some photos showed my exposed breasts, some showed my crotch. None of the photos showed my face, but of course I recognized my hair, my body, my bed, my sheets. I could tell from the photos that I was asleep when the photos were taken, my body was completely limp. Had I not known it was me, I would've assumed the person was dead. In one picture, it showed my jaw and a hint of my lower lip. My mouth was open as if I'd been snoring when the photo was taken.

"He sneaks in your house to take pictures," the young man said carefully.

I was speechless. I felt his eyes watching my reaction, for a moment feeling my pain. I got the sense that in his mind, the whole "joke" had gone too far. Yet, he still had naked pictures of me on his phone.

"How did you get these photos?" I asked.

"Email," he answered.

"Are there more?" I questioned, not really wanting to know the answer.

"Yes," he said softly, staring at the ground.

"You have to show these to the police!"

He backed up a few feet, looking up at the sky as if he were searching for the right thing to say. "Look lady, I'm just here to get some things before I deploy for basic training in the morning. I'm not trying to get involved. I just think you needed to know the truth."

"What am I supposed to do?" I asked incredulously, tears welling up in my eyes.

"Lady, you need a team," he said, exasperated, as if I hadn't figured that out on my own.

"Good luck," was the last thing he said as he turned and walked away, nervously running his hands over his hair.

Watching him leave, I could tell he wasn't sure showing me those pictures had been the right thing to do. He was already regretting it.

The truth that came at me that day was so big and painful it would be years before I ever truly allowed myself to process it properly. Until then, the reality of my situation had knocked me into the abyss of fear as deep as the Grand Canyon and as endless as a Montana sky.

I drove home stunned and fragmented. I felt nothing and everything at the very same time, as if a war of the senses were taking place inside my head. The memory of the night in the hotel rushed back into my consciousness as if it had only happened yesterday. The images captured on the man's phone seared themselves into my brain, tattooed there for life.

After I pulled into our driveway, I sat in the car unable to move. It was then that I felt something leave my body, rising through my core, evaporating like steam in the sunlight. At the time, I couldn't place the feeling, the loss.

I now know it was hope.

When hope leaves the body, its absence is felt immediately. Your mind becomes deathly silent, aware that the glue that holds you together doesn't have its elasticity anymore. I walked into the house forever altered.

When fear strikes, it strikes hard, delivering its message like a Mike Tyson punch. Fear isn't looking for friends—it's looking for hostages. My fear didn't come from all the things I knew, my fear came from the things I didn't.

Few things are scarier than the unknown. Mysterious, clouded, intangible, and unruly, it makes us come dangerously close to accepting our own powerlessness, our frailties, the truth of how small we really are when measured against the enormity of everything irreverent and uncontrollable. It's like dark matter, something you can't touch or see, yet it changes the nature of wisdom itself, twisting all you thought you knew into a joke you played on yourself.

Let's talk about fear. Fear is the bone crusher of life. Fear is the vampire of destiny. We all have to deal with fear at some point in our lives—its energy is prevalent and undeniable. Learning how to conquer fear is a pivotal step toward the state of internal freedom because it is fear and fear alone that will always be the most formidable opponent on your path toward dreams and light. Fear's job is to test how bad you want something and then punish you for wanting it at all.

Please know that the only thing in the universe that never dies is love. That's it. Everything else decays, surrenders, or perishes. This means that fear can die too.

What kills fear? Confidence. Confidence is the exterminator of fear. Think about it, aren't you less afraid to take a test when you're confident you know the material? Less fearful of losing your job when you know you have marketable skills? Less afraid to be by yourself when you have the confidence to enjoy your own company? Less afraid to try when you have the confidence to believe in yourself?

We must learn how to move through moments of fear just like we move through any other challenge in our lives—by facing it head on, staring it straight in the eye, slamming it to the ground like an active shooter. We kick fear's ass when the confidence of our will proclaims that we're not listening to fear's bullshit anymore.

When you project confidence when confronting your fears, it's fear's turn to be intimidated—fear becomes afraid of you.

But this is 20/20 vision pulled from yesterday's pain—this is what I know about fear now. That day at CVS, I let fear banish hope, then

I tripped into the darkest period of my life. Once hope left, fear did what it does naturally—it expanded.

For a very long time I allowed the fear of the unknown to render me utterly frozen. The state of being frozen is the complete surrender of the mind. In this harsh and unforgiving landscape, life feels meaningless.

The challenge of my lifetime wasn't learning how to defeat Cain, but learning how to defeat fear.

I just popped the last succulent blackberry into my mouth, letting the flavor wrap my tongue in ribbons of summer. I've ordered a double espresso to help with the long drive back home.

My work here is done. For quite some time I dreaded the idea of talking about the memories found in this letter. I suppose that's why I felt the need to write in a setting that feels like a Jimmy Buffet song, helping to cajole my thoughts into a calm release rather than a frantic purge.

I try to end my letters on a high note because that's how I've chosen to live my life for many years. It's good to reflect and process, it's healthy to talk about painful things, but we must learn how to draw the water from the rock. Every experience teaches us something.

I want to return to the central theme of my journey—the light. Walter's message spoke of two haunting facts: I had a big problem and things would get worse before they got better. But his most poignant observation was one that, during the black years, I'd swept under the rug thinking it didn't matter much: Walter felt I was smarter than Cain, but Cain didn't know it yet.

How sweet those words are to me now. This simple statement would prove to be delightfully accurate. Even though it's true that for a very long time I suffered from Cain's fascination with depravity, it's also true that one day I would split the night wide open when I came to know the power of my own strength. When my confidence took control, it reduced the saga of fear to nothing more than a pothole on the road to lightness and being.

When fear changed hands, fate changed course.

Sending positive energy across the miles and holding you close in thought,

Your Loving Mother

SEVENTEEN

Summer 2019

On the porch

Dear Sparrow,

I'm sitting on the front porch with my suitcase that's full of beads, spools of colored wire, silver notions, and other samplings of creative merriment. I took your advice and rented a booth at the upcoming arts festival. Now I'm in a mad dash to put the finishing touches on my decorative birdhouses. The colorful rhinestones outlining the tiny doors and windows are firmly set in glue and I'm threading a garland of beads for the roofs. Then, it's just a matter of securing the twinkling lights so it looks like the birds are throwing a party.

If even one person buys one of my outrageously silly birdhouses, I'll call the event a success. I'm not trying to peddle Phyllida Barlows on a street corner—art that makes you think. I'm just trying to make people laugh.

When you suggested the idea of the arts festival, I realized you're concerned I have too much time on my hands. Of course, you aren't aware that I spend so much time writing. My letters gather in a cedar box lined in lavender satin with sprigs of maple, the tree of offerings, and sprigs of ash, the tree of higher awareness. I added dried roses and yarrow as symbols of love and a bouquet of dried hydrangea, the flower of understanding. I sprinkled petals of daffodil and white lilies as a declaration of new beginnings and devotion. The acorns symbolize power and spiritual growth, and the moonstone, the stone of healing waters and sacred feminine energy, symbolizes the natural rhythms of life—a talisman of the inward journey.

I haven't decided yet when I'll give these letters to you. I guess I'll know when the time is right, just as you'll know when the time is right to read them. Until then, the written story of my life remains my secret to keep.

I enjoyed my road trip to Pensacola Beach. I was glad I made it through those memories without feeling like I needed to rent a bulldozer and demolish an unsuspecting water treatment facility. After I gathered up my things at the restaurant, I drove home listening to a Dave Matthews CD, followed by some Jill Scott, letting the wizardry of a pumpkin-and-sanguine sunset serve as the light show while my fingers danced on the steering wheel.

After the sun disappeared from the horizon, I slipped in my Lynyrd Skynyrd CD, listening to "Free Bird" on repeat. I always listen to that song with the volume up high—the jam session at the end is like care-free with an electrical charge.

I'm taking a break from my birdhouses. They're delightfully silly, but their assembly is tedious—tiny couches, tiny tables, and tiny pictures on the walls. When I first got the bright idea to decorate the inside of the birdhouses, I thought I was brilliant. Until I had to build them. It's funny how a bright idea looks so much better in our heads, free from the forces of gravity and restrictions that our inner genius never stopped to consider. A dozen little fireplaces later and I'm eager to step away from my bright idea for a while.

I've poured myself a glass of lemonade; now I'm ready to return to the spring of 2008. That's when the exhaustion set in. That's when I started making too many mistakes. That's when our world slipped off its axis.

Sometimes lost is a state of mind, and sometimes it's a place of being. When it's both, the only thing you can count on is complete exhaustion. After the joys of life have abandoned you, exhaustion longs to be your constant companion, making even a blanket of sunshine seem like a cold cement floor.

Stage Four is the exhaustion stage. This should come as no surprise since only exhaustion can follow prolonged anxiety. Anxiety is when the brain is firing a thousand rounds per second; exhaustion is when it isn't firing at all. The soul comes to feel like a lead balloon tied to a paper string—even breathing becomes a chore when you're tethered to an anchor that can't support your weight.

Here I'll lean on "The Seven Stages of a Stalking Victim" to help convey my experiences: "During the exhaustion stage, the stalking victim begins to completely unravel. The victim trusts no one—least of all herself."

As her mental health deteriorates, her physical body continues its descent into chaos. She experiences insomnia followed by days of lethargy and extreme sleepiness. Her appetite, digestion, and heart rate have changed. Her nervous system is no longer receiving normal communication from her brain. The victim's thought process becomes cloudy, her judgment impaired. Her prolonged stalking ordeal is no longer just an emotional roller coaster, it's now part of her physiology.

The stalker experiences the exhaustion phase, too. But it doesn't weaken him, it energizes him, feeding him from his victim's agony as if it were his life blood. Draining a body of life becomes his sole objective; he wields fear as though it's the scepter of a determined warrior. Exhaustion foreshadows surrender. And surrender wins the game.

By late the spring of 2008, we found ourselves an inch away from being homeless. I'd run out of money after cashing in my 401(k), and my ability to cope mentally, physically, and financially was limited. I began having panic attacks whenever I was in large groups of people—I simply couldn't handle the feeling of someone coming up behind me. Adding to my growing paranoia, I found it impossible to keep a regular routine out of fear that Cain would capitalize on it.

I'd had no success trying to find a job that fit within my mental limitations. Working with the public was out of the question, having a set schedule was out of the question, working with large groups of people or at a place with a large parking lot was out of the question, too.

I'd tried to overcome these fears, accepting any job I could find because we needed the money, but each time I started at a new place I had trouble focusing. If people stared at me, sizing up the new girl, I couldn't help but wonder if they were staring at me for darker reasons. I kept telling myself I was overreacting, but the stressed-out woman inside refused to listen. The more failure I experienced, the more depressed and exhausted I became.

I knew I had to do something, we were about to lose everything. I even considered stripping or prostitution. I would love to tell you that I never reached a place of such desperation, but I vowed to be painfully honest—even at the risk of my pride. There was a period of my life when I thought prostitution was the answer to all my prayers. I didn't give a shit about morality or condemnation—we needed money.

Thankfully, I didn't have the guts to go through with it. Not because I didn't want to (well, maybe the word *want* is over-reaching a bit), but because I feared karma would try to teach me a lesson if I even tried. I was convinced that if I sold my body, I'd lose my car. I'm not sure why I was certain it would be my car that karma claimed, but at the time, it seemed the most likely since I had nothing else to offer. The thought of losing my car paralyzed me. A person can't escape without a car.

The ability to escape a situation is how I analyzed everything during the black years. I didn't like being sandwiched in the middle of a long line because I might not be able to escape. I didn't like sitting at the back of a restaurant because I might not be able to escape. I didn't like going to the movie theatre because I might not be able to escape.

My sense of personal safety no longer revolved around my ability to protect my safe zone, it completely revolved around how quickly I could escape a danger once my safe zone had been violated.

I rarely appeared with you in public anymore and I never went anywhere during a business's busy time, hoping to make it in and out of a store in less than thirty minutes. I always dressed in inconspicuous, drab-colored clothing with my hair tucked under a ball cap. Bright colors were too easy to spot—my goal was to look as beige as possible.

I became a Cleveland Cavaliers fan out of necessity, making sure I always knew their game schedule. Cain was a huge Cavs fan, and I suspected that I could leave the house in relative anonymity whenever the Cavs were playing. Many people like LeBron James for his phenomenal skill; I like LeBron James because he kept Cain's attention focused on something other than me.

It's an odd sort of existence to only emerge from your house in short bursts or when a basketball game is on TV, but our lives were odd in so many ways that I stopped seeing my battle as odd. Feeling normal wasn't normal anymore. Feeling tired, confused, alienated, and defensive had become so ingrained in me that it came to feel natural; strange was my constant, so strange stopped feeling strange after a while.

After I lost my job, I knew it was only a matter of time before I couldn't afford to live in our house anymore. I did my best to hold on for your sake, knowing your friends in the neighborhood and your school were the center of your world. I did my best to shield you from our reality so your life could feel uninterrupted for as long as possible. Thankfully, preteen girls are the most self-absorbed beings in the galaxy, so hiding my truth required little to no effort.

Privately, however, I saw the house the same way I saw my old job—its safety had been violated and its vibe had been contaminated. Strangely, after the day at CVS, Cain stopped sneaking into our house, but I didn't know how long it would last. No matter how I tried, I knew I would never feel safe in that house again. And in my heart, I knew you weren't safe there, either.

For a very long time, I tried to convince myself that Cain was stalking only me, but in reality, he was really stalking both of us. Any trap he set for me, he set for you, too. I tried to communicate to family that I felt we were in danger, but I think the whole scenario sounded more like a sign of mental illness on my part than an intricate scheme on Cain's. The problem had been going on for almost three years at this point—I think it was reasonable for a normal people to feel as though the situation should've corrected itself by then.

It didn't help that I tried my best to appear normal whenever I was in the presence of family. If I felt my mask slipping, I made an excuse to leave. To me, the stalking had become an elephant in the room. I didn't feel safe talking about it, and no one ever asked.

After the incident at CVS, there was little doubt in my mind that you were a part of the collateral damage. The last picture I'd seen, before I looked away to spare myself any more pain, was a photo of me standing just outside my shower wearing a thin, plastic grocery bag over my head. The photo was somewhat blurry, as if taken while I was in motion. In the photo, I'd seen myself from a side view with one arm holding the towel to my chest and my backside completely exposed. I'd just emerged from the shower and appeared to be drying off.

As soon as I saw that photo, a memory came rushing back to me. I remembered a day shortly after we'd first moved into the house and Cain had unexpectedly stopped by. We'd stood in the kitchen talking while I unpacked groceries, and Cain began sorting the bags with an odd sort of smirk on his face. Then he passed me a pile of neatly folded bags and said, "These ones don't have holes," chuckling to himself. I didn't think much of it at the time because I didn't know Cain well enough to know if it was his habit to sort plastic grocery bags, so I'd dismissed the encounter as meaningless.

In the photo of me fresh from the shower, I had a plastic grocery bag around my head. I often used one instead of a shower cap because shower caps mildew so easily. But it was my well-kept secret because I knew I looked ridiculous wearing a plastic bag on my head.

Cain's sorting and folding, followed by his sly grin, was his subtle way of letting me know he knew my embarrassing secret. Had I not been so distracted with groceries, maybe I would've realized that Cain was actually revealing the location of one of his hidden cameras.

And then I remembered the picture frame Cain had given me as a housewarming gift. At the time, I was extremely touched by the gesture since the frame was so beautiful, with metal flowers and rhinestones decorating the border. I'd placed the frame on those built-in bathroom shelves next to the vase of dried flowers and the stack of *National Geographic* magazines.

I'd long since forgotten about the frame. It's funny how, after a while, we overlook the objects we see every day around a house. We'd notice if they were missing, but for the most part, after we grow accustomed to them, they become part of the muted background. When I saw the photo, I knew from the angle the photo was taken from that the camera had to be buried somewhere on that shelf.

After I returned home from CVS, I immediately went to the picture frame. I expected to find a hidden camera behind it. I didn't. Of course, I was still under the impression that a hidden camera would be easily visible once you knew where to look. Little did I know that surveillance equipment had become so small it could easily have been hidden within the frame itself. Even though I didn't see an obvious camera, I dropped the frame into a bucket of water, letting it sit overnight, then wrapped it in a towel, stuck it in an oversized purse, and threw it in a dumpster when I stopped at a gas station.

Even though I was sickened by the fact that Cain had been secretly recording me while I showered, used the bathroom, or changed a tampon, the most mind-bending part of Cain's invasion into my privacy was the fact that he would have been recording you as well. You often used my bathroom. And you were only thirteen years old.

Even now, my mind must hurry past this memory. I have a difficult time sitting on top of my thoughts in an effort to keep them calm. There are simply no words to describe the revolting, perverted, sinister, and feeble-minded recklessness of a man so entirely weak and disturbed. I've had many miles and many years to process this event in our lives, and I've come a long way in tempering my rage. That being said, I can't dwell here for long for fear that the disdain I feel toward Cain will overpower my God-given sense of peace, threatening to weaken me once more.

I almost didn't reference this event in my letters. This pain sits at the very deepest part of my well. However, I feel you deserve to know why I felt so strongly that you were no longer safe living with me. Until the crisis was behind us, I had no doubt that whatever Cain dished out to me, he dished out to you, too, and he'd already proven he had no ability to restrain his macabre curiosity.

For many reasons, I saw losing our house as a blessing. Perhaps I wouldn't have used the word *blessing* back then, I would've used the word *relief*. But like I said in an earlier letter, the art of life is knowing when to say when. You can do your best to try to overcome obstacles, but in the end, you can't match wits with crazy. All you can do is protect those you love, and yourself, as best you can—even if that means accepting that you can't protect anyone anymore.

The darkest moment of my life came when I had to admit that you needed a safe haven I couldn't give you. I felt like I'd failed at being a mother, failed at being a person, failed at being anything resembling someone capable and decent. I wasn't entirely sure what would happen to me, but I didn't care. I only knew that you had the right to live a life free from the madman who hunted me. Some days I hoped that our separation would be short-lived. Most days I feared that it wouldn't.

Running parallel to this time in our lives, your grandmother had retired, becoming a full-time caretaker for your two cousins during the work/school week, spending far more time at Charlotte's house than she did at her own. This meant that there was often more than one adult in Charlotte's house and the house rarely, if ever, stood empty. I liked the idea of you staying with Charlotte until I could figure out plan B, especially since you could stay in the same school.

Thankfully, Aunt Charlotte had plenty of room, plenty of help, and plenty of love, so she willingly agreed to let you stay with them for a while. I hadn't told anyone the true magnitude of our situation, fearing that if I did, they wouldn't want either one of us near them.

After we moved our belongings into the storage unit and you were living at Charlotte's, I was supposed to stay with your grandmother. But I didn't feel comfortable there for reasons that had nothing to do with her. She had worked hard to enjoy the benefits of a gorgeous house in the country, rightfully viewing it as her sanctuary, her safe place in the world. But I knew it wouldn't be her safe place for long if I stayed there for any length of time now that my life had become the equivalent of a contagious disease. You were safer being away from me, but I couldn't put your grandmother more at risk.

As I mentioned before, during the black years I viewed every situation for its potential threat level, and her house unnerved me. Instead of seeing a beautiful home, I saw a myriad of vulnerabilities easy to exploit: There were too many large windows that were never covered so the sunlight always felt welcome, there were too many sleepy neighbors who wouldn't notice a thing, and there were too few lights on at night, leaving acres of darkness. I was also aware that your grandmother had the habit of leaving her keys in her unlocked car at night. I'm sure this was a perfectly convenient solution for knowing where her keys were, but thanks to Cain's disastrous presence in my life, leaving keys in an unlocked car was the same as handing Cain a key to the house. Though your grandmother had a security system, she often didn't use it. I suspected it wouldn't take long before Cain found the weakness in her habits.

Once I began living without you, I began to loathe myself. I had difficulty sleeping, and the vomiting increased to an unprecedented level. So did the drinking. Then the blame game started. I blamed myself for everything. I blamed myself for Cain's sickness. I blamed myself for Cain's choices. I blamed myself for being so naïve and stupid and inept. I called myself worthless and unlovable. I called myself ugly, hopeless, crazy, and vile. I felt deep within my heart that the reason I couldn't be saved was because I wasn't worth saving.

Enter Stage Five: the self-blame stage. Following so closely on the heels of anxiety and exhaustion, this stage is the most damaging to the victim's psyche. I felt this stage as if it were my second skin—you could've fit my self-esteem through the eye of a needle and still had plenty of room left for a camel. I felt miserable inside, and blaming myself for everything was the only thing that made sense.

The summer of 2008 marked a turning point in our lives. It came to pass that after you moved in with your Aunt Charlotte, I drifted, trying to avoid your grandmother's house as best as I could. For the most part, I considered myself homeless since I often preferred living in my car in remote locations far away from Columbus. I knew if I wasn't there, Cain would leave both of you alone.

I would drive until I lost the radio station signal, hoping that Cain's GPS would lose signal, too. Then I kept on driving, hoping Cain wouldn't follow. I tried to believe that his fascination with me applied only when I was nearby, as if obsession is ruled by convenience, as if nut jobs adhere to the proverb "out of sight, out of mind." I was foolish to believe I could cure his addiction by layering miles between us, but I didn't know what else to do. So, I kept driving until even I didn't know where I was anymore.

Running scared, living on coffee and carefully rationed cigarettes, I was tired, I was overwhelmed, and I was out of options. With my back against the wall and a wolf at my throat, I began my life on the run.

Fear deafened me.

Blame was the only voice I heard.

My mind returns to my birdhouses. I must admit, they're pretty charming even though they no longer have any room left for, well, birds. I doubt any self-respecting bird would want to live in them anyway. Too flashy and too many colors. Perhaps I'll call my birdhouses fairy houses instead—fairies love bling.

I hope at least one person at the arts festival is looking to make adequate provisions for their homeless fairy. After all, it's become abundantly clear that a fairy who feels neglected can become quite a problem—they tend to spin chaos just to get people's attention.

If Donald Trump has taught me nothing else, he's at least taught me that.

Sending positive energy across the miles and holding you close in thought,

Your Loving Mother

EIGHTEEN

Summer 2019

At the coffee house on the beach

Dear Sparrow,

I'm enjoying a cup of coconut-pear tea with a slice of artichoke heart and sun-dried tomato quiche, staring at the Gulf while I reflect on the arts festival this past weekend. I did fairly well. Apparently, quite a few people were looking for a home for their fairy. I had no idea so many fairies were homeless—it's almost an epidemic.

I sold most of my fairy houses and all of the wind chimes. The wind chimes (I decided to embellish them with quartz, agate, amethyst, and carnelian) got a favorable reaction, glistening in the sun like colorful snowflakes playing Ring Around the Rosie. It's always interesting to me how many people have no experience with crystals yet are so drawn to them. People from all walks of life stopped by my booth to admire the beautiful gems and listen as the dancing copper chimes shaped the sound of the wind.

Humans' love affair with crystals is primal, resonating deep inside us, an eternal vibration connecting us to the very core of our planet. As energy moves upward from the core through the mantle, it crystalizes with elements and compounds, becoming the DNA of the earth. Crystals hold the blueprint of their journey, emitting an energy that is captivating and tangible, infused with timeless properties that gather our senses, realign our inner world, remove impurities from our thoughts and the spaces around us.

Even if we don't speak the language of crystals, the earth speaks it for us, unconcerned that man has moved on to more conservative forms of harmonizing that generate bigger profits. Crystals are the most stable matter in the universe, created over millions of years, so it should come as no surprise that the energy stored inside the stones feels healing and touched by something exquisitely divine.

Your great-grandmother Margaret was a woman who knew her way around a garden and the Bible. She believed that hidden in plain sight are the keys to unlock every sickness known to man. She had absolute faith in the power of holistic healing found in herbs and medicinal plants, the cleansing properties of natural elements, the value of opening yourself up to the infinite and the untamed.

Science often has much to say about the credibility of metaphysical realms, but keep in mind, not so long ago, science declared that animals don't have feelings and lobotomies were a perfectly good idea. Sometimes science is the proof of something before it can be proven otherwise.

One gentleman came to my booth looking for a birthday gift for his wife. I sized him up as a no-nonsense sort of character, as if the word *silly* had never been used to describe him. He studied my wind chimes with a doubting-Thomas expression on his face. I began telling him about the purifying properties of quartz, the intuition of amethyst, the uplifting aura of carnelian. He shook his head as if to dismiss my gibberish, saying, "The good Lord doesn't need rocks to make you feel better."

I laughed in agreement. "You are correct, sir. The good Lord doesn't need music to make us feel better, either, yet He gave it to us anyway." He snorted as if he was stifling a laugh he didn't want to offer.

"The symbolism of crystals and gems is biblical, sir. A gift from the earth, just as the earth is a gift from God," I stated gently, hoping to dispel his assumptions about New Age thoughts, even though it's hard to consider something "New Age" that's as old as the earth itself.

Then I posed a question. "If faith allows you to believe that the good Lord had the ability to place the Son of God in a humble manger, then what keeps you from believing that He couldn't place some feel-good in a humble rock?"

His face changed expression, my comment landing on home plate. Suddenly, he looked at my wind chimes with a new set of eyes. The protective layer of crust built around him wanted to cast me off as a clever snake-oil salesman, but the child inside him longed to believe. He stood staring at the wind chimes, with his back to me. After thinking it over, he bought two wind chimes, one for his wife and one for his adult daughter. Later he returned and bought one of my fairy houses.

After I passed him his change, I said, "Be careful when you invite fairies into your life, sir. There's no telling what they'll do."

He burst out laughing at the mere thought of it. He was still chuckling to himself as he walked away, his energy far less stiff and guarded. I smiled knowing the crystals had already begun to release their ancient magic.

After you moved in with Aunt Charlotte, I spent most of my days wandering aimlessly. I experienced fear as if it were a mind-altering drug, intensifying my symptoms—I couldn't think clearly, I couldn't eat, I couldn't sleep, and I couldn't find a resting place that I considered safe. I existed, but only in the most skeletal sense of the word.

I would spend hours staring at a tree, my mind completely disengaged, just staring into the distance at a fixed object without really noticing the object at all, hovering in the quiet space before consciousness, lost in the grotto of the mind.

When the mind is spent, fear becomes the sun that all other thoughts revolve around. I found myself in a chronic state of panic and worry. I began having dizzy spells. My muscles felt weak and my reflexes were dull. I knew I wasn't making good decisions, but I couldn't figure out how to make better ones. I tried to force my way through my depression, but exhaustion is a toddler that refuses to listen.

Trauma traumatizes, it's just that simple. I don't need a degree to understand that trauma is a soul wound. You can stuff trauma for a very long time, pretending that your essence is well, but when trauma forces its way to the surface, it bleeds like no other. I believe that during this period of my life, I was experiencing symptoms of PTSD, but I was under the impression that PTSD only affects soldiers returning from war. I never stopped to consider that my symptoms were the result of wounds dating back decades, stacked on top of each other like unsteady Jenga blocks, triggered by long-term stress and mental exhaustion—the automatic release mechanism on Pandora's unstable box.

I only knew that I had way too much shit on my mind and my internal systems were declaring mutiny, leaving me to cope without any kind of safety net.

I continued to avoid staying at your grandmother's whenever possible because I started to suspect that Cain had already begun to infiltrate her safe zone. Suddenly, the next-door neighbor's gardener took a keen interest in me even though for many years he'd never seemed to notice anything that went on beyond his employer's fence. Also, a small group of what appeared to be preteen boys began congregating at the riverbank just behind your grandmother's house. I assumed they came from the apartment complex on the other side of the river. I'd never seen them before.

This gaggle of knobby-kneed boys had tried to get my attention one afternoon as I sat on the back deck. It almost seemed as if they were calling my name, but I couldn't be sure due to the sound of the wind and water. Sensing something wasn't right, I went inside and locked the door. I'd been through this scenario too many times before to be fooled by these seemingly "random" encounters. I suspected that Cain had already established the weak links in my mother's sur-roundings—most likely, the bored tweenagers and the overly curious gardener were actually Cain's shiny, new toys. So I began staying inside or venturing only as far as the screened-in back porch whenever I was alone at your grandmother's.

And predictably, since I wasn't giving Cain the attention he re-quired, he turned up the heat.

One afternoon, I returned to your grandmother's house after many days living out of my car. I desperately needed a shower, a hot meal, and a warm bed. Showering had become a real problem for me—I felt extremely uneasy in the shower, convinced that cameras could be anywhere.

On this particular day, I knew your grandmother was at Aunt Charlotte's house. Even though I didn't like arriving when the house was empty, it was broad daylight and the neighbors would most likely be outside, so I felt I could probably relax enough to get some sleep.

As I walked through the front door, I was overtaken by the strong smell of cologne—unmistakably Cain's signature scent. The familiar smell hung heavy in the air and I could pinpoint its place of origin as being just inside the back door, recently sprayed and lingering like a visit from an overzealous Avon lady.

I froze. I'm certain all the blood rushed from my head. *He's here*, I said to myself, fearing I wasn't alone. Feeling lightheaded, I reached for the kitchen table in an attempt to steady myself. I was quite literally gobsmacked.

Still to this day, I can't begin to explain the soul-crushing weight of this experience. I desperately wanted to believe that Cain, or one of the dumb-dumbs working on his behalf, would never go so far as to enter my mother's home—I wanted to believe it was sacred ground and that even sickos respected maternal boundaries.

I was wrong. Clearly, Cain would stop at nothing to prove that he was everywhere and anywhere he chose to be.

I wanted badly to convince myself there must be a logical explanation for the strong smell of Cain's cologne engulfing the air, but I knew I'd be lying to myself. Cain was following his familiar habit of corrupting the outside of an environment and then moving inward.

I looked into the backyard toward the river. I realized how easy it would be to slip inside the house completely undetected. If you picture your grandmother's old house, sitting so close to the thin slice of woods bordering the river, you can see what I saw that day as I stared out the back door. If you remember, the river was often shallow—one could easily cross it with their pant legs rolled up to their calves. Since the back of the house was so secluded, I had no doubt that a parade of inebriated clowns could've frolicked their way through the backyard and into the house if they had the motivation and a key.

I now suspected they had both.

I engaged the security system and left immediately. I contemplated calling the police, but once again, I feared that calling to complain that I smelled cologne in my mother's house was the phone call of a fruitcake. You and I know that your grandmother didn't have male visitors when she wasn't home, but how do you prove that to a cop? I also considered calling my father or Vince, but I suspected there was zero chance they would believe me. In their safe world, people don't break into people's homes just to make a point. In their safe world, people in their right minds don't spend time practicing the tenets of gaslight manipulation.

After I left, I drove to a nearby church, taking refuge in a gazebo tucked inside a blanket of trees, and sat staring into the woods. Too dumbstruck to cry and too numb to pray, I sat perfectly still like a wooden soldier with painted eyes staring blankly into the distance. I stayed there until night fell, then made my way out of town. I drove into the blackness of a new-moon sky until the exhaustion became so overwhelming that not even coffee and fear could deliver me from its colossal trance.

Only now as I write of this experience can I finally begin to understand the magnitude of the devastation the stalking had on my life. It was crushing to think my child wasn't safe being around me and that my mother had become part of Cain's game. I felt like toxic waste.

I told myself I was a problem my family didn't need and my life had become a burden to them. The more I believed these thoughts, the more exhausted I became. The blame game can be so delirious.

There's a difference between personal accountability and blaming yourself for things beyond your control. I shouldn't have spent a minute of my time beating myself up for Cain's madness. Instead, I should've spent more time taking ownership of my reaction to Cain's madness. Self-blame is a very creative energy. It turns people into misfits and losers, not because they are, but because feelings of stupidity and worthlessness paint with the colors of shame and regret.

Homelessness isn't for sissies. Living out of my car wasn't easy, but it felt safe in many regards. I was no longer predictable in any form or manner—I moved like the wind. As a result, the stalking stopped. As in, "slam on the brakes" kind of stopped.

Being homeless felt like a strange kind of freedom. Of course, Bobby McGee would tell us that freedom's just another word for nothin' left to lose—my feelings of weightlessness came from having no one looking over my shoulder and no one listening at my door. So it wasn't the "kick up your heels" kind of freedom, but it sure felt like a relief I really needed at the time. I guess even freedom experiences the nature of light and dark.

Sometimes freedom is a man who owns nothing, sometimes freedom is nothing owning the man.

Food was a problem. I had very little money left and no idea how long my meager holdings would last me. I tried to make wise choices regarding my spending, but living wild has a tendency to rearrange a person's perspective. From the viewpoint of homelessness, the world is scary; from the viewpoint of hunger, the world is cold.

I slept in short bursts during the day in hotel parking lots and tried to keep moving at night. I never stayed in one place for more than an hour or two before feeling the urgent need to get moving again. To me, sitting still equaled getting trapped. I came to believe that constantly changing my location was the key to my survival.

For the most part, I hovered near the Ohio/Kentucky border. I don't know why I chose this region as a makeshift home base other than it was only a few hours' drive to Columbus to see you, yet far enough away to be inconvenient for Cain to bother me.

It was my blessing that I didn't fit the stereotype of a homeless person. I had a newer car and decent clothes, was easily able to disguise myself as a woman traveling alone rather than a drifter. I became part of the fluid scenery. As a result, I could slip into a pricey hotel offering a breakfast buffet, fill a plate, then disappear out a side door. I came to move like a cat: I never spoke, I preferred to go unnoticed, and my eyes challenged anyone who would dare stand in my way.

I still had a few friends back in Columbus, but none of them knew I was homeless. I often showered at Adia's. She knew I had anxiety issues whenever I showered, so she probably assumed I preferred to shower at her place with Quinn standing guard. Eventually, Adia offered to let me stay with her. This was an act of complete selflessness on her part since I had no job and a stalker, and my mind was a jumbled mess. She would've known better than anyone the risk she was taking because she'd heard Walter's warnings straight from his mouth.

Adia had recently returned from a stint at a rehab facility after battling alcoholism for years. She was focused on staying sober, and no doubt my presence was a threat to her sobriety. But she offered me a room anyway. After I moved in, the constant drive-bys began immediately. The notes, being followed in public, weird greetings from creepy strangers, thefts from garages and vehicles nearby, and disappearing mail and trash became a daily event in both of our lives.

It helped tremendously to have someone to talk to who was now experiencing the true scope of Cain's stalking campaign, but Adia quickly became overwhelmed. Liquor seemed to help.

Before long, we were both drinking heavily, hoping to dilute our reality. It took no effort whatsoever to blame myself for her return to alcohol. She tried her best to reassure me that she was trying to escape her own demons, but I was never certain she was being truthful, I suspected she was just being kind.

At some point, fresh on the heels of exhaustion, fear, and too much alcohol, I made the ridiculous decision to begin seeing Cain again in an attempt to calm the situation. I feared that if I didn't pacify him, I would lose the only home I had. Offering Cain access to me had worked the last time, so I hoped I had the guts to carry through with it again. Adia thought it was a good idea, too, believing the gesture would bring an end to the haunting. Neither one of us was thinking clearly, we only knew we had a big problem that needed a Band-Aid quickly.

I don't remember how many times I saw Cain after I moved in with Adia, but it was only a handful because being in his presence disgusted me. More than once a shudder ran through me as he spoke. I always made a point of seeing him in a public place in an effort to keep our meeting short and safe.

Regardless of how suave and debonair Cain tried to present himself, I could only see him as a mentally deranged lizard with lifeless eyes and a mean streak so wide it needed its own ZIP code. I hadn't slept with Cain again yet, I'd only permitted visits so we could catch up—as if he hadn't been pursuing me like a rabid dog.

It soon came time for Cain's birthday. I remember it clearly—the date was October 4, 2008. I'd agreed to spend his birthday with him. Adia and I invited him over to watch college football, and Adia ordered two large pizzas. I suppose I knew in my heart that if my charade of "I like you no really I do" was to remain believable, I'd have to sleep with him that night.

Knowing what my evening held, I began drinking the minute I woke up. I went through over half a bottle of whiskey before noon hit—I was so liquid I could have poured myself into a cup and passed myself off as a glass of Amy Winehouse. By the time Cain arrived, I was staggering and slurring my words.

I remember Adia leaving to pick up the pizza. I was alone with Cain for the first time since he'd hit me. And then I did what drunk people do: I told him the truth. I told him I was only going to sleep with him because I felt like I had to, but that the idea literally made me so sick that I had to get really drunk to even look at him.

Then I said, "It's shameful you can't find a sober woman who wants to fuck you." This sudden need to purge my soul wasn't in the script—he was mortified.

I remember the look of utter shock on his face, as if I'd just told him I was seriously considering becoming a pelican. It was clear Cain thought my desire to see him was hidden love finally revealing itself. After the initial shock wore off, he looked devastated. Then a look of contempt spread across his face, tightening his jaw, clenching his teeth, curling his upper lip in a sneer. He turned and left, slamming the door behind him.

By the time Adia returned with the pizzas, I was already passed out in bed. This would mark the last time I ever willingly saw Cain again.

Yet the stalking would continue for another ten years.

Adia reached a dark place in her life after this incident, probably feeling trapped by a saga that wasn't hers to bear. One evening, she barged into my room so drunk she had trouble opening the door. She insisted that I call someone in our family and ask for help. She seemed convinced our family had done nothing to remedy the stalking situation, and she claimed they had "their heads buried in their ass."

I knew Adia felt an enormous amount of pressure. She had begun receiving phone calls from strangers threatening to expose her secrets (I don't know what these secrets were, only that she seemed panicked at the thought), she knew someone was privy to her private conversations, and her car was being rummaged through on a daily basis. She had come to feel just like I did—in way over her head.

As Adia stood in my room firing off insults, I did my best to defend our family. They had tried to help, but they were out of their league. She declared that their help was the equivalent of "offering a grain of rice to someone dying of starvation." She was angry that I'd stopped discussing the situation with our family, and she was angry that they'd so easily stepped aside. She demanded that I pick up the phone immediately and call someone. I refused.

Adia was adamant that Cain wasn't feeling enough pressure to stop, so the problem was only growing bigger. Of course, none of this was news to me, but apart from doing my best to not entertain his craziness and making sure you were out of the line of fire, I didn't know what else I could do. I sat there wondering why she didn't call Walter if she felt so sure I needed more help than I had.

After Adia showered me with her frustrations, she stormed out of my room with the words, "You know, my family may be dysfunctional, but your family is useless," trailing behind her.

The following day, I came home to find an eviction notice left on my pillow with a note that read, "Walter thinks you should leave."

Our family helped move my things into a storage unit.

I drifted once again.

The quiet of the woods surrounded me. The perfect kind of silence only nature can offer. A silence so deafening it makes you feel exquisitely solitary, yet not at all alone. In the sanctuary of the woods, I never felt empty or without. The troubles of the outside world felt waning and distant, allowing me to find a calm place in my head. I came to seek the woods like a sinner seeks the cross.

By the spring of 2009, I was homeless again. Only this time, I didn't live out of my car. I made a campsite deep in the woods in Hoosier National Forest, just west of Louisville, Kentucky. Just like before, I preferred a location a few hours' drive from Columbus so it wasn't convenient, yet close enough so I could still spend time with you.

I suppose hearing that I lived in the woods sounds rather extreme and sad. Let me reassure you that it was not. The woods became my monastery, offering me a peace I hadn't known since my stalking ordeal began. I had room to breathe, a place to rest, and most importantly, the cadence to free my mind.

I felt safe in the woods. Though some might consider sleeping in a darkened forest the stuff of nightmares, I found it to be the stuff of dreams. I always awoke feeling refreshed. The longer my stalking experience remained idle, packed away like a funeral dress, the more the spirit of the woods wrapped me in the splendor of ohmness where fear didn't exist. I felt the yellow of the sun and the silver of the moon, heard the whisper of the wind and the conversation of birds, smelled pine and cedar seasoned by earth and stone. I tasted the freshness of wild onion and hickory nuts, let the satin of rippling water caress my hands and feet with a sensation that felt spiritual and quietly rejuvenating.

Whenever I had to leave my campsite, the fear struck like a lightning bolt. I feared someone would stumble across my hidden bungalow, stealing the few possessions I had. I feared someone would follow me back into the woods and learn my secret location. I feared Cain would be hot on my trail.

There came to be a huge division between how I felt whenever I was alone in the woods and how I felt when I wasn't. Outside the woods, I was a stalking victim. Inside the woods, I was a woman learning how to save herself.

As the summer rolled by, alternating between time spent in Columbus and days spent in the woods, I spoke less and less, which is odd since the word *verbose* fits me remarkably well. Whenever I was in the woods, days would come and go without ever hearing the sound of my voice. It always startled me if ever I caught myself thinking out loud, words filling the quiet space around me like pebbles thrown against a metal door. I came to prefer the silence.

The woods represented my willful separation from the world. I'd been through so much in my life (even more than I mention in these letters), that I gladly threw up the white flag of surrender, escaping to a place that didn't hurt, didn't judge, didn't see my tears in terms of strong or weak. I was just another vibration blending into the ambient sounds of the forest. Animated and intimate, the spirit of the woods began to live inside me.

And that's when the process of healing began.

Viewing my stalking experience from a distance for the first time, I can see fear was forced to step aside for a while, allowing me to bring forth the anger I'd been denying. Fear is a narcissist that demands all of our attention. It surprised me when I realized how angry I was—at everyone, at life in general, but mostly, at myself. My anger was voluminous, I was pretty sure I'd lose ten pounds if I could at least reduce my anger by half.

It felt remarkable that I'd been carrying around so much anger without ever realizing it. How could I begin to reclaim our lives with all this muck swimming around inside me? I wanted to like myself again. I wanted to trust myself. I wanted to be someone you could be proud of, not a fearful, angry, woman too nervous to live anymore.

Let's talk about anger. Anger needs to speak its truth. It's that simple. You get to choose how and when, but anger isn't going anywhere until it's had a chance to express itself.

It's perfectly normal to be angry when someone hurts you. Incredibly angry. But anger has a way of wandering irresponsibly, attaching itself to everything in its path. You can start off being angry that a check didn't arrive in the mail, and before you know it, you think the mail carrier is a complete asshole.

Anger has a way of getting ahead of itself, so anger needs a babysitter. You have to stay on top of your anger before it runs and hides, or you'll be cleaning up unnecessary messes for the rest of your life.

Anger needs to be identified and isolated—you have to take the time to figure out who you're mad at and why. Then say it out loud, let it vent; scream it if you need to: "I'm angry that I didn't get a pony for my eighth birthday! I'm angry that my boss is an idiot! I'm angry that life is unfair and all my favorite foods are fattening!"

It doesn't matter how trivial or insignificant your anger may seem, it will morph into something major unless you release it.

That summer, I spent some time sorting through my muddled anger, trying to figure out who sucked and who didn't. Bit by bit, I began chipping away at the blackened tumor eating a hole inside me. I decided I wasn't angry at Adia, I was hurt, but I couldn't begrudge her the need to save herself—she needed to save herself.

I wasn't angry at our family, either. I knew in my heart they didn't understand. Our family is a wonderful assortment of good people who love beautifully. But love doesn't mean you can make every boo-boo go away. And some problems are a whole lot bigger than one family can fix.

It wasn't fair to be angry with the police, either. Cops spend their whole day dealing with lawlessness and tragedy, so I'd imagine a call about footprints in dirt and face prints on glass might seem less than urgent.

I was hurt that no one could bring an end to my ordeal, but I was wasting precious energy being angry about it.

Thanks to the therapy of the forest, my ball of anger got smaller and smaller until only one nugget remained: I was pissed at Cain and Cain alone.

This epiphany was huge, and it cleared out a lot of head space. Once my mind felt lighter, I was able to enjoy just being for a while. Without fear at my throat and all that extra, angry weight, I could just be. I was quiet and calm and momentarily centered. It felt like the "nothing owns the man" kind of freedom.

And that's when I felt it—the absence of hope. My world had been so crazy, I'd never noticed that it'd gone missing. I knew something made me feel vacant inside, but I hadn't been able to put my finger on it before. When I'd lost hope that day at CVS, I never went searching for it again. Yet suddenly, sitting among the constellation of trees, resting on a blanket of leaves and awareness, I felt the hole it had left in my heart.

I wanted hope back. I wanted the joy of life back, too. And I wanted to reconnect with God. I decided that Cain could have my mail, my journals, my trash, he could even have pictures of me with a bag on my head, but he couldn't have my kid, my mom, my sanity, or my faith.

That's the beauty of surrounding yourself with nature—the experience helps you see the universe in everything, even yourself.

In the following weeks, I spent a lot of time alone with God at my campsite in the forest. I didn't know it then, but I was beginning to learn the art of healing. I had a long way to go before I put the simple formula into practice, but opening my heart and my mind to the vast corridors of silence, surrounding myself with the luxury of feeling well, I experienced the comfort of reassurance that whispers like amazing grace.

As I sit writing these memories, I believe I was guided into the woods, a place where I felt comfortable, for bigger reasons than just trying to escape an idiot. I was sent there so I could focus on the inside, not the outside, because the inside is where life happens.

We all need to find our quiet place in the world. And we need to visit it often. Since where we're at externally has such an impact on where we're at internally, we need to seek a softer environment so our feelings have a chance to make better choices.

Feelings can't change colors without a refreshed palette. We can paint our world in charcoal if we want, but white, yellow, and green are powerful choices, too, helping us relax our vibrations and regulate our energy flow.

It's not enough to just want peace within the noise—we have to be willing to paint it into existence.

Sending positive energy across the miles and holding you close in thought,

Your Loving Mother

NINETEEN

Dear Sparrow,

I spent the last few days rereading some of the letters I've written so far. It felt like standing in a wind tunnel, the story of my life speeding past me like a train wreck in a hurry. It's odd to see yourself through the reflections of a distant memory, reconstructed so the significance is pronounced, yet lacking the in-the-moment intensity that made it feel so real at the time.

I think I'll add a sprig of white pine, the tree of peace, in my box of letters so its energy can wrap itself around my words like the tail of a contented cat.

When I first came home and began writing these letters, I thought I would spend a lazy week sitting under a beach umbrella, effortlessly rattling off a few dozen pages. I had no idea my letters would require so much thought, so much soul-searching.

Through my writing I've come to discover that life doesn't always stay inside the margins, and it's more visceral than most sentences can handle. Since the Aquarian nature of my soul is free to beat loudly in my chest, speaking of myself in terms of stupidity and suffering has been a pie-in-the-face I never really saw coming. But I'd forgotten so much until I put pen to paper. And I'm different now.

The tremendous memories that have worked their way onto these pages feel like the skeletons of a past life. I'd like to say that these memories don't fit me at all anymore, but without them, my evolution wouldn't be so meaningful. My inner strength would have no motivation to hang around quite like it does.

Strength likes to takes naps. It will sleep for years if you let it. But once it's pleased with itself, once it gets to experience its own glory, it's not so quick to close its eyes knowing that darkness is forever lurking.

The man who turns a blind eye has more to worry about than blindness.

Humans have a natural inclination to pretend that who we are when we find ourselves is who we've been all along. It's a humbling experience to admit that you haven't always been brave, wise, or resilient. Sculpted by experience, the evolution of a soul is found in its growth rings. Just like a tree, as we move though each season, we add another ring. A long growing season results in a wider ring. A soul reaches a higher level of consciousness when it comes to understand that the knots the rings produce are really the steps of enlightenment, the staircase to a whole new being.

So even though I'd like to distance myself from all of these memories, the truth is, these memories are the medals of a dynamic warrior. We don't live a meaningful life by accident. We earn it.

In this letter, I will return to the year 2009. It was a long growing season. Much of 2009 is forever lost to me because I spent a fair amount of time feeling great anger toward Cain and drinking way too much. I'd like to tell you that I regret both of these transgressions, but I can't. The drinking fueled the anger and the anger fueled the fighter.

A good poetry reading and a latte have never triggered a woman's inner Athena. Athena rises when the rage within can no longer be contained; her anger becomes her sword and shield. No longer willing to demur herself to the forces of the outside world, she declares herself fully awake.

Stage Six is the anger stage, the stage of fury and fighting back. Anger focuses your attention, gets the blood pumping again, throws the mind into action. Anger is how we discover our personal boundaries—when something makes us angry, we draw lines in the sand, warning those around us, *Caution: Danger Ahead, Enter at Your Own Risk, I've Had Enough of Your Shit*.

Prolonged anger is highly acidic, but anger that sets limits is a healthy form of protection. Sometimes it's hot and sometimes it's cold; sometimes it's loud and sometimes it's brewing; but anger is an energy to take seriously because it's always a game-changer.

During the anger stage, the victim becomes critically aware that the stalking experience has her life in a straightjacket. She's willing to do anything to stop its progress. She has come to understand the unfortunate truth that every stalking victim must accept: Law enforcement is under-trained, under-funded, and incapable of solving her problem for her.

The key to her salvation lies in her own two hands.

Meanwhile, the stalker realizes that the victim is fighting back and resorts to more threatening behavior to solidify his position in her life. Her anger has dwarfed her fear—he needs her to be afraid again. The stalker hasn't the foresight to comprehend the time-tested truth given to us by Mark Twain: "In a battle of wills, it's not the size of the dog in the fight, it's the size of the fight in the dog."

When I emerged from the forest the last time, I walked away from the experience feeling angry and clever. A red-hot fire burned within me, aimed at Cain and Cain alone. Suddenly, I wasn't tired anymore, I was energized. I had no idea how I was going to stop the madness, I only knew that I wasn't going to lay down my life without a fight.

The woods had steadied me, speaking a truth I needed to hear: In the natural world, it's not always the biggest or the fastest who guarantees their right to survival, it's the one with the most capable mind.

A skillful opponent has the ability to turn their adversary's weakness into their own strength. And since most people are unwilling to identify their weaknesses, they do a piss-poor job of protecting themselves.

I don't suppose I ever took the time to know Cain very well, but one thing I did know was he always demonstrated a clear disposition for the Libra side of life—he was so Libra he didn't know how to be anything else.

You and I have often discussed the signs of the Zodiac. I believe it would be fair to say that we agree that astrological signs are a window into the nature of how we operate when we operate by instinct alone. Instinct is action without thought, unpolished by logic and reason. Our signs are who we are when we're in harmony with the core of our inner self because it's the inner self that paints the world around us.

I know many people doubt the validity of signs, while others claim them to be the work of the occult. In the most literal definition of *occult*, I would have to agree with them. However, I only agree with them because *Webster's Dictionary* defines the term *occult* as: "not easily apprehended or understood; not manifested or detectable by clinical methods; mysterious." Using this definition, you could place spirituality, space, the ocean, and the human brain in the same classification.

I've never considered astrology to be the brew of witches, warlocks, or Satan worshippers, although I have no doubt that anything can be twisted until it becomes a darker version of itself. Ancient astrology was birthed in the elements of creation—earth, fire, air, and water. And wherever there is providence of creation, light and wisdom can be found.

God's a math guy. He likes formulas. I find it impossible to believe that God, who carefully considered everything from the cosmos to an atom, threw up His hands when it came to the nuances of man and said, "I really have no idea how to make this work." I believe it's far more probable that God's recurring theme of balance applies even to man himself.

We have four seasons, four directions, four main phases of the moon, and four elements of creation. Our planet is composed of four layers: the inner core, the outer core, the mantle, and the crust. The human brain is divided into four lobes, and the human body is divided into four main parts: head, arms, trunk, and legs. A sturdy foundation needs four sides, a stable chair needs four legs.

When God sought balance, it sure seems like four was his go-to number. I tend to believe that astrology is just an extension of this formula. By separating man into four main personality types, each with its own set of strengths, when unified, the world is balanced. Could it be just a coincidence that signs flow so purposefully? Maybe. Yet I've never known God to be much of a coincidence kind of guy.

Our governing sign lays the foundation for our thought process. We think how we think on a level that's complex and organic, a harbor of imagination in the sea of emotions and analytical responses.

You often hear the phrase "like-minded individual" tossed about when trying to describe someone whose thought process feels comfortable. I would venture to guess that the people we refer to as like-minded are actually a compatible sign or share similar experiences viewed from the same perspective we do, cushioned by the innate reflexes of how we interpret the world.

When we say, "I just don't get that guy," we're usually talking about someone governed by a sign whose thought process feels foreign to us. Of course, we aren't truly governed by our signs. The word *governed* implies compliance without will. We're always free to separate ourselves from our instincts whenever the mood strikes. So perhaps it's best to say that our signs are merely a tool we can use to better understand each other and ourselves.

Let's face it, God likes it when we understand each other, so it doesn't surprise me that he left a recipe for how to do so.

Acknowledging a person's thought process is central to understanding the person. Each sign carries its own personal anthem that is central to its being—an undeclared statement that guides our motivation. As an Aries—a fire sign—your inner anthem gravitates toward concepts regarding independence and self-assertiveness. As a result, Aries are usually quite confident and natural-born leaders. Aries are passionate, curious, and creative spirits with a youthful enthusiasm toward life. This is not to suggest that other signs don't enjoy these same attributes, but they probably don't *feel* them quite like an Aries does.

I can compare this analogy to people with red hair having a sensitive relationship with the sun. Redheads tend to burn and freckle easily, but this doesn't mean that brunettes and blondes never burn or freckle. It only means that redheads experience the sun differently than the rest of us.

Likewise, a Pisces—a water sign—is known for its tendency to go deep, analyzing matters quite meticulously. I'm not suggesting that other signs don't have deep thoughts, but a Pisces is more likely to ponder more deeply and for a longer time until they feel confident their decision is a sound one.

Understanding a person's astrological sign also helps us identify when a person is living in the dark side of their sign—when they're swimming against their own tide. And we all do it. Each of us is a shining example of our most honest inclinations, with a tendency to reveal their antithesis.

For example, a Scorpio is famous for their need for honesty and transparency, yet the shadow side of Scorpio shows us they're often the most secretive of all the signs. This information is helpful when you find yourself dealing with a Scorpio who is notoriously playing their cards close to their chest. If you knew it was in their nature to do so, you wouldn't take their behavior quite so personally.

I don't remember giving much thought to the Libra in Cain. Although he always struck me as unapologetically Libra, I don't suppose I ever considered using the wisdom of astrology as an insight into his vulnerable underbelly. As an air sign, Libras tend to live in their heads. They're often complex individuals, yet emotionally immature. Libras are famous for seeking balance in their lives. This proclivity toward balance makes them excellent diplomats. Libras also have a love affair with all things beautiful. I suppose we all love beautiful things, but a Virgo for example—an earth sign—would rather see things how they really are than with a coat of paint hiding any imperfections. Not so for a Libra, who thinks the more paint, the better.

As an Aquarian, also an air sign, the art of balance doesn't motivate me much at all. I naturally gravitate toward freedom as my central theme—freedom of thought, freedom of expression, and freedom of movement. As a result, my life is often terribly lopsided. If I'm pursuing a goal or idea, everything else in my life has to wait patiently in the corner—these letters are a classic example. The shadow side of my need for freedom is found in my hesitancy toward commitment. Commitment feels restrictive, suffocating, a shallow trap with arthritic sides.

Knowing that a Libra is geared toward partnership and symmetry, I suspected that a Libra would begin to unravel if a relationship turns obnoxious or ugly. And since Libras naturally find comfort in fairness and balance, then breaking rules and going off script is a sure way to create problems in the Libra mind. Chaos weakens the Libra.

So chaos is what I created.

After I left the woods, pieces of my life began to come together. Your Aunt Charlotte had decided it was time for you to live with me again, so we moved into that disgusting hotel, becoming one of the many fly-by-night characters who live day to day. Obviously, it wasn't an ideal solution, but it was all I could afford at the time. A room with dingy sheets and a stinky carpet was one helluva motivator though, forcing me to land a job and stick with it no matter how I felt inside.

I was delightfully surprised when I discovered that I actually liked working at that collection agency just up the road. I'd never been a skip-tracer before, but I found that the investigative side of my work kept my mind busy. I loved working in a small office that required the swipe of a security badge in order to enter the building, and my little cubicle sat in the far corner of the room, so I never felt like someone could walk up behind me. The parking lot was barely large enough to accommodate the employees' vehicles, so I didn't find my eyes scanning for spies like I always had before.

These simple factors, irrelevant to anyone else, felt like blessings dipped in dark chocolate to me. Before long, I was able to move us into that pricey, extended-stay hotel for a ridiculously low weekly rate— thanks to the kindness of the manager. The hotel never operated at maximum capacity so perhaps the manager thought a discounted rate was better than an empty room. Even though we were still living in a hotel, it felt more like a day spa, offering a nice swimming pool, a sauna, a state-of-the art workout facility, and rooms like plush one-bedroom apartments.

I know you hated the idea of living in a hotel. And I know you were angry at me for losing all of our belongings in the storage unit when I couldn't afford the monthly payment. You had every right to feel that way. I was angry at myself for letting you down. I could only hope that I was on the road to reclaiming our lives and that one day you would forgive me. I wanted to believe that everything we would gain would mean more to us than everything we had lost.

Since you were a freshman in high school, you were completely allergic to spending time me, engrossed in your own interests and your large circle of friends. So I found myself with a lot of free time on my hands, but I was still hesitant to leave the safety of the hotel with all of its security cameras and controlled entries.

I began passing time by working out at the hotel's gym. It was there that I met a man named Finn who had recently relocated from Minneapolis. Finn was a fitness fanatic with a muscular build, Scandinavian features, and a disciplined air about him. Even though he held the enthusiasm of a wet cardboard box, I felt comfortable around Finn for two important reasons: His favorite topic of discussion was himself, so he didn't ask a lot of prying questions; and knowing he was new in town, I felt he would have no connection to Cain.

We struck up a friendship over cardio equipment and conversations about electrolytes and protein bars, neither one of us looking for a partner, just an end to chronic boredom.

I'd told Finn that I had an unstable ex, feeling a moral responsibility to alert him. I didn't go into great detail, just giving him the *Reader's Digest* version, stopping short of sounding paranoid or schizophrenic. Finn didn't seem at all bothered, probably because he didn't see me as a girlfriend. It was refreshing to know that Finn didn't see me as a pariah, so we continued to spend time together, coordinating our schedules so we had a workout partner.

Then came the day when someone destroyed Finn's beloved sports car while it sat in the parking lot at his job. Someone had smashed the windows and removed three tires, and the front bumper was missing entirely. The vandal had left a note on his windshield. I don't know what the note said, all I know is that Finn immediately called me, demanding Cain's name and number. I gave it to him, but I suspected that Cain was too much of a coward to deal with Finn directly.

A little while later, Finn showed up at the hotel in a taxi while I sat outside waiting for him. As soon as our eyes met, I knew our friendship was over. Finn could hardly stand to look at me.

"Are you okay?" I asked hesitantly.

"Pussy wouldn't answer," he replied through clenched teeth.

"I'm so sorry," I said, feeling the weight of the world on my shoulders.

He passed by me as if I were a beggar on a street corner as he headed toward the front entrance, then he stopped abruptly and turned around. Looking in my general direction, but trying hard to avoid eye contact, he spoke to the top of my head and said, "Look, I can't get involved in this, okay? I got kids I need to think about."

Without waiting for a response, he walked into the hotel like a bull seeing red. By morning, his hotel room was empty and all his things were gone.

After the incident with Finn, combined with all the endless bullshit Cain had put us through, I was so angry, I would've done anything to level the playing field. My inner Athena demanded that I wage a counterattack before fear had a chance to make me trip again.

Cain's attempt to euthanize my growing independence didn't make me want to retreat into the woods or pick up a bottle or call the police. Instead, it flamed my anger into an idea that sounded twistedly appealing: If Cain was insistent that I didn't have the right to choose my own friends, I would begin choosing his.

Over the course of the next several weeks, every single time a strange man approached me to say something off-color or call me Mrs. Cook, I passed him my number and told him I thought he was cute. Cain's suckerfish stared at me in disbelief, yet they always secretly called. Cain came to believe that I was devouring his network. And I was. Before long, battle lines shifted, loyalties became blurred, and his cast of malleable fools began to dwindle. The change in atmosphere created a great deal of anxiety for Cain.

"Ol' boy doesn't know what to do," said one man, chuckling as if it pleased him that Cain was thrown off his game.

"He stays drunk," said another.

His "friends" seemed to enjoy his unraveling, phoning me regularly to tell me what was going on in his life. I learned that he'd gotten a woman pregnant, had hoped she'd have an abortion, then drank even more when he found out she wouldn't.

The men also began to tell the curious tale of Cain's younger brother, Ryan.

Ryan, it seemed, possessed what was described to me as "street credibility." He was a small-time drug dealer, earning the respect of those traveling in the same circle. Knowing Cain's family enjoyed a rather prominent reputation in the community, I was surprised to hear that his brother had criminal ties. I'd been under the impression that Cain was the black sheep of the family, but as it turns out, they were a small herd.

I'd never met Ryan, but I came to learn that Cain and Ryan had a competitive, often tumultuous, relationship. Even though Cain was seven years older than Ryan, he'd never gained his brother's admiration. Ryan privately viewed Cain as a drunk and "a family embarrassment."

Ryan was well aware that Cain was targeting me, often playing a role in many of my experiences. When the brothers were getting along, Ryan and some of his closest friends helped Cain, as if tormenting me was a bonding experience. When they weren't getting along, Ryan tried to get Cain to stop.

In the end, it would turn out that Ryan was almost as much of a problem for me as Cain was. Had I not befriended their friends, I never would have known.

By the turn of 2010, Cain was cracking mentally. He couldn't seem to tame his obsession, and he no longer knew who to trust. Rumors began spreading that Cain was going through jobs like water, developing a reputation as a problem in the workplace. A friend of theirs, Travis, informed me that Cain, desperate for a job, had applied at Travis' father's local newspaper but had been turned down for the position of delivery boy due to poor references from former employers.

"He just leaves in the middle of the day and never comes back," said a former boss.

"Somethin' ain't right," said another.

Dismantling Cain's team was a stroke of idiot-genius on my part. I knew I was rubbing elbows with a nefarious crowd, but Cain had already placed them in my vicinity, so I figured it behooved me to use them to my advantage. In doing so, I tipped the scales in my favor, throwing Cain into a tailspin.

Adding to his problems, I actually came to like some of the men in Cain's inner circle once I came to see them as people and not just weirdos following me around a store. I don't use the phrase "I came to like them" in the sense that I added them to our Christmas card list, but it became clear that Cain's army was more of an "I'll scratch your back if you scratch mine" partnership than a secret society of deviants.

Many of Cain's associates came to like me as well. He had painted me as a slut and a "crazy bitch," but after getting to know me, they realized I was neither. Cain came to look like a liar and a deceiver—even among his own tribe. When I revealed to them that Cain had snuck into my house to take nude photos and filmed us in the bathroom, many of his associates were genuinely surprised to learn how deranged his obsession had become. They wanted out. Word spread that Cain was "hot," meaning gathering too much attention. His network began to crumble even more.

And that's when the problems really started. When Cain could no longer get a stool pigeon to do surveillance, he was forced to do it himself. He applied to work at the company where I was working and at the hotel where you and I were living. Thankfully, neither one hired him. I learned that Cain had begun fraternizing with a man awaiting trial for murder. To make matters worse, the man accused of murder applied at my company, too. When my boss ran a background check, the accused murderer was banned from the property.

Even though I'd made significant progress by disengaging Cain's support system, the situation took a more ominous tone once a very drunk Cain began executing fear and intimidation on his own.

One evening while I was on break at work, I called Adia to complain that a co-worker sitting in the cubicle next to me was obviously masturbating under his desk. He had a reputation for doing this, so I didn't feel like his habit was directed toward me, but the smell sickened me. I would soon regret having this conversation on my personal cell phone.

Within an hour of that phone call, the entire office looked out the window and watched helplessly as the man's car burned to the ground. It literally went up in flames. Multiple fire trucks showed up. It was later determined that an accelerant had been poured on the ground, ignited by a burning cigar. No one could prove that Cain was the culprit, but I certainly had my suspicions.

Next came another incident of great concern. Very early one morning, I was making my way home after staying the night at a friend's. She and I had stayed up talking well into the night, enjoying a few glasses of wine, so I had rested on her couch for a couple of hours before making my way home.

As I traveled down a main road through Columbus, I noticed a dark SUV following closely behind me. It was one of the very few cars on the road, so its hovering proximity alarmed me. I moved into the other lane, the SUV followed. Suspecting a tail, I quickly turned into a neighborhood that wasn't familiar. The layout of the neighborhood mimicked a tic-tac-toe grid—long streets running north and south intersected by shorter streets running east and west. I began making a series of turns trying to outmaneuver the threat behind me. The SUV stayed hot on my tail. I began to panic.

The neighborhood, I quickly realized, was a dangerous place to be even in broad daylight. Many of the houses had boarded-up windows covered in graffiti, mattresses on the front porch, and trash piling up in the yard. Most of the streetlights were burned out or pulled from the pole entirely. Realizing I'd definitely turned into the wrong neighborhood, I began to panic even more, cursing myself for my own stupidity.

I began trying to find my way out of the neighborhood when I noticed the SUV come to a complete stop on the street running perpendicular behind me. I kept driving down the short, little street until I noticed a second SUV come to a complete stop on the street intersecting in front of me. I immediately stopped, hyperaware that I was trapped, boxed in from all sides. My heart began pounding wildly. I sat very still, frozen almost, unsure what to do next. Minutes passed like hours. The SUVs didn't move.

Aware that I was a sitting duck in a skirt and flip flops with no weapon of any sort, I had the presence of mind to trigger the car alarm on my key fob. Thankfully, my car alarm was loud and obnoxious, slicing through the quiet morning like the wail of a screaming banshee. The SUV behind me didn't waste a second, accelerating so fast the tires spun. The SUV in front of me drove away slowly. As soon as they were gone, I put the car in reverse, backed into a driveway, and headed out the way I'd come. I pounded my car horn all through the neighborhood in an effort to create a scene until I was back out on the main road.

I made it home safely.

This incident haunted me. For days and days, the feeling of being so vulnerable and surrounded rolled around inside me like concrete in a cement mixer—anything could've happened.

As I've mentioned before, it's the fear of the unknown that's so disruptive to the human psyche. Cain was plunging further into his own madness—applying at my company, befriending a murderer, possibly torching a car, cornering me on a darkened street. He was becoming more dangerous, and because drunk people rarely consider the consequences of their actions, I felt fear rising in my throat. I came to believe that I might never be able to reclaim my life until Cain was sober, dead, or in jail. A sense of dread began to fill me, the progress I'd made in the forest began to slip away.

And then came the dream.

One night, shortly after the incident with the SUVs, I was alone in the hotel room while you were spending the night at Sara's. I had a dream that changed the course of everything.

In this dream, I found myself in a faraway land, alone in an enchanted forest sprinkled with moon glitter. My skin was glistening. My hair was weaved with stardust. The vegetation around me was different from anything I'd ever seen before—tropical and fragrant, a place where macaws swooped and wild orchids sprung from a bed of ferns and plumeria. The air was deliciously sweet, smelling like mangos and honey. I closed my eyes and breathed deeply. I felt beautiful inside.

In my dream, I wore a simple, shapeless, white nightgown with billowing sleeves. The wind stroked my hair, sending it flying around my face. A sense of peace wrapped around me like a shawl made of clouds. I felt spectacularly alive. Stepping barefoot through the forest, I came upon a magnificent, old tree. I spread my arms to embrace it, and when I did, night turned to morning. I felt the warmth of dappled sunlight shining through the forest canopy like a curtain of divine light. I closed my eyes again, embracing the wonder of sheer joy. I smiled. My smile turned into laughter. I laughed and I laughed and I laughed.

And that's all there was to the dream.

Nothing more and nothing less.

After I awoke, I lay in bed with my head on the pillow, trying to wish myself back into the dream. I wanted to return to that place of perfect peace before it was lost to me forever.

Then I heard a voice. As God as my witness, I heard a voice.

The voice was soft and rather low. It seemed to come from everywhere, as if in surround sound. The voice said only one word and did not repeat it.

The voice simply said, "Go."

I sat up in bed in disbelief. "What?" I asked, looking around nervously, bringing the comforter closer to my chin.

"What?" I asked incredulously, waiting for a reply. A reply never came.

I lay in bed wondering if I'd imagined the voice or if I'd heard it in my dream. But in my dream, I hadn't spoken and no one had spoken to me—it was a dream of sights, smells, and feelings, not a dream containing words or conversation. I very much wanted to believe that I was mistaken about the voice, but something told me that I wasn't. I can't begin to speculate who spoke to me that morning, I can only tell you that something unexplained, something rare and comforting, softly said the word *go*.

Without hesitation, I instinctively knew the meaning behind the message.

I don't know where I was in that dream—I'd never seen it before or since—I can only tell you that I was somewhere I felt safe. I felt lovely. I felt whole. I interpreted the message as this: If I couldn't find my peace in Columbus, then I needed to go someplace where I could. The dream spoke of hope, the voice urged me to find it.

Something awoke inside me as I processed what it would feel like to put my past behind me and live with a sense of dignity again. I imagined a place that offered new opportunities and a chance to start over free from fear and threat and harassment.

Could such a place even exist? I wondered. *Could I really just walk away from Cain and his convoluted obsession?* The more I thought about it, the more enticing the idea became. What began as just a simple word morphed into a stream of consciousness overrun with gleeful satisfaction and energized possibilities.

Resting my feet on the floor and drawing my bathrobe around me, I held tight to the wonder of the moment. I took several deep breaths as I walked over to the widow and watched the cars driving by, imagining myself in a whole new word, a whole new frame of mind.

I lit a single white candle and said the words, "Let it be."

Then I brewed myself a pot of coffee and began planning our escape.

My mind is heavy with thought, remembering myself on that June morning as I sat in the comfortable silence of our hotel room hoping that I could actually change the course of fate. Banking only on the word *go*, I believed I had a chance. Hope needs room to dance, it felt exciting to feel hope turning again.

I thought of you. I knew you wouldn't share my vision and would detest the idea of leaving, but now that you know more of the behind-the-scenes drama, I hope you can see that staying wasn't even an option. You were getting older, more beautiful with each passing day. I felt like we had to take a shot at beginning a new life where you could be free from the madness, too.

Who knew how much our lives would change over the course of the next few years? I'm so grateful that time proved that the bond between us, the strength within us, and the light above us was more than enough to turn our misfortune into an opportunity for misfortune to experience its exact opposite.

When dreams speak, listen.

Sending positive energy across the miles and holding you close in thought,

Your Loving Mother

TWENTY

Summer 2019

A day of painting

Dear Sparrow,

I took your advice and began painting again. I love the idea of selling my work from a booth in the French Quarter—it sounds so romantic, doesn't it? I'll borrow the words of the French artist Émile Zola, who said, "If you ask me what I came into this life to do, I will tell you: I came to live out loud."

Selling my art in New Orleans seems a lot like living out loud.

I decided to do a series of paintings of the tree of life, surrounded by a forest alive with metaphysical energy. I'll do my best to capture the essence of that magnificent tree from my dream. The significance of that special tree has come full circle: Once the tree was a symbol of our future, now it's a symbol of our past.

Like most people who pick up a paintbrush, I paint out of a need to express myself. As you know, my approach toward art is a light-hearted affair with a definite folk-art vibe to it. If I took my art more seriously, it would take all the fun out of the process. My paintings may never hang in a distinguished gallery, but I hope they make a bathroom wall feel like a real winner.

After my last letter, I came to remember the tree from my dream. As I look back on it now, I realize my experience with the dream, and the voice, was a blessing in its most peculiar form—the kind you don't talk about in congenial company for fear eyebrows will rise and snickers will make you doubt the certainty of your own knowing.

Of course, when I was planning our escape, I wasn't certain of anything. The word *go* has never been enough to convince a reasonable mind beyond a reasonable doubt that a better future awaits if they dare to follow the surreal advice dropped from a ceiling in a hotel room.

I suppose I took a Nestea plunge into faith that fateful morning. Not because my faith was impenetrable—I was deeply concerned I wouldn't have the necessary funds or fortitude to find our happy place.

We left because nothing else was working. We left because the fear of the unknown seemed more manageable in a place out of sight and utterly new. And the voice telling me to go reassured me that somewhere, on the other side of fear, angels were trying to help. But I'll be honest, I fell into faith not because I was certain that God would fix everything, but because in the absence of all else, faith was all I had.

Remembering this moment, reflecting on my decision to leave Ohio, I'm faced with how impulsive and scary it all must've seemed to you. You must have felt so powerless to stop the madness. My heart grieves thinking about everything you gave up so that I could escape the addiction of a lunatic. I tried my best to convince you that we would return to Ohio as soon as the crisis had passed. Your eyes told me that you didn't believe me. My stomach told me that I didn't believe me, either. Years later, you thanked me for bringing you to Mississippi. That is the most emancipating thank-you I've ever received.

You asked me how I had the guts. It wasn't guts, child, it was the nature of brokenness. When your world is collapsing around you, you change or you succumb. Guts really have nothing to do with it. In life, we can either run toward something or run from something. Might as well chase a dream—your past can live on without you.

The moon was full on that June day in 2010 when we packed everything we owned into our Ford Taurus and headed south. We drove into the night with a fistful of money (courtesy of your grandmother); a heart full of prayers; and our beloved cat, Tuck, curled up on your lap.

I'd told as few people as possible that we were moving. There were no bon voyage parties held in our names, no long goodbyes, and precious few indications that our lives were about to change forever. As we drove out of town, a stillness settled into the car that stayed with us the rest of the trip. Every mile felt like a question mark, every state line was a one-way ticket to the unknown.

We spoke very little, lost in our own thoughts. I watched as you stared out the window, knowing your life would never be the same, yet unable to understand why. I knew one day I would owe you a better explanation than "home isn't safe anymore." One day, I would have to answer for your pain, your confusion, your loss.

I almost turned the car around a hundred times. I cursed myself for following a hunch that held no guarantees. The voice I heard telling me to go was all I had to keep us moving farther and farther away from the only home we'd ever known.

I stood on the shore staring into the loneliness of pitch-black water. The ebony of the endless sky stained the clouds with midnight, the vast openness engulfed me. The symphony of darkness felt threatening. Panic seized me. The wind twisted my hair into thin pieces of rope, battering my face like a whip. I scanned the horizon for any glimmer of hope—a twinkling star, a passing ship, a lighthouse in the distance. But as far as my eyes could see was a blackness indifferent to my presence, my longing, my wish for a sign that everything would be all right.

I'd predicted that as soon as we arrived in Mississippi, I'd feel better immediately. I was wrong.

Once we finally made it to your Aunt Mindy's house, I already felt like I'd made a mistake. She handed me a beer as soon as I walked through the door, introducing me to the two men lounging on her couch as if they were throw pillows, comfortable with the feel of her living room and hospitality, fixtures in her house. She seemed to view us as welcome additions to the party rather than two wandering spirits in desperate need of a place where we could decompress.

In the days immediately following my decision to leave, I'd bought a cheap, pay-as-you-go phone, hoping to keep our plans private. Then I called Mindy hoping she could help, knowing the cost of living in Mississippi is notoriously low, the lifestyle simple. And since your father had recently relocated to Denver, Cain would never think to look for us there.

When she offered the extra room in her house until we got settled, it felt like a lifeline. Since Mindy was retired from the Navy, always had a gun in the house, and had a tendency to take life seriously, I felt her home would be a good safe haven until we found our own groove. It wasn't until after we'd arrived in Gulfport that I realized that after Mindy's divorce, she'd become everyone's favorite party girl. It seemed that life and too much beer had faded her staunch colors.

After settling you in, and once Mindy's throw pillows made their way home, I drove to the Gulf, trying to ignore the knot in my stomach, desperate to touch the face of all that I'd been reaching for.

Staring into the night, I tried my best to listen to what the ocean had to say. The womb of the earth tells the story of timelessness, of a world beyond, life in a liquid state of mind. She is feminine primordial, and her song stirs the soul. But her silence felt profound. The magnitude of darkness made me feel locked inside my own foolishness. I began to wonder if the voice had lied—or if I'd even heard it at all—anchoring me to the weight of another dumb choice, another false lead, another dead end.

I don't know why this moment, when I went to the water's edge the very first time, felt so unsettling. I suppose it was there, with my Northern spirit resting its feet in Southern sand, that I faced the reality of starting over. It seemed so daunting, so unexpectedly impossible. Starting over is terrifying. Standing on the edge of our future, being a stranger in a strange land, didn't feel liberating at all. It felt like a mistake with a better view.

I screamed toward the sky, "I'm frightened!"

The waves gobbled up the sound of my voice like a penny dropped on a subway. I screamed louder. The ocean didn't notice.

I stood there feeling completely stupid. Exhausted. It didn't take long before I tasted the saltiness of my tears. They tasted like regret and stale hope—I knew the flavor well. I watered the sand for a while until I felt a neutralizing grayness flow through me like a river shapes a rock—I felt numb again. Before long, my tears dried up and I found myself staring out into the nothing as if it were the mirror of my mind.

I left the beach feeling weary and drove back to Mindy's house on autopilot. I'd wanted the water to reassure me, to offer me the feeling of something I couldn't find in Ohio. But it didn't. I lay in bed staring at the ceiling until morning broke through the bedroom curtains. Once I heard you rustling about in the kitchen, I pasted on a happy face and we stepped into our brand-new life.

Days came and went like shadows on rooftops, and before we knew it, we were being absorbed into the honey of Southern living. Everything felt so different from anything we'd known before—life moves like a polite sloth in the Deep South, doesn't it? I've heard it said that Northerners live frantically because they have to pack a whole year into six months. Southerners, by comparison, enjoy life more gingerly because every day is an opportunity for warm air and sunshine.

I'd never realized how much a person's geographic location determines their mindset; we are extensions of our natural surroundings as much as we influence our natural surroundings. We absorb vibrations seasoned by the earth around us, and they become part of our being; he who sees mountains and trees becomes steadied and ambitious, he who sees oceans and tides becomes thoughtful and relaxed, he who only sees buildings and concrete really needs to move.

I came to enjoy the laid-back vibe of a small city nestled on the shores of the Gulf of Mexico. I found it terrifically kismet that a place that once caused me great suffering now offered me a taste of the slower, calmer side of life. It just goes to show you that everything contains its own yin and yang, its own light and dark, its own purpose and serendipity.

I'm well aware that I came to appreciate our new lifestyle much more quickly than you did. While I basked in the therapy of ancient oaks, sandy beaches, and the healing powers of the Gulf, you found it to be insufferably boring and not enough like home. As you remember, we came to Mississippi while you were still in your full-blown "goth" phase. I'm sure you felt alienated from your peers because as a Yankee cloaked in black, it probably seemed to them like you were trying to channel a vampire.

I have no doubt that you experienced the beginning of our new journey feeling angry and homesick. It's not that I didn't notice, it's not that I didn't care, but I felt we'd come too far to turn back. I knew I had to stay focused on the bigger picture. That being said, if I had a nickel for every time I doubted my decision, and myself, I would be writing this letter from a mansion rather than a bungalow on stilts that looks more like a tree house than it doesn't.

As the months went by, school started, you found a group of friends, you wore less black and less make-up, and you courted less of a "screw the world" attitude. You transitioned from a sullen, moody teenager into a young woman who was learning how to embrace a side of herself she'd never met before. You came to say "y'all" as if it felt natural, you came to say "soda" instead of "pop." You ate crawfish, shrimp and grits, and Cajun delicacies as if your Northern roots had been denying your Southern palate. You grew to love spending time with friends at the river, fishing off the dock. Before long, you were talking about all the things you liked about Mississippi instead of all the things you didn't.

By then, we'd moved into that little apartment just outside town. It wasn't much to look at, and it was hard to consider it a home since it only had one bed and one folding chair, but it felt like living inside a blank canvas—what it lacked in color it made up for in possibilities. I'll admit, sitting on the floor Indian-style while we ate dinner and decorated the house with our imagination was the hope I needed to keep me moving forward.

We grew incredibly close during this season of our lives, two sisters of the moon on a life quest. We stopped worrying about what we didn't have, focusing more on our growth and our goals. Life can feel so luxurious when it's simple, sweet, and safe. It wasn't home, but it was an adventure we shared together. And together felt like happiness with the freedom to flower and grow.

I don't know exactly when I began to suspect that Cain had followed us. I believe I sensed his presence in Gulfport long before I saw him for the first time. I suppose I'd revisited Stage One, the denial stage, finding it impossible to believe he was so weird/icky/obsessed that he was willing to travel a thousand miles just to watch me live so quietly and frugally that I was absolutely no one's version of interesting.

In the years since, I've had time to process this "what in the fuck is wrong with you" turn of events. The best way I can grapple with his relentless obsession is this: If you were terribly, hopelessly, and thoroughly addicted to sludge, and the only place to find sludge was a thousand miles away, you may very well consider the tremendous distance a small price to pay in order to satisfy your addiction.

This is the only rational way I can explain why Cain continued to pursue me even though I went to the ends of America—quite literally—to avoid him. I would later learn that it's not uncommon for a stalking victim to try to place distance between herself and her stalker, and sadly, it's not uncommon for a stalker to travel across the country (even across continents) to find her.

Cain was very discreet at first, quietly learning the layout of the land, getting a feel for the place, forming friendships, excavating new ways to wage psychological terrorism. He didn't move to Mississippi, but he began making regular trips down South, often in the company of his brother, Ryan.

I was none too eager to believe that Cain had found us. Before we moved, I'd consulted a website on how to disappear on a budget and followed its advice as closely as I could.

At that time, my biggest source of anxiety was our car. I'd never found Cain's tracking device—I wasn't even sure our car had one—but if it did, then leaving it on our car was the equivalent of giving him our new address. I'd spent several days going over every inch of our car, inside and out, trying to find a hidden GPS. I never found one, but when you're unfamiliar with the components of a car's engine, even a dishwasher part would seem like it belonged.

Maybe it was a tracking device that gave us away or maybe I didn't do as good a job covering our tracks as I thought. Regardless, so fresh on the heels of positive change and healing, when I first began to suspect he'd found us, I very much wanted to believe I was only sensing ghosts that weren't really there.

Then came the day that I saw Cain sitting in a truck outside the post office and I was forced to accept the horrific truth.

I don't know if seeing him face to face in downtown Gulfport was a stroke of dumb luck, an unwanted gift from heaven, or a carefully executed scare tactic on Cain's part. But it doesn't really matter who deserves the credit because the reality stung just the same.

On that morning, I was positioned next to the curb, dropping a letter in the outdoor mailbox, when something caught my attention out of the corner of my eye. I looked over to the line of cars parked just outside the main doors of the post office. Sitting in a beat-up, maroon pick-up truck was Cain. He smiled at me with a devilish snarl as if he were the most clever crustacean to ever lumber forth from the sea. His smugness sent my blood into a boil. I did a double take to make sure it was him.

It was. Cain was sitting there as if he'd been waiting for me.

I'm thankful that the first time I saw him in Gulfport, I was in the safety of my car. Had I been walking, I surely would've tripped over my own feet as if I'd just seen a headless horseman. I drove slowly past him, trying to memorize the car, the license plate, the wretched smile across his face. Perhaps I wanted to etch the moment into my brain so I would never try to dismantle it in an attempt to convince myself it was all in my imagination. Unmistakably, Cain was in Gulfport. And he wanted me to know it. In slow motion, this memory comes back to me, reminding me of my anger as if it happened only yesterday.

Everything changed that day. Everything. I became frightened of my own shadow. I began vomiting again. I rarely left the house. I suffered panic attacks in public. It's a sad state of uselessness when you can't force yourself to be around people you don't know in a place where you don't know anyone.

It could be said that after I saw Cain Cook in Gulfport that day, a bubble burst in my brain. Or maybe my brain burst like a bubble. Either way, I could no longer fool myself into believing that we would ever be safe anywhere.

Perhaps a more diligent person would have considered the life-changing move to the shores of Mississippi as an extreme waste of time, but I never believed this to be true. I believed that Cain's willingness to follow us meant that I would *finally* be able to prove beyond a reasonable doubt that he was a legitimate threat in our lives. Who could now deny that I had a serious problem? Being followed around the streets of Columbus may have been easy to explain away, but being followed to Gulfport clearly illustrated the ways of a genuine stalker.

I had a stalker.

I must have repeated this putrid sentence to myself at least a hundred times before it finally sunk in. I was never willing to fully accept this fact until Cain showed up in Gulfport.

Even after all you and I had been through, I couldn't force myself to believe that Cain was a full-blown, no-doubt-about-it, no-other-way-to-explain-it, textbook-crazy stalker. I'd always tried to rationalize his behavior as something just shy of stalking, unwilling to believe that his obsession had grown beyond his ability to control it.

To admit that Cain had lost control of himself, that his urges dictated his actions, was too frightening to comprehend. When you hear about serial rapists and murderers, you get the impression their sickness can't be cured because their wickedness is no longer a matter of choice. That's what makes them so scary—knowing they couldn't stop even if they wanted to.

To accept that Cain's obsession ruled his entire life was a crushing blow to my psyche. The cold, hard truth felt polarizing, cruel, dirty, and singed by the reality of death.

The final stage in "The Seven Stages of a Stalking Victim" is acceptance. It's the saddest stage of all. A victim can no longer pretend that everything is going to be okay. The acceptance feels like a prison sentence, the statistics hit home. She no longer sees things in terms of getting through something and coming out stronger on the other side—that dream belongs to denial, bargaining, anxiety, exhaustion, blame, and anger. The victim sees herself differently now, realizing she was never really a victim before, she was a woman struggling against the madness.

But she'll be a victim soon. She's a dead woman walking.

After my first sighting of Cain, I began to see him on a semi-regular basis. Weeks would go by without my seeing him at all, but he would invariably turn up, blatantly parading himself, knowing his presence in Gulfport was meaningless to everyone but me.

I returned to a chronic state of hyper vigilance. My nerves sat on razor blades. The vomiting escalated. I never considered calling the police, fearing it would expose us to Cain's unstable anger.

After a while, I began to see Cain in the presence of a woman. I remember the first time I saw them together—Easter morning in 2011. They drove by our house, clearly dressed for church, turning into the apartment complex next to where we were living.

This would be the first time I realized he'd set up shop so close to us, acclimating himself to our surroundings as if it were his turf. He seemed so comfortable, so at home, so "church and ham and collard greens," so "I'm a dickhead and I love it."

Cain no longer left notes on my car, and I didn't receive strange phone calls anymore, but his habit of showing up wherever we were continued just as it had in Columbus. I would often pass him in traffic or see him sitting in the back of the parking lot at the grocery store or library. The mere the sight of him made my skin crawl, sending me into a deep depression.

The more I saw him, the more I retreated into my own world. I seldom slept, my eyes began to look lifeless, my skin felt like parchment paper. The concept of death invaded my thoughts like a magnet drawn to my worst fear. I wrote a will, not that I had much, but I wanted to make sure you got whatever I had. I stuck it inside the wooden box where I kept my keepsakes—the one lined in emerald-green velvet. I knew you'd find it after I was gone, wanting to connect to the things that had been most special to me.

A thousand miles away from home, with few established connections in Gulfport, we were so vulnerable. Fear spiraled like a tornado. *He's here*, is all I could manage to think. "He's here," I said over and over until the words turned black on my tongue.

I will lay down my pen for the day and pick up my paintbrush. The tree is waiting for me. I hope I can do justice to the magnificent tree by capturing its sparkle and reverie. After all, a tree isn't just a tree, it's a doorway into another realm, existing above and below, like things made of mystery and magic always do.

I will lay down my thoughts for the day, too. But before I do, I'd like to share with you what I've learned about the nature of wild winds, since it was wild winds that carried me into the next season of our lives. Wild winds have taught me this: When things get deathly quiet and the mind is so troubled that even the trees seem to have lost their green, it's important to remember that the winds of change haven't abandoned us. They've moved ahead of us with purpose, clearing a better path, making room for light to shine so the colors of life can feel meaningful again.

Sending positive energy across the miles and holding you close in thought,

Your Loving Mother

TWENTY-ONE

The painting continues

Dear Sparrow,

We're drawing closer to the birth of your daughter. This thought is so fantastic, it feels like my excitement is doing cartwheels. I often find myself daydreaming about her, imagining what it will be like to wear the role of grandmother. I'm trying to keep myself busy—I write, I create, I putter, but these tasks don't consume me like they did before, they only serve to channel my restless energy while I ponder the beginning of a brand-new chapter in our lives.

I have complete faith that you will be a kind and gifted mother—you've always held the essence of a teacher, a listener, a healer, and a friend. You will be focused and playful, patient and wise. Your daughter is blessed to have you as her mother, just as I'm blessed to have you as a daughter.

Becoming a grandmother has made me stop and think. What can I offer the child? How do I become a grandmother, anyway? How do I find that delicate balance between loving with all my heart, yet letting the mother do the mothering?

Throughout my life, I've loved many things: people, idiots, animals, nature, words, and ideas. Sometimes, I've loved well. Sometimes, I've loved foolishly. I've always been more of a rough draft than a completed version of anything, taken by the idea that as long as I keep putting my love out there, eventually I'm bound to create a masterpiece. But knowing how close we are to the birth of my grandchild, I feel the need to gather myself together quickly, trim my loose edges, so I can be the grandmother that your grandmother was to you.

Thinking of your grandmother, who always has a pleasant smile sitting on her face as if it never has a reason to leave, I can't help but feel like she's the incarnation of what a soul feels like when it's completely content with itself. She's always carried the spirit of a dancer, moving through life with great care and intent. Perhaps the thing I love most about my mother is that her heart is spectacularly sincere—it's easy to be around her, even when life doesn't feel easy at all.

I've always admired my mother, drawn to women like her, women who embrace the stuff that really matters, like the importance of kindness and humility. She finds joy in simple beauty, like morning glories weaving their way around a pumpkin, or a jar of antique buttons. She lives elegantly, authentically, encouraging others to do the same. Knowing that I will become the matriarch of my own herd, I hope to handle my responsibility as gracefully as she does.

After your phone call last night, I sat thinking about the name you've chosen for your daughter: Scarlett Rowan. It's lovely. I need to remember to thank you for choosing such a perfect name. I could say her name a thousand times and never grow tired of hearing it. Your great-great-grandmother Scarlett is probably dancing on a cloud somewhere, buying a round of brandy and smoking a cigar, daring all the men to play her in a "friendly" game of cards. And even though it's heaven, the men will still lose their shirts because even though it's heaven, she's probably still very Scarlett.

If your daughter is anything like her, she will demonstrate an unparalleled zest for life. Scarlett never did anything on a small scale. The fibers of her being were progressive and brave, she wore the badge of a strong woman with a sense of inner nobility while shooting a mean game of pool. When other women were home knitting and ironing, Scarlett was running her own business and daring anyone to tell her she couldn't.

The name Rowan was unexpected, but it sings to me. The spirit of the rowan tree has always captured my attention. Affectionately known as The Goddess Tree, it symbolizes the vibrant, protective energy of the feminine spirit.

The symbolism of trees is such an ancient wisdom, a mystical language of forgotten lore. It's unfortunate that the more advanced we become as a society, the more we lose the wisdom of the old ways. Some still believe that a child named after the earth will walk peacefully with it for all of their days. I'm so grateful that you chose a name that speaks of our heritage as well as our belief that the earth shares her secrets in all things growing and wild.

The closer we get to Scarlett's birth, the more sentimental I become, misty-eyed and gushy as if my daydreams were made out of marshmallows. So maybe this is how you become a grandmother—by letting your Sky Woman make her way to the surface, the Ancient One of the female structure who lives eternal in every woman's soul.

I'm in a peaceful mood this morning. I'll take this opportunity to continue sharing my reflections of the black years—we're almost through them, so there's no point in stopping now. I'm eager to satisfy this calling, this need to tell my story, so that once Scarlett is in your arms I can focus on the joy right in front of me rather than the memories behind me.

So let's go back to the place in time when darkness tried to seize our light, when fear waged its final war until I simply didn't have the strength to fear anymore.

Never underestimate the healing power of a dog. Seriously. God is great, therapy and forgiveness work wonders, wine is always an option, but only a dog has the ability to calm a mind like a lollipop calms a boo-boo. Dogs are like furry angels who pee in a corner and gnaw on your favorite shoes while restoring your equilibrium through uncondi-tional love.

Humans like to believe we've mastered the art of unconditional love, but we haven't— we're still trying to connect the dots. Our love often comes with invisible strings and unspoken expectations even when we try our hardest to give our love away for the sake of love alone. Only a dog has the ability to fully love someone in spite of their flaws and stupidity. Cats hold grudges, fish couldn't care less, birds are the craziest creatures on the face of the earth, and trying to impress a farm animal is like trying to snort oatmeal. In the end, the faithful, loyal, loveable dog deserves the title of man's best friend more than any other creature that walks, swims, flies, or creatively ignores you.

After I got evicted from our little apartment (money is hard to come by when you can't manage to leave the house), I thought mov-ing into that broken-down trailer miles away from town was a helluva good idea. I realize that you were none too pleased about my return to the chronic depression that led us to lose our first step toward in-dependence. Your anger was incredibly justified—I wasn't keeping up my end of the bargain, allowing Cain's presence in Gulfport to reduce me to Jell-O. Again.

Our positions had shifted: I wanted to leave Mississippi and you wanted to stay. Being so low on funds and hope, I took advantage of the offer to move into the trailer rent-free, promising to clean it up, rid it of weeds and debris, and turn it into someone else's version of a redneck Holiday Inn.

I know you considered the trailer another epic embarrassment, but I considered it a blessing. Keep in mind, child, at that time in our lives, I was emotionally distant from everyone so I'm not sure how the landlord ever concluded that a person with so many ghosts, so many reasons to run, could ever be of some use. Maybe because he was a deeply spiritual man. I often wondered if he offered us a helping hand because he felt it was the right thing to do more than he thought I was a sure bet.

The best part of moving into that dilapidated trailer was the trees and land around it. It called to me—the silence, the oak trees, the shy pond under the willow tree, the earthy taste of well water drawn from an underground spring. It was a perfect setting for a spiritual connection. And it meant I could finally get a dog. I needed a dog. I needed Quinn and privacy and space.

Enter Radar—amazing, intelligent, good-natured Radar. I remember going to the Humane Society that Saturday morning "just to look around." I came upon him in the very last cage in the very last row of cages. I knew instantly he was the dog of my dreams. He reminded me so much of Quinn, my head felt dizzy. I couldn't believe such a majestic animal could ever end up in a place for unwanted dogs. I'm sure a less frightened person might have thought twice about adopting a full-grown pit bull who tipped the scales at 85 pounds, but his muscles and his wide mouth didn't intimidate me at all because his eyes told the story of his nature: gentle and genuine.

A volunteer at the Humane Society had given him the nickname Radar because he seemed permanently on patrol—the name fit him like a glove.

I stared at Radar in his cage, unable to take my eyes off him. He stared back at me with his big head tilted to the side as if to say, "What are you waiting for?" I asked to walk him in the little courtyard outside. They leashed him up and he happily dragged me around the courtyard, stopping every now and again to lick my entire face. I felt so safe with him, like walking a machine gun. I knew immediately that I wanted to spend the rest of my life with Radar by our side.

I was crestfallen when I found out that a man and his son had already submitted paperwork to adopt Radar, choosing him over the selection of hound dogs available, wanting him for a hunting companion. My heart sank. I couldn't believe I'd finally found my best friend only to discover that a stranger—a hunter (Little Dick Syndrome)—now stood in my way.

I went out to the car and nervously smoked a cigarette, trying to process my options. Then, I started to pray. I asked God to intervene. If Radar was meant to be my friend and if God thought he'd be a good fit in our lives, I prayed that God would allow me to adopt him. I sat in the car a moment longer, not wanting to leave without him. I decided to leave my phone number in case Radar didn't work out for the hunter and his son.

As I stepped back inside the Humane Society, the volunteer came rushing toward me.

"There you are! Good news! They decided to adopt another dog. Radar is yours if you want him," she said, passing me an application.

I was speechless. I couldn't believe it. "Thank you, God!" I said aloud, tears welling up in my eyes. The volunteer smiled and winked.

After I filled out the paperwork and paid the adoption fee, Radar officially became part of our family.

In the weeks and months after Radar came home, my mind terrain began to change drastically. I began to sleep better, think more clearly, and venture out of the house a little more often. Radar was a hearty listener, sensing the anxiety within me. If ever my mind began to drift to dark places, Radar would quietly sit beside me as if he were there to absorb my feelings. I think Radar loved me because I needed him and loved you because you wanted him.

We took Radar with us everywhere we went, his big head sticking out the back window as if he were mayor of the road. The three of us formed a special bond, and he became the man of the house without hesitation or a formal request. I would like to say that I became brave after Radar came into our lives, but I don't deserve the credit—Radar was brave for me.

After Radar showed up, Cain stopped following me and strangers began following me instead, making it clear that Cain's empire in Gulfport was growing. Unlike before, however, this new cast of characters never attempted to speak to me directly. I suppose none of them was dumb enough to breach the protective barrier that Radar's presence had placed around us.

I now realize that Radar was the beginning of the end to my stalking nightmare. Of course, I still had many years and many miles left to go—Radar didn't make Cain go away. But he created a necessary safe zone, allowing me to step back into myself before I lost too much ground.

And so it was that even in spite of Cain's presence in Gulfport, I came to believe that I'd finally found a capable ally. I still believed that one day Cain would take my life, but I was thankful to have a friend with loving eyes, powerful jaws, and a reputation that preceded him.

Next came J.D. As you remember, J.D. was the closest thing to a human friend I had in Gulfport. Had it not been for the fact that he was an officer in the United States Army and his parents lived next to your Aunty Mindy, I don't suppose I would've ever allowed him into my personal space. Truth be told, I welcomed his friendship for one simple reason: I needed someone in my life who had an understanding of the underbelly of Gulfport, since it's in the underbelly of a city that people like Cain Cook tend to thrive.

J.D. grew up in the streets of Gulfport with ties to family and friends who kept their ears low to the ground, knowing things an outsider would never know. Like Emory-James, J.D. was a lone wolf and I liked that about him. He spoke slowly, carefully, as if his words had value. He carried a book with him wherever he went, always tucked under his arm as if at any moment he might sit down and read a few pages.

As our friendship evolved, I eventually told him the truth about why we'd moved to Gulfport. He didn't seem the slightest bit concerned, yet he stayed in touch more regularly once he found out. Also as with Emory-James, J.D. and I spent much of our time having deep, philosophical conversations about God. Having been raised Southern Baptist, his God was a little more fire-and-brimstone than mine, but our conversations were engaging, each of us sharing thoughts on God the other had never before considered.

Radar loved J.D. as if they were kindred spirits cut from the very same cloth. J.D. had never owned a dog, never loved a dog, so his affection for Radar caught him off guard. He felt sorry that Radar was carrying the sole burden of our safety. Even though Radar patrolled our property like a T-Rex, J.D. feared that the first casualty in Cain Cook's infantile war would be Radar.

After J.D. became more of a constant in our lives, Cain did what bitches do: He began a campaign against J.D. Before long, J.D. was experiencing slashed tires, items stolen from his locked garage, and strange phone calls. He also caught someone following him on more than one occasion.

Big mistake on Cain's part.

It wasn't in J.D.'s character to sit back and do nothing. Though he had a calm and reserved disposition, within J.D. was the essence of a fighter, a demagogue, the hand that turns the wheel. Pressure began to pile up inside him—he couldn't bear to stay in our lives, yet he couldn't bear to walk away.

Soon J.D. gave me two choices: Go talk to the sheriff before someone got hurt; or give him all the information I had on Cain, including everyone Cain knew back in Ohio, so J.D. could find him and kill him.

In J.D.'s mind, these were the only two reasonable options. J.D. was disgusted that the situation had grown so big in the first place, reconfirming his Southern belief that Northerners are all a bunch of sissies, so self-absorbed they can't see beyond their own needs. J.D. felt Cain's behavior was a sign of complete disrespect, which in J.D.'s mind meant Cain's actions must reap equal amounts of fire, fury, and wrath.

I tried to talk J.D. into a less drastic solution, knowing he didn't know the scope of Cain's true crazy, but he wouldn't be deterred.

"You've been sitting still for too long," he said in his baritone voice, so rich with timbre I could literally imagine his vocal cords were made of gravel wrapped in heavy velvet. "No more waiting. This fool needs to learn he should've kept his bullshit up North."

Once talk about death and killing came to occupy space in our conversations, I knew the whole situation had reached a boiling point. The endless question, "What's next?" now had its most unfortunate answer: Bodies would begin dropping.

Of the two options J.D. presented, I didn't like either. I'd long since given up on law enforcement's ability to stop the insanity invading my entire life. And I was deeply concerned that if I took my case to the police and they did the equivalent of absolutely nothing, their indifference would further empower Cain—he had already proven that his favorite people in the world were the ones who looked the other way.

But the latter of the two options would be even more devastating. As eager as I was to rid myself of the problem, murder seemed like an enormous leap into the unknown. If J.D. took matters into his own hands, it would carry a life sentence beyond Cain's life alone. It opened a door to the possibility that the people I loved the most could get hurt in an attempt to settle a score. Both options sucked entirely. I tentatively agreed to try law enforcement once again, but I only said this to buy some time, hoping that God or angels or Athena would intercede and calm the storm churning in J.D.'s mind.

For a while, I stalled, making one excuse after another as to why I hadn't spoken with the sheriff yet, terrified of the idea that the police would think I was certifiable, and that I'd fall into a funk I couldn't escape.

But J.D. is a persistent little shit, and one day he showed up at our house with his laptop. He asked me to write down everything I could remember about Cain, how it all started, including any information that the police might find useful. I stared at the laptop for days, leery of its presence as it sat on the kitchen table like a game of truth or dare. I quite literally didn't have the energy or the stomach for all the remembering I'd need to do or the emotional risk I'd have to take, sorting through all my experiences that I felt needed to stay stuffed if I had any hopes of moving forward.

Early one morning, I sat on the front stoop watching the sunrise with Radar napping across my feet. I watched as the first rays of morning threw bursts of pink and periwinkle across a sailor's red sky. Something in the air felt right that morning, as if energized by eucalyptus and conviction, and it surprised me when I found myself walking into the trailer and opening the laptop. I pressed the power button and refreshed my coffee while the computer buzzed to life.

Then, I sat down and began writing.

Without effort or tears, my story came tumbling forward as if it had been waiting seven long years to finally tell its harrowing tale, the words spilling across the pages like an opened damn. As I look back at it now, that beautiful morning sky was an oracle of hope being offered to a woman who was willing to risk it all to stop the progression of a disease spinning out of control.

J.D. sat in the car drinking a beer.

I was unnerved that he'd decided this was a fine time to catch a buzz. He hardly ever drank, yet there he was, casually slurping a beer as if we were on our way to a family BBQ.

"Dear God, can't you wait to have a drink? We're in the parking lot of the flippin' sheriff's office in case you haven't noticed," I said, irritated that he seemed so ambivalent.

"Do what you need to do. This isn't about me," he said calmly, staring out the window as if his eyes were pruning the trees.

In retrospect, J.D. probably did feel like he needed a beer. As I stood outside the car gathering my nerves and my loose pieces of paper, it never occurred to me that J.D. might know more than he was telling. I would later learn that J.D. was aware that Cain and his brother had become successful drug dealers on the Gulf Coast, establishing a web of connections and safe houses, an army of soldiers willing to keep their secret. He also knew that there is absolutely nothing Northern about Southern law enforcement—once I identified myself as the reason why Cain and his mini cartel had set up shop in our city, there was little chance law enforcement wouldn't move heaven and earth to stop it.

In case you didn't know, the Interstate-10 corridor has task forces designed specifically to address the influx of drugs being moved from Mexico through our southern states on their way to cities all throughout America. These task forces are well trained and well funded, and they take down drug dealers as easily as a burst of dynamite takes down an outhouse.

J.D. knew everything was about to change. From this point forward, I would have a constant police presence in my life. And he would be asked to defend his decision to help make it possible. The code of the streets can be vicious. J.D. knew that once I took my case to the sheriff, his allegiance to the friends and family he knew from the underbelly would be questioned, tested, abolished.

Of course, I knew none of this as I stood outside the car trying my best to collect myself. In a fit of disgust, I slammed the car door shut, walking toward the building completely unaware that I was walking toward my destiny.

I stepped inside the sheriff's office, walked up to the reception desk surrounded by bulletproof glass, and hesitantly stated that I needed to speak to a detective, as if I weren't sure. I tried to hide the fact that my hands were shaking. I tried to hide the fact that I felt like I was going to throw up. I knew from past experiences that appearing like an erratic mess or a detached zombie didn't attract the help I needed, so I did my best to appear calm and rational. I took several deep breaths, trying to convince my insides to act normal. *You can throw up later*, I promised my stomach.

An officer instructed me to take a seat and wait until someone called my name. As the moments passed, I shifted in my seat like I was sitting on a porcupine, second-guessing my decision. Surely, Cain knew my car was sitting in the parking lot at the sheriff's office. He would be angry. Who would pay the price for his rage? And what if law enforcement found my complaint completely ludicrous? After all, I had no physical proof that Cain had followed us to Gulfport. I had no proof of anything beyond the fact the Cain simply refused to leave us alone.

As the moments ticked by, my anxiety felt like it was filling the entire room. I almost walked out the door a dozen times, certain I was wasting my time. *They're never going to believe me*, I told myself over and over until soon I felt ridiculous for sitting on a porcupine in a sheriff's office.

When I heard my name being called, it jolted me back to reality. I looked up to find a fit, middle-aged man wearing a dress shirt and sensible tie. He motioned me to approach him. He introduced himself in a voice that sounded steady and firm. Within his greeting I remember hearing the name Masterson, but for the most part, I paid no attention to his words, looking deep into his eyes for any sign of compassion or kindness. His eyes pleaded the fifth, but his body language told me he'd never been considered weak a day in his life, holding the spirit of an old-west Texas lawman. I felt strangely calm in his presence.

He guided me into an interview room and I began to tell my story. In the telling, I began to feel more a little more confident, surprised to hear the words coming from my mouth sounding organized and reasonable. Nothing I said seemed to surprise Investigator Masterson;

he wasn't shocked, he wasn't doubting my experiences, he never made me feel like I was crazy. He quietly listened, took notes, asked a few insightful questions, and filled out a report.

During our conversation, I came to view Investigator Masterson as a no-nonsense, "stick to the facts" type of guy. His quiet ruggedness made me feel safe, and it was easy to find respect for him—he looked me in the eye, he treated me like I had a right to be concerned, he made no attempt to minimize my situation, and he seemed to sense that I'd been through a lot. I began to believe that for the first time since my stalking ordeal began, I was laying my burdens in front of a man who had the inclination, and the ability, to make a difference.

After our meeting ended, I walked out of the sheriff's office feeling a huge sense of relief. I wasn't convinced that Investigator Masterson would be able to stop Cain Cook's advances, but I felt confident that if for any reason Cain took my life, Masterson would do his best to seek justice.

I can't quite put into words the peace that comes to a battered mind when you gain the assurance that your death won't be reduced to another unsolved mystery. It gave me a great sense of comfort to think that I wouldn't be just another body found bound and gagged in a river or discarded like trash in a dumpster, one whose story is never known, their last moments never told. I could now consider myself a woman who had done her best to name her killer before she died. The relief I felt as I clenched Investigator Masterson's business card in my hand touched the deepest part of my inner pain. I didn't feel so vulnerable anymore.

I'd never realized until that moment the identity of my most unspoken fear: that I would die at the hands of a madman who no one believed was real. I can't say for certain that Investigator Masterson believed my claims at face value, but I can say for certain that he pledged to get to the bottom of it, altering the paralysis of my deepest, darkest fear.

I wasn't aware of it at the time, but on that day back in October of 2012, I stopped living like I was dying and started living like I had a future worth reaching for—even if it didn't last very long. I believe my inner Athena was truly born on that day. She'd made appearances before, but I couldn't seem to hold on to her. But after my meeting with Investigator Masterson, I felt affirmed and empowered, as if I'd walked into the sheriff's office with papers in my hand and walked out wearing a cape.

Life was about to get really, really good.

I think I will spend the rest of the day painting. I feel warm inside. I think of Radar. Everything within me grows tender at the memory of such a fine animal. Of course, one day we would lose him, but not before he came to save me in a way I never thought possible.

You were the connection I needed toward love. Radar was the connection I needed toward life. J.D. was the connection I needed toward faith. Investigator Masterson was the connection I needed toward hope.

Finally, I had a team.

Sending positive energy across the miles and holding you close in thought,

Your Loving Mother

TWENTY-TWO

Summer 2019

At the coffee house

Dear Sparrow,

I'm enjoying a lovely view of the Gulf this morning. My green tea with honey and ginger is the perfect complement to my cheese grits and fruit salad. I'm in no rush to paint today. My thoughts are elsewhere.

I spent the last few days wandering around inside myself as I painted, trying to write this letter in my head before putting my words on paper, hoping I could figure out a way to say it right. Of all the letters I will write, perhaps this one is the most meaningful to me. This letter will speak on a subject matter close to my heart, declaring a truth I want you to know—need you to know.

The recipe for an abundant life is found in this letter, including a list of necessary ingredients. But like all recipes, you can make it your own by adding a pinch of style and a dash of personal perspective. I ask that you read this letter with an open mind and open heart, giving the seed I hope to plant the chance to germinate. I want it to grow so full and luscious that it can feed you for the rest of your life. You'll need this information while you're here on earth if you dare to experience the bountiful side of life.

Watching the pages of my life come alive before me, viewing my journey from a safe distance as I sort through each chapter, each experience, each failed attempt to find my one true north, I have reached the point in my story where I feel compelled to speak on bigger things.

After I formed what I believed was a capable team, the belief opened a passageway to a new line of thinking, reconnecting me to the clarity I'd once found in the forest. The more confident I became, the less I feared. It didn't take long before I was opening myself up to vibrations I hadn't been able to tap into before.

Through osmosis more than intent, I began brewing the recipe for an abundant life, finally understanding that I'd had the ingredients all along, I just hadn't known how to put them together. You know the part in *The Wizard of Oz* when Glinda tells Dorothy she'd had the power to go back home whenever she wished, but she'd needed to learn the lesson for herself? For years, I never understood that part of the movie. It made Glinda seem less glittery, almost careless, but I get it now.

Discovering the secret to a life worth living, a life of meaning and free will, isn't really a secret at all, but you have to travel your own road before you're confident enough to make the recipe come out right. So let's talk about positivity and choice, abundance and self-creation for a while—let's talk about the art of living.

Within each of us lies a love for people, places, and things, a sense of spirituality or preferred life philosophy, and a desire to prosper— these are the intimate doctrines guiding our internal compass, the rudders steering our ship. Lying below these personal truths is an ocean of thought, floating in the amber of who we really are, connecting us to the galaxy of everything.

The mind is humankind's only superpower. We need no other. Our thoughts are pure energy: potent and powerful, authoritative and transforming, the alpha that shapes the omega. Our thoughts are the genesis of every experience, every interpretation, every invention, every state of being, and every story our souls will ever tell. Before we cast light or shadow, a thought exists in an embryonic state, incubating in the vortex of our minds, feeding on our intentions before making the transition into a manifested reality. We do not speak things into existence, we *think* things into existence; our thoughts are the architect, the craftsman, of our reality. The universe is everything God ever thought of, the earth is everything man ever thought of, the light emanating from the individual is everything the individual ever thought of.

We can't separate fate from our thoughts, they're rhythmically intertwined, weaving themselves around the tree of life like a vine braids itself through a trellis. Thought and fate have a symbiotic relationship—the artist inspires the paint while the paint inspires the artist. Our thoughts create our words, our words create our actions, and our actions create our character. From there, a soul begins to experience itself.

If it's true that the art of life is knowing when to say when—when to take a fork in the road and when to stick to the path you're on, when to find happiness with what you have and when to seek happiness elsewhere—then it could be said that the art of living is found in the *how*.

Masters throughout the ages have left us the recipe for how to live joyously, how to claim our own destiny, how to live a life of plenty and peace. Their words and symbolisms are found in religious texts, sacred documents, oral folklore, poetry, and songs. Sages and scholars, mathematicians and scientists dating back to antiquity have added layers of insight helping us unlock the matrix of a vibrant and rewarding life, hoping to get us to understand that the art of living isn't complicated or imposing, it's simply a matter of consciously choosing where our thoughts lead us.

We take control of our life when we take control of our thoughts, because at the end of the day, we live the life we imagined.

The first ingredient needed to create an abundant life is an understanding of how our superpower works. Since our thoughts are pure energy, our minds have their own electromagnetic force field, attracting and repelling the energy around us just like a magnet, seeking vibrations that resonate with our own. Everything flowing from us and to us is regulated by the energy stored inside our minds.

We can do little to alter the bullshit that comes our way, but we have complete control over how the bullshit affects us, how it moves us, how we rank its level of importance, and whether we attach our energy to the positive or negative vibrations of the bullshit.

Energy likes to pal around with energy that feels the same way, so when we send out negative thoughts, they multiply with the negativity around us. Equally, when we send out positive thoughts, they invite positivity over to play.

I realize this concept sounds like an esoteric cupcake, but the science behind it is very real. Albert Einstein once said, "Everything is energy and that's all there is to it. Match the frequency of the reality you want and you cannot help but get that reality. This is not philosophy. This is physics."

I've heard this phenomenon—often referred to as The Law of Attraction or The Principle of Resonance—explained many different ways and called different things in different cultures, but none made more sense to me than "The Legend of The Two Wolves Within," passed down by the Cherokee Nation. I will share it with you now.

The Legend of the Two Wolves Within

An old grandfather said to his grandson, who came to him with anger at a friend who had done him an injustice, "Let me tell you a story.

"I too, at times, felt great hate for those who have taken so much, with no sorrow for what they do. But hate wears you down and does not hurt your enemy. It is like taking poison and wishing your enemy would die. I have struggled with these feelings many times."

He continued, "It is as if there are two wolves within me. One is good and does no harm. He lives in harmony with everything around him, and does not take offense when none was intended. He will only fight when it is right to do so, and in the right way. He is joy, peace, empathy, love, humility, kindness, benevolence, generosity, and truth.

"But the other wolf, ah! He is full of anger. The littlest thing will set him into a fit of temper. He fights everyone, all the time, for no reason. He cannot think because his hate and his anger are too great. He is envy, sorrow, regret, greed, arrogance, self-pity, false pride, superiority, and ego.

"A fight is going on inside of me and sometimes it is hard to live with both of these wolves," said the grandfather. "Both are trying to dominate my spirit."

The grandson thought for a moment. "Which one will win?" he asked, staring into his grandfather's eyes.

The grandfather smiled and quietly answered, "Whichever one I feed."

Each of us feeds a wolf within, deciding which will thrive and which will perish, which will dominate our thoughts. It often seems like life is making the decision for us, but that's the convoluted tale the dark wolf wants us to believe. Fear, hate, ego, and pain are unable to feed themselves, so they have to trick us into believing we have no choice in the matter. Remember, child, darkness is a desperate wolf. And a desperate wolf lies.

For a very long time, I believed the lie. I thought I was unlovable, so I tainted my own ability to feel loved. I thought I was stupid and inept, so I settled for a lesser version of myself. I thought I wasn't worth saving, so I became hopeless—even suicidal. I thought Cain would kill me, so I came to feel dead inside. I allowed my thoughts to feed my fear, sending fear out into the universe, so all I got back was more fear. I unknowingly gave away all my power to the least deserving energy on earth.

Sometimes we unintentionally hand over our own destiny to the energy doing its best to eat us alive.

You must be vigilant in choosing your thoughts, or others will be happy to do it for you. You must make a conscious choice to feed the white wolf. The dark wolf's eagerness to lie and deceive makes it a diabolical opponent to the mind asleep at the wheel. So stay awake, child, and choose your thoughts for yourself. Your thoughts are the energy connection to everything good and wonderful, presented to you through the superpower of a mind consciously involved.

The wisdom of the ages tells us this: Whatever we believe, we become. Belief is a very powerful thing—it's thought with a lot of confidence. Believing in something generates remarkable kinetic energy—energy that is in motion.

And the act of believing is the second ingredient in the recipe for an abundant life—believe that whatever you want is entirely possible. How do you get the belief ball rolling? It's simple: State an intention, see it in your mind, send your thoughts and feelings toward it, and believe with all your heart that it can happen.

It probably won't happen overnight because becoming is a process. You might have to convince the universe (and yourself) that you truly want what you say you want, conveying your intention with steadfast resolve, proving you can stay focused on the goal no matter what comes your way. But remember, stating an intention is powerful magic—a declaration to the universe of who you are and who you wish to become. So wish wisely, because from the mouth of history we have learned: Be careful what you wish for because you might just get it.

My life changed forever once I found the recipe to my own liberation: Feed the white wolf and reject opportunities to feed the fear and pain. My becoming was a freedom like no other. All those years of suffering completely lost their nourishment as soon as I had the confidence to empower myself with thoughts of strength, determination, and the singular goal of declaring myself queen of my own life.

It's a glorious state of being when you finally realize that life handed you a coloring book. Situations beyond your control may dictate the outline of your life, but you have complete control over the colors you choose to decorate the picture with. A lighter shade of being may sometimes seem like an impossible task, but that's only because the dark wolf senses the change within and his hunger begins lying to you again.

A lovely Chinese proverb says, "Now that the barn had burned down, I can see the moon." Even when joy seems terribly out of place, a spirit can adorn itself in its own imagination when first it has the courage to hope and believe.

By the spring of 2013, I began to feel better. Much better. The dialogue inside my head began to heal itself, sending out the vibrations of a survivor. My new stream of consciousness began connecting me to the radiant energy around me, and before I knew it, I began attracting positive results.

Life began flowing more smoothly. Seeing Cain no longer rattled me to my core, instead, I began to see it as an opportunity to face my fears. And that's all it took for me to begin finding humor in the whole, pathetic situation. Cain's ever-present smugness stopped making me feel like he knew a secret he wasn't sharing. Instead, it made me laugh because a lunatic with an overinflated ego and a cone head looks a lot like a circus clown. The more ridiculous I saw the situation, the lighter I became. I wasn't ready to run down the beach naked with a kite in my hand, but I began stepping back into life again. My positive thoughts were chasing off my negative ones. Soon, my negative thoughts had nothing left to eat.

I'm quite certain that it was our blessing that Investigator Masterson had the misfortune of showing up to work the day I walked through the door—I attribute much of the change within me to his involvement in my case. Your love and support had been a constant, the cornerstone to my success, but until the big dogs showed up, we were little more than puffs of dandelion blown by the wind. Investigator Masterson helped me identify the source of my darkest fear, and once that fear hit air, it began to evaporate.

He also helped temper my distrust of law enforcement in general. For years, I'd been convinced that they had let Cain's sickness grow without borders. And every cop-gone-rogue story splashed across the headlines only fueled my suspicion that our heroes aren't always heroes. I've had many years and many miles to ponder my reluctance to turn to the police—even when it was clear Cain had followed us to Gulfport. I've decided that it was irresponsible of me to throw all cops into the same pot as the ones who I felt let me down.

I mean, I've met some pretty shitty delivery drivers, plumbers, and dentists who seemed to have graduated from The Jaw-Dropping Institute of What the Fuck, yet I didn't cast off the whole lot as unreliable and useless.

I owed it to you to keep trying.

Law enforcement is often a convenient punching bag whenever justice fails or we don't get the results we feel we should have. But where would we be without them? I've come to understand that beyond the attention-grabbing headlines lies a quieter, more prevalent truth than the one America is being groomed to believe. Most members of law enforcement are the stuff of courage, integrity, and commitment to the greater good. The pain caused when a weak cop makes a weak decision is devastating to a society, and shame on them for betraying a trust so many died to protect. But it serves no one's best interest to view all of them in the same light as the ones who didn't have the nuts to walk the line.

As I've stated at least a thousand times, I believe things happen for a reason. Maybe Cain's stalking campaign, and his ego, needed complete freedom to grow as big and ugly as they wanted before the good guys (and women) had enough meat to bite into. Equally, maybe I needed to grow into a more skilled and focused advocate for my own cause. Laws regarding stalking are flimsy at best, so until our laws evolve, a victim better bring her A game to the table.

Maybe the police in Columbus wished they could've done more, but maybe they also wished I'd done a better job of gathering the evidence needed in order for them to build a case. Instead of viewing law enforcement in the negative, I could've chosen to see them for what they really are: good people doing their best to make a difference in a world going batshit crazy. Feeding the latter opinion would've gotten me further much more quickly.

Investigator Masterson held true to his Texas lawman nature, carrying the torch for all the heroes just like him—doing the right thing simply because it's the right thing to do. And best of all, he returned my phone calls and never made me feel like my experience was too outrageous to believe. I began feeling comfortable enough to report any incidents I found noteworthy. This connection to a badge greatly affected how I perceived my ability to become a driving force behind my own freedom.

As my thoughts changed, I changed.

Shortly after I first met with Investigator Masterson, I grew suspicious of a little, used-car dealership near the airport on the main drag in town. I could never figure out how Cain had access to so many different vehicles, never considering that he might have access to a car dealership, until the day he made the mistake of repeatedly driving by our house in a car that stood out from the rest.

The car was an Easter-egg blue Toyota Land Cruiser. The vehicle caught my attention due to its obnoxious color. After I saw it pass by our house a few times, I positioned myself in the row of trees lining the road, hoping to get a better view of the driver. It didn't take long before the car drove by again, and there was dumb ol' Cain sitting in the front seat like a clown driving an Easter egg. The car's license plate read SASSAFRAS—the name I'd wanted to be called when I was a little girl. The word *sassafras* had too many characters for an ordinary license plate, and the last letter wasn't lined up with the rest. This was the first time I became aware that Cain was altering the license plates of the vehicles he drove.

As fate would have it, I had an errand in town later that day. Of course, I was on the lookout for the ugly, blue Land Cruiser. As I passed by the used-car lot, I noticed an Easter-egg blue Toyota Land Cruiser sandwiched in a row of cars for sale, but it didn't have a sticker price on the windshield like all the others. As I sat at the light waiting for it to turn green, I scanned the cars at the dealership, realizing that I recognized many of them as ones I'd seen Cain driving. I phoned Investigator Masterson to tell him I had my first solid clue as to how

Cain could have access to so many different vehicles, thinking he must have some affiliation with that dealership.

Investigator Masterson promised to check it out. And knowing Investigator Masterson, I have no doubt that he did. I can't report what information he discovered—if any—but the beauty of having a good cop on your team is this: Once you give a good cop your information, you can let go and continue on with your life.

And so I did.

By and by, I became a more capable version of myself—I drank less, sang more, and took walks in the woods with Radar by my side. Cain continued to make a fool of himself, but his relentless behavior became a positive in my mind, providing endless opportunities for law enforcement to verify that he was in Gulfport. What I needed most was solid proof linking his presence to me. Thankfully, my wish attracted an idea I'd never thought of before.

One day, while scrolling through the TV channels, I came across Nancy Grace proclaiming, "You know what they say, if you're trying to catch the devil, you better be willing to go to hell to get some witnesses."

Her comment hit me like a stroke of genius borrowed from the mouth of a savvy prosecutor. I wasn't willing to go to hell, but I was certainly willing to go to Office Max.

I printed fliers asking "HAVE YOU SEEN THIS MAN?" and featuring a photo of Cain's face that I pulled from the internet. I offered a reward to anyone who could positively place his whereabouts, hoping to generate interest. I distributed the fliers at places I felt Cain was most likely to frequent—car dealerships, barbershops, car washes, bars, a few select apartment complexes, and the community rec center where a large group of adults gathered each Saturday for a game of basketball. Through these fliers, I obtained useful information I was able to pass on to Investigator Masterson.

I discovered that, in an attempt to form alliances, Cain and his brother, Ryan, were claiming to be born and bred Mississippians—even fabricating a story about riding out Hurricane Katrina. As you and I both know, Southerners are slow to accept Yankees, and talk about Hurricane Katrina is still a regular part of casual conversation. Cain and his brother assumed fake identities, making it appear as though they were just neighborhood good ol' boys. Once they established a level of trust and familiarity, they began moving large amounts of drugs.

One young woman who identified Cain from the flier called to say, "He's a dope boy, ma'am. He likes to act like his shit don't stink. He stays over in the hood on Mississippi Avenue."

Before night fell, I had a flier at every house on Mississippi Avenue.

J.D. would later inform me that my fliers created a ripple in the streets, garnering the attention of people who aren't fond of the spotlight. They came to see Cain as a liability they couldn't afford. Suddenly, Cain had a big problem on his hands. So, he did what he does best: He disappeared into thin air. My guess is that he headed back to Columbus with his tail between his legs, hiding under a rock until the crisis passed.

The tables were beginning to turn, but I didn't know it yet. I only knew that changing how I saw myself, and running effective offense instead of defense, felt like the energy my life needed most.

After Cain stopped renting a room in my brain, I was able to focus on the more important issue of carving out a future from the dust and rubble of my past. I came to believe that my new outlook on life ensured a fresh start. Now that I had a team and a new attitude, I hoped I could somehow turn my ship around and sail toward calmer waters.

And so I did.

It's always hard to start over when the economy is in the tank. I don't suppose you were aware of it, but back in 2013, when my evolution first began, no one was hiring—least of all hiring a transplant from up north with a sketchy work history. I'd been fortunate enough to land odd jobs here and there that helped keep a little food on the table and the light bill paid, but we were so poor I was rationing toilet paper as if it were papyrus from the Dead Sea Scrolls.

My lack of education and bankable skills showed up to kick me in the ass. Even though I'd made great progress in my head space, I wasn't ready to step back into the world like a normal, functioning adult. I still had old wounds that were festering and baggage I was dragging around. I felt better, but not yet whole.

Every day I searched the help-wanted ads for anything that could bring in some money. I cleaned toilets, I chauffeured a Vietnam vet to his doctor appointments and ran his errands, and I helped a neighbor with her catering business whenever her daughter landed herself in jail again. I was extremely grateful for the opportunity to work, but nothing was moving the needle toward greater security and independence.

I noticed that there were always plenty of positions available for nurses and truck drivers. At first, I dismissed both of them as the equivalent of applying for a job of as a deep-sea fisherman—I lacked both the skills and the interest. So I kept scrubbing toilets and chauffeuring vets until one day a thought came to me with a new set of eyes: *A truck driver, hmm. I think I could do that*, I said to myself. The more I thought about it, the more plausible it seemed. And the more plausible it seemed, the more beautiful the idea became.

Becoming a truck driver solved every problem I faced—it was good money, I didn't have to work with the public much, and I'd never be in one place for very long. I figured it would be impossible for Cain to follow me around America, and if by chance he even tried, he would end up leaving a paper trail that Masterson would be sure to sniff out. Truck driving would offer a stable income, allowing us to move closer to town now that you were getting ready to start college. And the wanderlust of my spirit welcomed the opportunity to see parts of the country I'd only dreamed of seeing.

Over the course of the next few days, I pondered the idea, turning it over in my head, twisting it this way and that until it resembled a Rubik's Cube with all the colors lined up. I felt confident it was a good fit for our lives. Of course, it never occurred to me that I would be a woman stepping into a "man's world." And when the thought finally did occur to me, I simply didn't give a shit.

"So what if it's an odd solution to an odd life," I reassured myself.

"So what if everyone will think I'm nuts," I laughed out loud more than once.

My decision to become an over-the-road truck driver was one of the best decisions I've ever made. I'm an unconventional spirit, so my unorthodox approach to problem-solving fit me perfectly. I once thought hope looked like a magnificent tree. Turns out, it also looks like a big rig rolling down the highway. Some might think my decision was outrageous, but I came to believe that not only could I handle my business at home, I just might find myself somewhere out on the open road.

And so I did.

I can't help but smile remembering the beginning of this chapter in our lives. Everyone has their own starting point in life—I guess mine was at the age of forty-eight. 2013 was a very good year. I can't quite say the wickedness chasing me fully understood that its heyday was over, but in retrospect, I can clearly see that when I began channeling light and feeding the white wolf, I threw my cage wide open and flew toward the power of me.

That's the magic of a person discovering their superpower—that's the art of believing. Hope feels so radiant, so abundant, that once the mind feels powerful, it's never willing to be held captive again.

The black years were over.

My thoughts had set me free.

Sending positive energy across the miles and holding you close in thought,

Your Loving Mother

TWENTY-THREE

Summer 2019

On the front porch

Dear Sparrow,

I awoke in the wee hours of the morning to the sound of a wolf howling. I'm serious. I couldn't believe my ears. I don't think wolves live in Mississippi anymore, so I'm pretty sure it must have been the long, slow howl of a dog baying at the moon. The sound of its lonesome call touched my inner wild. I, too, wanted to stand beneath the moon and intertwine with the night, connecting to the Athena within me. It's always wise to keep your inner warrior fed, because she is the essence of the rare fire that has served us well for eons. She is the anthem of our inner mythology, and every now and again, she probably needs to howl at the moon.

Dresses speak softly but carry a big stick, don't they? It may well be in a woman's nature to adorn herself in garments that celebrate her femininity, but the ways of silk and stilettos are only perfume, never to be mistaken for the spirit of a woman, a spirit more ferocious than any other creature on earth.

Women were not sent here to be the playthings of men just because we're beautiful. We are the crucial element to life itself. We are the drum and the sword. Not the stream, but the ocean, the fire and the mist, the granite and the chisel. Our mothers and grandmothers—and all women before them—dedicated themselves to carving our rightful place in history using diligence and intelligence, a telescope and a microscope, a needle and a thread, a hammer and a saw, humor and patience, the mind and the muscle, sacred stories and healing hands.

While wearing a dress, we've studied the stars, invented machines, made discoveries in math and science, plowed fields, bore young, and traveled through uncharted territory in pursuit of our most courageous dreams. We've held down homes, turned boys into men, empowered freedom, fought for justice, turned the soil, fed the soul, and silenced the mouth of ignorance. The spirit of a woman holds the essence of the bear, the tiger, the elephant, and the eagle. She is a force of nature, a law unto herself. And she gives the most dazzling display of brilliance and blaze when she feels her moment has arrived.

Anyone viewing women as the weaker sex has spent their entire life with their eyes closed. Character isn't determined by chromosome, and a penis isn't the international symbol for strength. Men once thought they could own us, tame us somehow, but only a fool or a dinosaur would think that now.

Whenever you come upon a woman struggling to find her footing, help lift her up—her dilemmas are your dilemmas. Whenever you come upon a woman who is fully alive in her own glory, help lift her up—her success is your success. Though religion, geography, and culture may separate us, we are connected by the same great warrior within.

The woman who allows herself to become badass is a woman the world takes seriously. Joan of Arc was badass. Nanyehi was badass. Harriet Tubman was badass. Madame Curie was badass. Ruth Bader Ginsburg is badass. Shirley Chisholm was badass. Jane Goodall is badass. Janis Joplin was badass. Fatima Zaman, Simone Biles, Emma Gonzalez, and Greta Thunberg are badass, too.

Badass isn't easy—it's a difficult title to earn and even harder to carry. The women I mention above are made of the same stuff we are—there's a badass in every woman, in every family, in every community, and every place all around the globe where people gather. A woman who has given herself the freedom to experience her own brand of badass is a woman elevated. Her strength is gorgeous.

Women represent half of the world's potential. That's a really big number. We have the right, and the responsibility, to demand our seats at the table. Not seat—*seats*. Collectively, we have the ability to shatter glass ceilings, change laws, stop oppression, elevate the dignities of human life, create meaningful dialogue that empowers change, and redefine priorities that serve only a precious few.

We owe it to our daughters to be the role models they're searching for—we owe it to ourselves to be the light we were destined to be.

It wasn't my intention to inject my thoughts on the Sisterhood of the Earth in this letter. I guess it's the energy of a Sunday that leads my mind to places a Saturday would never take me. I think it's important to speak on sisterhood because sisterhood is so important—we are powerful when we rise, we are unstoppable when we unite. So forgive my tangent, but don't abandon its message. I encourage you, sweet sister, to see yourself, and your daughter, as part of a team that is destined to save the world.

I'm sipping persimmon tea out of my new teacup, bought at our favorite antique store. I went there to buy a jar of local honey and a jar of that pecan apple butter we love, thinking I would add them to the basket of goodies I'm gathering for the woman down the street whose son recently died. I decided to add an antique teacup to the basket, just for the joy of it, and I'll probably add some flowers from my garden, just for the joy of it, too. I don't know if she's a "teacup and fresh flowers" kind of chick, but when a heart is hurting, simple human kindness can look like anything and still feel stabilizing.

Soon I'll put away my thoughts of howling wolves, women of strength, baskets filled with love and busy myself getting ready for your grandfather and Aunt Charlotte's visit. As eager as I am to see both of them, I'm terrifically eager to see the family cradle again. I can't wait to run my hands along its polished wood, slipping back in time to when you began your life nestled in the family cradle and I was a new mother peering down at you, certain that everything I ever needed was right before my eyes.

Scarlett will be the eleventh child to sleep in the cradle your grandfather made. Having it near us again is a beautiful reminder that her birth is imminent. Writing those words makes me feel a little breathless, a little drunk with joy.

I think I'll pour another cup of tea and share this moment with the prettiest teacup I've ever seen. I bought three: one for me, one for my neighbor, and one for Scarlett—I'll save it for when she's old enough to have tea and blow bubbles in the garden, our feet in the soil, our hands washed in the green of tender leaves.

I can't wait to see Charlotte. I always feel good when I'm with her. Her enthusiasm is infectious, isn't it? With her loud and hearty laugh, she's a happy soul if ever there was one. I've always admired her ability to plow straight into life. There are those who go wherever the day takes them and there are those who take the day with them wherever they go. Charlotte is what *carpe diem* looks like when it has plenty of office supplies, a minivan, and a will of iron and sunshine.

Charlotte has always followed the rulebook, choosing to walk a very safe mile. She has carefully, thoughtfully, hand-selected her version of joy. It's really quite amazing to watch someone practice the art of living as if it comes naturally to them.

When we were younger, she annoyed the shit out of me—I couldn't understand her need to be so damn happy all the time. But now I admire her ability to always choose the lighter shades in the crayon box, never feeling like she needs to wander through Oz or walk through hell in order to learn the importance of staying positive. It's funny, all those years I thought Charlotte should've been learning something from me, I really should've been learning something from her. Never underestimate a woman who methodically feeds the white wolf. She is a force the dark wolf runs from.

Charlotte was the first person I told about becoming a truck driver, and without hesitation, she encouraged me to forge ahead. When she arrives, I think I'll open a bottle of wine and offer a long overdue toast.

Her optimism helped fuel my dream, encouraging me to believe in the one thing I wanted to believe in most of all: Seek and ye shall find.

I stepped off the Greyhound bus at 3:00 a.m. in Dallas, Texas, carrying only one small duffel bag filled with sweatpants and flannel shirts. My purse was sparsely outfitted with a few bottles of water, a few protein bars, a few packs of cigarettes, a few twenty-dollar bills, and one new driver's license bearing a Class A CDL endorsement. I was fatigued from the long bus ride. I'd never been on a bus before, besides the one I rode back and forth to school as a child—it was certainly an eye-opening experience. The insane asylum on wheels had leaned and sputtered, smelling like fermented urine and unwashed bodies, weaving its way toward Dallas one never-ending stop at a time. I'd stared out the window watching the towns roll by, snacking on a bag of popcorn and thinking of home.

As soon as the bus left Gulfport, I was already missing you. You ran through my mind as if you were on horseback, galloping through my thoughts, leaping over rivers of the unknown and fences of uncertainty.

Once again, it was faith alone that gave me the strength to board the bus, leaving you and Radar to manage without me. I don't know how I ever did it. I don't know how I ever had the resolve (or was it the foolishness?) to leave you in the care of angels while I hit the road. Had it not been for Investigator Masterson and Radar's presence in our life, I never would have left—the leaving felt too much like abandoning you. I know that's not how you saw it, but that's certainly how it felt to me.

As a young woman ready to start college, you probably thought it was a fine idea to have your mother out of your hair for a while. However, given all the variables in our life at the time, I wasn't sure my leaving was the smartest choice, but I knew staying would never bring us closer to our goals.

I spent a good portion of the bus ride talking to God. I asked Him to wrap you in a bubble of protection and kiss you with grace in every breath, every step, every day. I reassured myself that I would be back home before I knew it, and that you and Radar would be fine without me.

I knew the stalking wasn't over. Even though Cain had disappeared into a cloud of smoke and embarrassment, he unexpectedly resurfaced the evening before I was scheduled to take the written portion my CDL test. Our paths crossed on the long stretch of country road leading to our house as I was making my way home after a day spent in class. When our eyes met, I was surprised to see a look of panic on his face. The smug grin was gone. I stuck my head out the window so he could get a closer look at the contempt coming from my eyes. He was the first to look away.

I have no doubt Cain resurfaced for one reason only: to throw me off my game. He probably wanted nothing more than for me to dissolve into a puddle of tears and spend the evening choking on his attempt to reintroduce me to fear. Thankfully, seeing him had the opposite effect on me—I was more determined than ever to nail my CDL test

I'd gone home and studied deep into the night, memorizing facts about air brakes, the components of a diesel engine, and laws governing truck drivers. I walked through the proper procedure to follow when inspecting equipment until I knew it like a faded pair of jeans. I studied a road atlas, memorizing the major highways connecting major cities. I practiced working my way through the pattern of a ten-speed transmission using an umbrella sunk into a potted plant until the rhythm felt natural. I repeated words *like glad-hands* and *weight distribution*, and recited hours-of-service rules until the study guide fell from my hands and my mind collapsed into sleep.

The next day, I was confident and focused as I sat down to take the test.

I scored highest in the class.

I was the only woman.

Before we knew it, I was on the Greyhound bus to Dallas. After the long bus ride and a long wait for a taxi to take me to the company terminal, I finally made my way to my hotel room. Knowing I didn't have time to rest before orientation began, I threw my duffel bag on the bed, inhaled a few cups of lousy coffee, arranged my hair into a long braid, and was the first person standing in line waiting for the doors to open.

Of the forty-some people in my orientation class, I was one of two women. The other woman, who I assumed was about my age, had flaming red hair that sprang from her head in wild tufts, making it look like Heat Miser was her personal stylist. She nervously chewed her nails, moving from one to the other as if her hand were a corncob. We sat next to each other in silent fellowship.

During the three-day orientation, we were given a statistic that surprised me: Only one out of every hundred new drivers will still be driving in a year. The turnover rate was astounding—some left due to the danger, some because of the long hours, and some because the sacrifice of being away from home and family proved to be too great. Regardless of the reason, it was predicted that only one of us would remain. Without any doubt in my mind, I knew I would be the one left standing.

And so began the season of learning how to become an over-the-road truck driver. I jumped on board my trainer's truck and we set out for parts unknown. The training portion of my new career was a miserable existence if ever there was one. Living inside the cab of a big rig was a challenge bigger than I'd expected—like living in a coat closet with someone you've never met. Imagine traveling around America for weeks on end with a complete stranger who never grows tired of talking about himself or picking his nose in front of you.

My first trainer was a ridiculous narcissist who believed he had the power to change stoplights from red to green with his mind. My second trainer confessed he took powerful sedatives to silence the voices in his head that told him to kill people. My third trainer was missing all of his teeth and sucked on cinnamon rolls as if they were a woman's breast.

It didn't take long to realize why so many new students headed home after only a week or two on the road—you had to escape to an alternate place in your head and turn up the music really loud in order to pretend anything about the lifestyle was safe or normal.

Thankfully, I'd chosen a good company that was willing to shuffle students from trainer to trainer until they found the right fit. It was my good fortune that my last trainer, Tugboat Jones, was an extremely likeable person who taught me everything I needed to know. Tugboat was a retired Marine who had been driving a truck so long he didn't know how to get a good night's sleep in a bed that wasn't rolling down the freeway. He was good-natured and endlessly patient, a true gentleman in every sense of the word. Since he was such a veteran of the road, he received loads considered the cream of the crop. Once I was on his truck, we were laying down miles faster than Santa on Christmas Eve, zigzagging our way around America as if the devil were nipping at our heels.

Trips from Jacksonville, Florida, to San Diego, California, took two and a half days. I scaled the Rocky Mountains, the Sierra Nevadas, and the Cascade Mountains, and I summited Donner Pass in a snowstorm like it was in my blood to crest mountains in a semi truck. I became a woman I'd never met before.

After I climbed on Tugboat's truck, my paychecks almost made me cry—they had so many pretty numbers and I'd worked so hard to earn them. I set aside just enough money to carry me through the week, sending the rest home to you. Sending money home felt like a victory. The grueling schedule, the infrequent showers in dirty truck stops, and the unexpected demands of the job seemed like a fair exchange for the opportunity to begin taking proper care of our life.

Before we knew it, I returned home after my three and a half months out on the road and we moved into this charming little bungalow. I remember sitting on our front porch for the first time, enjoying homemade biscuits smothered in blackberry jam from Oregon, telling you stories from the road. The laughter came easy that day, didn't it?

As time went on, I grew excited each time I was able to add another layer of comfort to our house—the new beds and furniture made the place feel more like a home. I loved wandering through the regions of our country, buying pottery from reservations, homemade quilts in Pennsylvania, that gorgeous stained glass window from a chic antique mall in Virginia. I fell in love with the paintings of wild horses I bought in New Mexico and that colorful tapestry from Montana. Bit by bit, mile by mile, our home came alive with the energy of America.

You had settled into your life as a full-time student with lots of friends, and I was learning my trade one breathtaking view at a time. We came to know the satisfaction of creating our own reality, then happily living inside it.

I can't say for certain when I first noticed the FBI's presence in my life. But that's not surprising since it's not like the FBI to announce their presence. By the time you figure out the agents are watching, you have no idea how long they've been there or what they've seen. You'd imagine that if you're a criminal, a terrorist, or even just a complete moron, nothing would strike fear in your heart faster than knowing you've come across the FBI's radar.

I must admit, I'd never spent a minute of my time thinking about the Federal Bureau of Investigation. They were an entity so high up in the stratosphere that I could never imagine being of any interest to them at all. In my mind, they were among the giants who fought the greatest battles on earth. I'd always been proud that America has such an elite assortment of commandos and operatives, but for the most part, the FBI was like a black panther—skilled, lethal, and elusive, operating in a world that never touched my own.

If I had to venture a guess as to when I began to sense that something strange, something big, was moving about, I would have to pick the spring of 2013, back when I was first emerging from my frightened state into a more pragmatic believer in the power of positive thinking. I remember feeling a change in temperature, like a storm cloud sitting lower to the ground on the outskirts of my life, but I attributed this change to the fact that I was beginning my climb upwards, causing Cain to lose his mind.

During the spring of 2013, I began to notice a change in the vehicles that were following me. The biggest difference wasn't the types of vehicles, but the manner in which they followed. Cain and his cohorts had always made a complete nuisance of themselves on the road—making sudden movements, drifting from side to side, running stop signs. But by spring of 2013, whoever was tailing me was much more discreet.

At the time, I thought Cain had finally learned how to stalk and drive at the same time. Never in my wildest dreams did I consider it could be the FBI. Had I known, I doubt I would've done anything differently. I never came to see their presence as a bad thing, just a peculiar thing, creating a long list of questions I've never been able to answer.

I once called Investigator Masterson to report I felt like the FBI was watching me. He didn't seem fazed by the suggestion, but he claimed to have no knowledge of their involvement in my case. After

I hung up the phone, I wasn't entirely certain he was telling the truth, but I was entirely certain that even if he knew the truth, he wasn't allowed to tell me.

Time went on. I got my own rig (gotta love a Kenworth, baby!), miles passed under me, states flew by me, I collected crystals and feathers, four-leaf clovers, five-leaf clovers, and gathered free-culled herbs from all around the country. By then I was certain the FBI was always in my vicinity—no matter where I was. They didn't try to hide themselves, often parked just outside a shipping facility or across the road from the entrance to a truck stop, yet they never approached me or asked me to talk over coffee, so I did my best to ignore them. The whole experience was kind of weird, but at least this weird was sane and carried badges. The only thing I couldn't figure out was why—what did they know that generated their ability to dedicate so much manpower and resources?

The FBI doesn't take a case unless it meets specific criteria warranting a federal investigation. I suspected that stealing mail, tapping phone lines, and crossing state lines in order to stalk me might be enough to meet the requirements, but Cain had never verbally threatened me (the tipping point in any stalking case), so I doubted it was the stalking alone that piqued their interest.

I tossed different scenarios around in my head, forming the hypothesis that the FBI probably hadn't shown up in my life to dismantle a stalker, but rather, in trying to flush out the bad guys, they'd come across me as one of the bad guys' favorite obsessions. There's an old police idiom that states, "Follow the butter and the bread shows up." I came to see myself as the butter, but I had no idea what else Cain had gotten himself into—identity theft, robbery, murder, child pornography? With him, anything was possible.

I gathered some facts about the FBI, hoping to understand it a little better, wanting to reassure myself that I was now in the company of heroes unlike any other heroes on earth. I discovered that the FBI isn't as opaque as the average citizen probably thinks—it even has its own website. Who knew?

In today's news, it would be easy to believe that the FBI is a collection of untouchable assholes, but that's just a spin that sells papers. The truth is, the FBI is composed of the best of the best, who receive extensive training in order to fight the crime that has the greatest impact on the American people.

The FBI cut its teeth taking down mobsters, organized crime families, and KKK imperial wizards, but it soon broadened its scope to include sleazy politicians and corruption at the highest levels of business and government. To date, the FBI has investigated some of the most notorious crimes and criminals ever to besiege our nation: spies, terrorist organizations, bombings, the attack on the World Trade Center and the Twin Towers, espionage rings, fraud schemes, gangs, drug cartels, kidnappings, murders, and hijackings. Most importantly, it works tirelessly to protect and deliver justice to the most innocent of all victims: our children. If ever there was an organization within the federal government that truly serves the good of the people, certainly the FBI should hold this title.

I know that some try their best to diminish the importance of the FBI's work, but usually, those are the people fortunate enough to never need its services. And some try to degrade its credibility, but perhaps a person's willingness to assault the FBI's character is the greatest compliment the FBI can receive. Let's face it: If bad guys don't like you, you must be doing something right.

If given a choice between believing the propaganda or an institution with the statistics to verify its service to the red, white, and blue, stick with what you know: Honor doesn't boast. But liars and charlatans always do.

I can't begin to explain why Cain, a man who considered himself invincible and street-wise, never seemed to notice that the FBI was watching his every move—perhaps his intelligence was wasted on a stupid person. Suffice it to say, Cain continued to operate as though he were invincible, seemingly oblivious to the fact that the walls were closing in on him.

As for me, I kept my mind alert and focused, I kept sending money and postcards home, I took note of the strange current swirling around me, and I kept on driving.

The sun high in the sky tells me I'd better get busy preparing for your grandfather and Charlotte's visit. I need to put away my writing, my easel, my pieces of barn door leaning against the couch and chairs like overnight guests in a frat house. I'll head to the farmers market to see what yummies they have for sale and gather some flowers for the table—nothing says welcome quite like a bouquet of flowers leaping out of a vase as if they're trying to hug you.

The cradle is coming! The cradle is coming! Said the smiling woman to her daughter.

Sending positive energy across the miles and holding you close in thought,

Your Loving Mother

TWENTY-FOUR

Summer 2019

At home

Dear Sparrow,

Charlotte and your grandfather left early this morning, eager to get on the road before sunrise. I enjoyed the time we spent together. It felt good to get out of my head for a while and enjoy the simple pleasure of being in the company of those who know me so well. It's funny how family can drive us crazy and make us feel wonderful at the very same time, almost like a guilty pleasure. Humans crave the family experience, yet it's humbling to be in the company of people who know how dumb we used to be.

The cradle looks beautiful in the nursery, like something out of a fairytale. My heart was the color of a ruby when I found you sitting in the rocking chair, staring at the cradle with such love in your eyes, as if you didn't want to leave it, wishing we'd go out to dinner without you. I will always remember holding hands as we prayed over the cradle. Your hands felt so light in mine, as if you were floating.

The hour is drawing near—I feel it in my bones. I suppose you feel it in your bones, too. I know the doctors predict you have a few more weeks left, but I respectfully disagree—Scarlett Rowan is ready to make the transition from womb to world. The moon will be full soon; the universe is ready to celebrate.

At this very moment, I feel like I'm wrapped in the essence of silver—a grandchild on the way, a visit with family, a plate of baked blueberry French toast, and my pen in hand as I set about the task of remembering a time in our lives when I started to become the woman writing these letters.

I guess it could be said that I became fully awake after I began driving a truck. It's hard not to—driving a seventy-two-foot semi through sprawling cities in rush-hour traffic, down narrow country roads, and over mountaintops is a sizeable risk, forcing you to stare your own mortality in the face every day. The benefit of this kind of white-knuckle awareness is it reminds you that every day is a gift: Life is a gift, time spent with loved ones is a gift, sleeping in your own bed is a gift, and the freedom to manage your own reality is quite a gift, too.

As the miles rolled by, I came to know the road very well. It wasn't my friend quite like I thought it would be—the road wanted to batter and bruise me. Any healing I'd hoped to attract, any seek-and-ye-shall-find, I'd have to earn the hard way. Crappy food, shitty coffee, too much exhaustion and too little sleep, ridiculous demands, split-second decisions, volatile weather systems, wobbly bridges, horrific drivers, the lingering smell of diesel fumes, roads that drove like rutted paths in third-world countries, and filthy truck stops became the only permanence in a journey of constant motion.

I woke up every morning wondering what state I was in until the fog of sleep dissipated, remembering that I'd shut down in Utah, Georgia, maybe the southern tip of Florida. The never-ending fluctuation of temperatures, seasons, time zones, and altitudes played tricks on my body—I often felt dizzy whenever I was standing still. Since I stayed on the road for months at a time, I came to feel like a visitor in my own life whenever I finally made it home again.

The battles of the road are inescapable umbrage in the life of a truck driver, so I decided early on that I wouldn't view these discomforts through a magnifying glass—they'd look too impossible. Instead, I took it all in stride as I made my way around America, letting the spirit of freedom and the wonder of discovery rise higher in my mind than the displeasures of a road hell-bent on trying to break me.

Shortly after my one-year anniversary, I'd been to all 48 states in the contiguous United States. My eyes took in scenery so divine it made the postcards I was collecting seem like a single sentence trying to tell a spectacular story. I was calmed by endless fields of sunflowers, the opulence of fall, and the glory of sapphire-blue waters surrounded by a halo of wilderness. My mind dove into the pristine beauty of mountains sprinkled in powdered sugar, overpowering the horizon like living monuments to the earth's ambition. I admired breathtaking views of the oceans, cascading rivers boldly carving their way through layers of cinnamon canyon, cathedrals of ancient trees rising into the sky like signposts to heaven. I witnessed a rainbow around the full moon and the total eclipse of the sun. I took in peaceful sunrises sculpted by nirvana and psychedelic sunsets sculpted by fire.

When the road was really generous, I would shut down for the night in the middle of nowhere, far away from the stale glare of city lights, and step out into the blackness. I would climb onto the hood of my truck, lean into a pillow resting against the windshield, and witness the miracle of a galaxy sharing the light of a billion stars.

The more I traveled, the more I came to feel the earth in a way I'd never before experienced. I felt a wondrous assortment of awe and yearning, making me realize that the world outside our windows is a world our primal self hungers to experience—I believe there's a cave-dweller, a tree-climber, a botanist, and an explorer in each of us. Unleashing our inner restlessness awakens the core of our celestial being; the untamed and the timeless become the canvas of the dreamer.

I fell in love with the Pacific Northwest. The lush, inspiring wilderness of Washington, Oregon, northern California, northern Idaho, and western Montana is unsurpassed in my mind. Everywhere you look is indescribable scenery that begs you to pull over and start taking pictures. From Douglas fir trees and giant sequoias, to sparkling waterfalls and mountain views that stretch for miles, this region of our country is a metaphysical masterpiece that triggers the most succulent part of our imagination.

Each time I drove the mountains in the Pacific Northwest or the Rocky Mountains in Colorado, it was a spiritual experience for me, connecting me to the radiance of heaven touching earth. Even though trucking is a solitary, bohemian sort of existence (and the endless miles sometimes feel like a punishment more than a pleasure), the moments when I could experience the healing elements of nature helped keep me feeling refreshed and thankful. I often couldn't believe I was getting paid to embark on the journey of a lifetime, like an archeologist who's paid to find bones but finds their peace instead. Some paychecks were truly a joy to earn.

By and by, I simmered in shades of yellow, blue, and green, blossoming in the light of self-reflection, attaining a truth I'd waited a lifetime to learn: I can live in the world without letting the world live in me.

Heading south down California's vivid coast, past wine country and picturesque cliffs, I came across the suffocating smog of Los Angeles. It jolted my mind to realize how much Hollywood had lied to us. Los Angeles wasn't the land of the rich and beautiful quite like movies want us to believe—it was tent cities under freeway overpasses, brown air, and dying trees. The Hollywood sign, nestled on the side of a hill, almost seemed embarrassed, as if it knew it was a landmark to a place that didn't really exist. The endless traffic and sensory overload suggested that among writers, actors, and those in search of fame, an assault of the senses is the appropriate obstacle course for a name destined to be in lights.

Heading through the desert southwest, I drove through the neon scream of Las Vegas, a city surrounded by miles and miles of open space that makes the city appear like a glowing mirage from a distance. Las Vegas has a lot to talk about, with its blinking lights and overstated bling, but its conversation didn't tempt me.

I much preferred the vibe of ghost towns discarded along the highway or the sleepy little train-stop villages dotting the landscape like candy canes on a Christmas tree. The buildings on the main drag of these sweet, little towns were often dilapidated, with roofs so exhausted you could tell they were dreaming of becoming floors, yet the storefronts were often painted in bright, festive colors. The cheerfulness of their façades seemed to suggest the town's overall philosophy: Life is what you make of it—better choose yellow, red, and purple.

I laughed when I saw a herd of goats gathered around the front door of a tiny post office as if they were expecting a package. The goats seemed annoyed by the sound of my engine, but not annoyed enough to scatter. They stared at me as if I were an unwelcome guest in a town overrun by enterprising goats, lively relics, and old men taking a morning snooze in folding lawn chairs outside the hardware store.

When I came upon the quiet resonance of a desert setting for the first time, traveling through the Mojave Desert, Death Valley, and the badlands of the Painted Desert in Arizona, I could understand why Georgia O'Keeffe was inspired to capture its severe elegance. Under a turquoise sky, a landscape burnished by the sun was haunting and visceral, offering unexpected bursts of color. Cactus, agave, and strange-looking plants clawed their way through the scorched earth like witch's fingers, contorting themselves into shapes I'd never seen.

The desert holds a hallowed vibe; its solitude feels sacred. Stripped of the essence of water, you are silent witness to life in its most primitive state.

A curious raven eyed me as I slowly passed by, keeping watch for the ancestors, their teachings intertwined with his feathers like crystals on a veil.

Moving eastward, as if my travels were like reading the book of America, I came to appreciate the quiet loveliness of cornfields and farmland in the Dakotas, Iowa, Wisconsin, Missouri, Kansas, and Nebraska. This region of our country is iconic America: a well-kept farmhouse with an American flag waving in the front yard, a lazy dog trailing behind an irritated rooster, a weathered wagon wheel leaning against a mature shade tree. It's Main Street USA, a covered dish at a potluck dinner, Friday-night ball games, and Sunday-morning prayers. My mouth dropped the first time I saw a team of Clydesdale horses grazing in an emerald-green pasture. The majestic horses seemed unfazed as I rumbled past. To them, I was nothing more than paparazzi.

I spent a good deal of time in Texas, the entry point of so many goods going in and out of Mexico. The pride in Texas is palpable. Texans embody the spirit that built this country: dusty dreams pulled from the earth; a rugged sense of self; and the never-ending pursuit of land, cattle, and freedom from a government that tends to overstep its bounds. Perhaps Texas, more than any other state besides Wyoming, seems to honor a belief so important to our founding fathers: Liberty is only worth something if people have the right to live and worship in a land of their own making.

I bought that string of rustic stars that hangs above my vanity in Texas, hoping to carry a little piece of the Lone Star State with me

proclaims in a lofty sort of manner, declaring man's innate desire to establish himself lord of his surroundings. The air is caffeinated with an insuppressible energy, day and night are interchangeable, life moves quickly, the passive makes way for the persistent.

Cities are old in the East. Buildings hold the secrets of our past, streets seem to moan and shiver, paved with the nuances of our pilgrim intent. The genesis of democracy, manifest destiny, commerce, and industrialization carved their place into our consciousness in cities that serve as the lighthouses of America. We are far from our puritan origins, but our origins aren't far from us.

As I made my way around America, appreciating the beauty and sampling the culture of its people, some realities were easier to face than others. Yet the wisdom of the road encouraged me to see the potential rather than the recklessness. I came to know the gentle ways of farm country and little towns with sweet smiles, the haunting stares of mothers doing their best to raise children in inner-city war zones or on barren Indian reservations. I smelled the salty brine of seaside villages and heard the impoverished weeping of forgotten mining towns. I tasted the luxury of fresh food from local farmers markets. I felt the stinging defeat of urban decay.

I made a delivery in Compton, California, at 3:00 a.m. and wrestled with the boroughs of New York City as if I had a lick of sense in my head. I felt the pulsating heat of Miami and the rhythmic Zen of Sedona. I experienced the complicated frenzy of life in the fast lane and the gilded simplicity of life in the slow lane.

I saw tarantulas, bears, and bobcats. I saw buffalo and wild mustangs. I saw dozens of bald eagles surfing the wind, and a moose jogging along the side of a freeway, trying to avoid the snowdrifts in the grass. I drove through blinding winter storms and torrential downpours. I battled fog, black ice, irreverent winds, and apocalyptic sand storms. I saw dozens of rainbows and shooting stars.

The yin and yang of it all made things begin to fall into place in my mind.

The more I traveled, the more enlightened I became, experiencing the mood and the marrow of America. From seraphic seas to saffron deserts, from majestic mountains to colorful canyons, and from moonlight monoliths to the mega metropolis, the United States of America is a land fantastically alive with flora and fauna, hope and potential. I came to have a greater understanding of America through my travels, and for the first time in my life, I was able to see for myself why our nation is so revered. As a people, we are creative, resilient, intelligent, and proud. We are the embodiment of all things strong, graceful, enthusiastic, and determined.

During my time on the road, I sat in more than my fair share of local diners, discovering that a diner is the best place to gauge the overall temperature of America. Listening to the conversations floating around me, I came to realize that we're all focused on the very same things: family, home, work, spirituality, holidays, and the opportunity to make a better life for our children and ourselves. We share a mutual concern over the state of the world, the integrity of our elected officials, and the division sweeping across our country. Through these dappled conversations, I realized that our inspirations don't separate us—they unite us. Our hopes and dreams are the same as those of our neighbors across the street, across town, across state lines, and all across America.

As a nation, we believe that each individual is an important part of our collective story, we take pride in our willingness to give, we all want a little more light in our lives, and we all wish everyone could be a little nicer to each other. We hold good moral character in the highest regard, we respect a strong work ethic, honesty, and integrity. We brag about the neighbor who helped a stranger, the friend who donated their time, the community that came together to make a difference.

And at the very heart of our unified belief system lies a truth that lyrically joins us: We all want love to win.

Some may say that America is in great turmoil, but we've always been in great turmoil—that's the shadow side of democracy. When people have the freedom to speak their truth, things can get a little messy. Americans are a passionate tribe, and passion is loud. We've always felt a need to express ourselves outrageously before streamlining our thoughts into a workable plan that adapts and changes, yet serves and protects. Our conflicts are the growing pains of a country crowned king while still in its infancy, doing its best to evolve in an ever-changing world, struggling to find a united path that serves such a rambunctious and opinionated population.

In my mind, the ingredient we need most right now is compassion. Compassion is like hot sauce—you don't need much to make a big difference. Compassion empowers decency, which in turn, empowers people. Our country is big enough, strong enough, already great enough to include everyone—there isn't a light we don't need.

I believe we have a moral obligation to debate with dignity to ensure the country we're shaping is a place we want our children to live. Modeling simple human kindness is the call of a nation that aspires to do more than just build a strong future, but longs to define a legacy.

From the viewpoint of the stars, we're all in this together; we are a global community. Other countries look to us for inspiration—they always have. It would be our downfall as a nation if we relinquish our place in history because we allowed the forces of darkness to paralyze our minds or turn us into people we don't like anymore.

I pray that the leaders we choose to represent us are worthy of the honor we've bestowed upon them. America has sacrificed too much to surrender itself to those who abuse public trust or govern like toddlers. We must be forever mindful that countless soldiers have laid down their lives so our liberties would feel real to us. You can't honor the fallen if you devalue the America they died for. Tearing to shreds people who don't agree with you has always been the path of a weak mind, so we must elect leaders who speak the language of progress through collaboration, success through inclusion, respect, and accountability.

Sometimes America turns a blind eye to the vomit spewing in Washington, D.C., mostly because we're fantastically busy with the task of living. Thankfully, we're not "stand in a straight line and be happy with gruel" kind of people. Perhaps this moment in time is nothing more than political correctness experiencing its exact opposite. Being too politically correct stifles the growth of the individual, while the complete lack of moral etiquette wounds a country. So though it's true that the pendulum seems to be swinging wildly, maybe it has to so we can find a more stable center.

I've heard it said that each of us must be the change we want to see in the world. At face value, that request seems overwhelming, doesn't it? I mean, who has time to change the world—we barely have time to water our plants. Perhaps the secret to success on such a grand scale is to start small: Cast a vote, find a cause you believe in and support it, don't participate in the insanity around you, be the first to show kindness regardless of the reaction you receive, and walk the walk a child can admire and emulate.

We begin to change the world when we begin to change our thinking. So let your mind guide you to a place of giving and compassion, respect and tolerance, and you will contribute to the change the world needs most.

And then came the art of healing and forgiveness. As the miles rolled on, I reinvented myself. I wasn't afraid anymore. I wasn't willing to self-sacrifice anymore. I was fearless, fierce, capable, and confident. I didn't have to pretend I was okay—I *was* okay. The story of America helped me rewrite my own story.

Staring into the infinity of a life forged from my thoughts, I began the necessary task of getting rid of my extra baggage. I don't remember ever thinking, *Time to sort through the bullshit,* as if it were the next item on my Things-to-Do List, it just happened naturally. The solitude, the scenery, the self-reliance needed to do my job effectively became the contractions of a woman waiting to be born. No longer numb inside, I began *feeling* the story of my life for the first time.

I've come to understand that sewing yourself back to together is done the old-fashioned way: one intentional stich at a time. And the process takes however long it needs to complete itself. For me, healing was a four-step formula, and I worked my way through Pandora's box following this method for healing.

Step One is Acknowledgement. Talk about it—get that shit out of your head! Don't be afraid to acknowledge what you've been through just because it might stir up unwanted emotions. Feelings happen. It's okay to feel them, even the yucky, catty, confusing ones. Feelings don't answer to logic, so they tend to get a little feral sometimes. But just because you felt something once doesn't mean you're stuck with it for the rest of your life. It's okay to let feelings move on.

The best way to encourage your feelings to move on is to let them express themselves. It's easier to take control of your feelings when you allow them to speak their truth in the safest way possible. So spend some time alone in your quiet place and scream, curse, pound, and cry your way into a spectacular release. Once your emotions feel validated, you'll find that they don't need you to carry them around anymore.

Step Two is Giving—sounds pretty cheesy, but it's true. Turn your pain into something that serves the greater good by letting your pain experience its exact opposite. Ask yourself this question: "If I could turn my pain into something useful, what would I want it to look like?" If you lost a beloved pet, volunteer at an animal shelter or drop off a bag of dog food or a few containers of kitty litter. If you suffered at the hands of an unhealthy relationship, send a care package to a woman at a domestic violence shelter. If you feel neglected or unappreciated, send the gift of thoughtfulness to a soldier overseas—a box of sunflower seeds, oatmeal cookies, beef jerky, and a note of encouragement would do much to restore their faith in humanity. Remember the children at St. Jude with donations or a personalized card and a puzzle or a toy, take a bouquet of flowers to an old-folks home, volunteer to coach little league, leave a painted rock outside an AA meeting, help raise money for a school.

Decide what you want your love to look like, then let it happen. And keep loving until you feel better, because sooner or later, you will. Sending kindness out into the world weakens pain, letting pain know it doesn't own you anymore.

Step Three is Letting Go. And letting go is hard, it's the act of your final goodbye. But if you've followed Steps One and Two, by now you're probably ready. The process of letting go is patching the holes in your *élan vital*—your creative life force. Pain and anger burn their way through your psyche, and the hole they create needs mending so more pain doesn't take its place. Because life keeps flowing and people aren't perfect and sometimes the dark wolf sneaks a bite.

No one's letting-go looks the same as someone else's, and there's no wrong way to get it right. After you've acknowledged your feelings and allowed them to experience their opposite, hopefully you can see your pain and hurt from a calmer place—this is an ideal time to let go.

When your memories and trauma feel a little more settled, it's time to let the fat lady sing—the show is over.

For me, letting go took the form of writing letters to God. I talked about all I'd been through and how it felt. Since I'd already purged my feelings, my letters didn't contain a lot of sting, they were covered in brutal honesty instead. I didn't worry about grammar or syntax or holding back or even hurting God's feelings, letting my thoughts flow through me however they felt they needed to. I said goodbye to the pain, I told God I was stronger now—I was ready to let go. Then I picked a place that felt right and left the letter behind, telling myself that once I let go of it, the pain in the memories was no longer mine to worry about.

I left my feelings of not being good enough stuck to a cactus in Death Valley—these feelings didn't deserve my attention anymore. I left my feelings of not being loveable tied to a sycamore tree in the Great Smoky Mountains—I sure hope squirrels can't read. I left my feelings of being responsible for the rape, the miscarriages, the abuse, the storm, the stalking in the textured walls of Antelope Canyon— these feelings had never empowered me, so I didn't want to own them anymore.

With each letter, a cleansing took place. The more I healed, the more I was ready to forgive.

Step Four is Forgiveness. It has to be. The greatest freedom you will ever experience will always come from the act of forgiving. Forgiveness isn't a gift you give to the person who hurt you, it's a gift you give to yourself. Forgiving someone doesn't mean the memory is any less real—it isn't a reset button. But in order to completely move on, you have to let go of the rope tying you to someone else's mistake.

How do you do it? You just say the words "I forgive you." And then you breathe.

You'll know you're ready to forgive when you start thinking about the pain less and yourself more. When you start visualizing a future that doesn't include unresolved hurt, a fractured spirit, a person dragging their soul behind them. That's when you know the time is right—you've found the sweet spot of forgiveness. You'll know your heart is ready when you have the strength to accept that forgiveness is really an act of self-love.

Once self-love became a part of my story, I knew my pain had experienced itself long enough. I left my bag of secrets, lies, and darkness somewhere out there on the road. I stopped worrying about yesterday and started dreaming about tomorrow. And after I sent kindness to people who didn't know me, could never thank me or repay me, after I completed my four-step process, I gave a gift to myself. I allowed myself the freedom to embrace the beauty, the relevance, and the mystery of me. A light washed over me.

Athena shined. The white wolf howled.

I was truly born.

The years flew past. I stopped spotting Cain. The last time I saw him was on Father's Day, 2016, near Louisville, Kentucky. I had a load going from Buffalo, New York, to Nashville, Tennessee, when I saw him hovering right next to me in traffic, looking as dumb as ever, going out of his way to make sure I knew he was near, too prideful to realize I could squash him like a grape if I wanted to.

I wondered about his children, who wouldn't spend Father's Day with their dad because he was too busy following a gypsy in a semi truck. As much as I wanted Cain to pay for all he'd done to us, there was also a part of me that wished he'd just go away so his children never had to find out how much time he'd spent being a weirdo instead of a father.

Sometimes justice makes pain go away, but sometimes, it just makes pain change hands.

After June 2016, I never saw Cain again, but he continued to try to infiltrate my world via phone calls, strangers, and emails from bogus accounts—classic attempts at catfishing. But by 2018, either he'd died, finally moved on, or begun sensing the FBI around him. I can't tell you what happened to him—I wasn't lying the last time you asked when I said I didn't know. And I don't really care what happened to him because he's not my problem anymore. All I can do is pray that he isn't anyone else's problem. I can only tell you that after I began feeding positive energy, after I became a truck driver, after the FBI came into the picture, after angels wielded the sword so I didn't have to, the stalking lessened and then abruptly stopped all together.

I'd always hoped that one day the FBI would show up at my door, declaring victory, ready to answer my long list of questions. It never happened. Maybe it will happen one day— federal investigations can last for years.

I've never had a clear understanding of why they're so interested in him in the first place, but at this writing, it all seems so far behind me now. I've already reached my pure space, my inner peace, without the satisfaction of justice in its most made-for-TV form. I had to learn how to heal without the benefit of indictments, courtroom drama, the word *guilty* followed by the slam of a gavel, or Cain being led away in handcuffs.

So I can't say for sure that the battle is over, and I can't tell you the name of the soldiers God asked to fight the war, but sitting here in the silver of my thoughts I can tell you this for certain: I'm okay and you're okay.

Love won.

Sending positive energy across the miles and holding you close in thought,

Your Loving Mother

TWENTY-FIVE

Dear Sparrow,

I'm sitting under the full moon, gazing into a mesmerizing fire, hypnotically entranced as I watch the flames reach skyward with the passion of a flamenco dancer. Its elaborate choreography celebrates a living energy; her ceremonial dance offered to the universe in recognition of her dominance over all earthly things. Only water can tame fire, but fire will always rise again because it's a phenomenon eternally summoned by the will of man.

Fire and water are not enemies—they are sisters. And they are most lovely underneath the Mother Moon.

I am at one with the mystical vibrations around me, nestled here beneath the oak, beech, and southern pine, sipping a glass of chardonnay while quietly toasting the events of the day. I feel a sense of perfect peace.

I have fallen in love with you all over again.

You shined today, child. You truly shined. You brought Scarlett Rowan into the world with incredible dignity, looking like a marble statue of fertility and femininity, channeling all the mothers of our bloodline as if their timeless verve coursed through your veins.

All I could do was hold your hand, thankful that I was able to witness the birth of a mother, the birth of a child. It was quite literally breathtaking to behold. I am in awe of the wonder of life and the eminence of the feminine spirit. Thank you, sweet child, for showing me the power of your brave.

When I held Scarlett in my arms for the first time, I knew I was staring into the brilliant blue eyes of a colorful mind. She's an old soul. She's been here before. Scarlett Rowan came into this world with plans already formed, a purpose already named, a destiny already known. Hers is a spirit driven to forge her own path and harness her beautiful wild as she lives the poetry of her own dreams. She is the stuff of legends—I feel it in my bones.

As evening fell and the moon rose outside the window, I watched you and Scarlett resting comfortably in the quiet glow of the hospital room. I leaned back into the reclining chair, wanting to absorb the tranquility of the mother/child experience. I let the silence speak, wishing I could stay tucked inside that moment forever—or at least carry it with me for the rest of my life, like a keepsake honoring the day when all three of us became something we'd never been before.

It's hard to put into words how I feel right now. If I had to describe the music of my heart, I would certainly choose Pachelbel's Canon in D. Uplifting. Angelic. It's not often that we get to watch miracles happen right before our eyes, but when we do, it feels like a symphony of pleasure that mirrors the very heavens that created it.

As I watched both of you sleeping comfortably, Scarlett swaddled in her first day of life, I knew I would come home and build a fire, pour a glass of wine, and relax in the serenity of thankfulness. Meister Eckhart, a German theologian from the Holy Roman Empire, wrote: "If the only prayer you ever say in your entire life is 'thank you,' it will be enough."

I'm pretty sure he's right—gratitude is impressive, especially when it's sincere.

So here I sit, right where I'm supposed to be on this night of perfect beginnings, thinking of you and Scarlett. I send my thoughts of love and appreciation to a God who gave us the gift of life in the breath of a remarkable child.

As much as I wish I were with you now, I know it's not my place. As soon as it's my turn to connect with the child, fully embrace her, I will do so with delighted abandon. But for tonight, while you're in the care of smiling angels and attentive nurses, I'm keeping company with the moon.

I'm writing you this letter just as I've written so many before, from the hearth of a mother's love that longs to awaken and reassure. This letter may not convey everything I'd like to say, but we have plenty of time to speak on mighty things like warriors named Athena, wolves that howl, and thoughts that connect us to our destiny.

We can even talk about the path we've traveled if you'd like, but I have a feeling that you don't need to heal from the past's wounds quite like I did. You've already found your place of peace—I saw it in your eyes when you held Scarlett in your arms.

You came into your own womanhood while I was on the road. I couldn't be more proud of you. I guess we both needed our own space so we could plant our own Eden. After you fell in love, I stopped talking about the road, preferring to listen to your heart-journey instead. When you told me you felt a sense of guilt that I came off the road to help with the baby, I did my best to relieve you of that worry.

Let me take it one step further by saying this: I made my decision for many reasons, and my favorite one was Scarlett.

After the brakes in my rig caught fire (determined to be due to a mechanical failure, by the way) and I almost didn't make it home for Christmas, I came to see the road differently. Then Radar jumped out the window of my truck to chase that group of bikers before disappearing into the woods, never to be seen again. After days turned into weeks without his microchip yielding the results we were hoping for, it felt like the end of an era. It was as if life had already turned the page.

By the time I got the call that you were pregnant, coming home felt right. By then, I'd already found my groove. The road had been a pivotal turning point in my life, but I was ready to move on. I'm sure it surprised you when I said I was coming home to stay, ready to begin my life as an artist and a grandmother rather than a philosophical trucker, but when fate opened the door, it was my destiny to walk through it.

When I came home, I began writing you a series of letters. In them, I did my best to explain my journey—our journey. I hoped I could enlighten you, empower you, feeling certain that you deserved some answers and that I had a responsibility to guide you to a better place—all so you could step into this new season with a more insightful version of wellness.

But after watching you today, I realize you don't need my letters. You don't need me to save you from anything, because you're not lost. And I don't really need to offer you my truth, because you've already found your own. You're already badass, child. How silly of me to think you needed my umbrella.

A box filled with these letters sits next to me in the grass. I'm aware that they're mine now—I guess they were never really meant for you at all. Perhaps I needed to write down the story of my life so

I could finally purge the last bit of residue from a strange and twisted journey, shaping it into chapters that finally make some sense.

It's funny how I started out with the intention of answering your questions, but in the end, I answered some of my own. So these letters weren't meant to be a gift to my daughter. Instead, they're a gift to myself.

For years, my journey jumped around inside my head like popcorn. I couldn't seem to make it sit still. I held a lifetime of stuffed pain that felt like Pluto circling around my brain—obviously a mass in my solar system, but downgraded to just a peculiar object floating in the farthest reaches of my galaxy.

While I was on the road, I experienced the therapy of freedom once I finally found the courage to confront the trials of my past. Somewhere along the way, I stumbled upon a formula for letting go that worked for me. I'd like to share this formula with you one day, but for now, I will tell you this: The one thing I couldn't seem to master was learning how to truly forgive myself. That is, until I wrote these letters. I can see my walk more clearly now. I can see my strength more clearly, too.

Of all the things we will ever do, forgiving ourselves will be the hardest task we ever ask our heart to handle. We are endlessly abusive to ourselves. Humans are far more likely to forgive a stranger than offer compassion to their own tender frailties.

I think of the young man who was able to forgive his brother's killer but could not find it in his heart to forgive himself for not answering the phone the last time his brother called. We are willing to murder our own soul as punishment for not being perfect. Then we dangle our imperfections over our head as a daily reminder that we aren't one of the "chosen ones" because we can't be trusted to be flawless all the time. This is the lie the dark wolf tells us. This is the lie we believe.

These letters were my inner voice taking charge. They rebuke the last remaining lie of the dark wolf. I'm now able to embrace a glorifying truth: Through all of my experiences—the ones where I tripped and the ones where I rose—I endured with as much sanity and grace as I could muster at the time.

I did the best I could.

And you know what? I'm okay with that. I'm at peace with the moments when I feared and fell, when I cried and denied, even when my weakness felt so strong. I can look back and see that I never, ever gave up. I kept working my way back to my destiny. Our destiny.

You once told me you thought I was brave. I'm thankful you see me that way, but truthfully, I'm no braver than anyone else, I've just had more opportunities to face my fears. And I kept facing them until I finally got it right.

Life takes an enormous amount of creative energy, and we're bound to trip along the way—mistakes are part of living because they help fuel our growth. We should never allow our fails to define us. Decorated soldiers are known by their victories—the mud, the blood, the tears, the scars become their sacred ground.

Wisdom is light that's had a chance to experience itself, so each time we fall and get back up, each time we dust ourselves off and keep moving forward, we show character the soul can be proud of.

I no longer view my story as a burden, but a blessing. It birthed a fighter, a dreamer, a dignitary, and a shaman. And my growth created a space for self-forgiveness to find its niche, because it was the falling that empowered the climb.

I highly recommend that you forgive yourself on a daily basis until forgiveness becomes a habit. A spirit that elevates its own value higher than it loathes its imperfections is one of the lightest beings on earth.

Self-acceptance gathers light, which in turn multiplies its light. Before you know it, you become one with yourself. The fear of failure lives no more.

As I sip my glass of wine with Tuck curled up on my lap, I consider this box of letters. I know I don't need them anymore. It's an honor to live long enough to let your face tell your story. My face, my hands, even my spirit, tell the tale of the roads I've traveled. I will let that be enough. So perhaps I'll throw these letters in the fire and let them burn one by one, joining the dance of the ages as they feed the fire that wrote them. It seems fitting, really—my journey isn't more significant than anyone else's. It is just one of many pages that fill the book of life.

I suppose we can all find a piece of ourselves in each other's story. Our stories may walk different, talk different, laugh and cry different, but we all come to know the ways of rust and glitter. The human experience is a colorful one—we've all felt a little yellow, a little green, a little gray.

My contribution to the book of life tells the tale of a bold spirit that has seen a wider world. I've felt the hands of wisdom and received her healing waters poured into a mind desperate with thirst. Universal truths are the melody of the cosmos. They teach us many things.

When we listen to the chorus of the stars, we realize we're all fragile and fantastic. Each of us is a weeping willow and a majestic oak, a wise teacher and an unsteady student, an idiot and a sage. There isn't a soul out there who isn't searching for something they can't seem to find—even if it's just their glasses. We are in the company of kindred strangers as we move throughout our days, each of us walking a path clouded in mystery that is meant to inspire rather than destroy.

You will go through your moments of great questioning, wandering, and stagnation, too. When these times come upon you, please remember to be kind to yourself. You're the best shot you have at happiness. You're the only hero your story will ever need. When darkness strikes, don't look down, look inward—that's where you'll find your guidance. That's where you'll find your gifts.

I suppose this night offers me a perfect opportunity to pass along some threads of knowledge that I've earned along the way. I can't pretend to be a mouthpiece of the heavens or even very good at expressing myself with the same passion with which my heart believes these truths, but if you find something useful in what I have to say, then it's certainly worth the ink it takes to write it.

I have come to understand that within each of us burns a rare fire. It is the living essence of who we are. It's rare because it's complex and unique. It's rare because it's celestial and infinite. It's rare because it's completely our own. We get to decide how our energy dances; we get to decide who we want to be in this world.

We have a primal need to discover ourselves and get lost in what we love. I encourage you to do your best to satisfy this need. When we suppress our fire, we deny our light. So walk your story with some brio—a vivaciousness of spirit that ignites your divine spark.

I've also come to understand that sometimes we radiate and sometimes we're terribly ashy. Life wasn't designed to be a smooth ride—it's under no obligation to use its indoor voice. Anyone who thinks life is supposed to feel like a bouquet of heather and baby's breath will be shocked when the dump truck shows up.

Since the world generates a lot of static, it's best to have a system in place for tuning out the white noise. There will be moments when you feel your peace slipping away. In order to remain grounded in the splendor of who you are, it helps to find your center. It's the place where you feel good even when life isn't perfect.

We all drift away from our north star. Storms happen. Waters get murky. Tides shift. Adulting can be painful. When you feel like you're moving further away from your *joie de vivre* rather than closer to it, make an immediate date with yourself. Schedule a wellness secession from your busy life before you begin to succumb to the madness.

I wish I could save you and Scarlett from a turbulent and toxic world, but I can't. Like everyone else, I'm still learning how to maintain my own Zen garden. I've made tremendous progress, but sometimes I have to revisit my healing formula, too. And when I do—when I make my inner world a priority—I'm able to realign myself with my center because I know what my center feels like now.

Tuning into our superpower so we can stay connected to the good stuff requires concentrated energy; flowing is an abstract concept rooted in specific intention. So whenever I start feeling overwhelmed, I know it's time for a mind scrub—I'm all about exfoliation of the emotional self.

It all starts with some deep, cleansing breaths—there's a difference between breathing and just taking in air. Deep breaths call up the warrior we call perspective. And she's both dynamic and persuasive when you let her speak her truth.

When your mind feels frantic, everything is a problem, even when it isn't. Enter the holistic benefits of empathy. Whenever you think your life sucks, remember the person whose life sucks worse. When you burn dinner, remember the person who eats dinner out of a garbage can. When you're late on your mortgage payment, remember those who hunker down in war zones. When your body aches, remember the person who can't walk. Or swim. Or carry their own cup of water. There are people all around the globe who would gladly trade problems with you.

People tend to believe that empathy is merely the act of being sensitive toward the suffering of others, but it's also a fabulous form of self-appreciation. Empathy for others has a way of balancing out the delicate ecosystem in your head, reminding you that you're better off than you think you are. When you keep things in perspective, the pressures of the outside world come to know their place, making it easier to preserve your center.

The goal of a good mind scrub is to protect your harmony. Harmony is the most precious gem in your crown and the one the dark wolf is trying its best to steal. When you're going through a long growing season, don't give chaos a platform. Chaos and hate need followers—they always have, they always will. So choose what you're willing to entertain. Invite it in. Then lock your door. And when people try to take a bite out of you, remember that they do so because emptiness feels fuller when it's feasting on someone else's joy.

I've also learned that stepping outside your comfort zone is a fantastic way to reset your compass. It's revitalizing. Did you know there's a woman living inside you that you haven't met yet? And you'll never meet her until you dare yourself to be something more than how you see yourself right now.

I have a dear friend who went through an extremely painful break-up—she was having a tough time moving on. For reasons even she can't explain, she decided to book a trip to England. Solo. She was her own best friend as she explored an unfamiliar country, relying on her own intelligence and grit, meeting a part of herself she'd never known before. She later claimed it wasn't a vacation—it was a pilgrimage. Each New Year's Day she does the polar bear plunge by jumping into the frigid waters of Puget Sound. She makes a conscious decision to refresh and renew. She offers sustenance to her inner Sky Woman; she lives her own fight song.

There will be times when you can't make it through on your own, times when solo isn't even an option. So when you need help, don't be too proud to ask for it—refusing to ask for help when you need it is a useless kind of pride that stumbles around with foolishness. We all need help sometimes. If we were meant to stand alone, God would've created more islands.

For me, a critical ingredient to staying on course is remembering that I am not alone. Neither are you. I've heard it said that if we knew who walked with us, we would never feel alone. I get it. I haven't always, but I get it now. I now view faith not as my last option, but as my most realistic chance. Then I wait with expectation—the key word here is *wait*.

We are a society addicted to instant gratification. We like our blessings to show up twenty minutes after we've placed the order. Unfortunately, God isn't a pizza delivery driver. And masterpieces take time. It may seem like God funnels our blessings through peanut butter, but the truth is, God is always ready to bless us abundantly. We just aren't always ready to handle it. Sometimes, there's work to be done first.

So, if you go through moments when you feel He isn't there, be still, child—the show ain't over yet. Don't give up just because the bad guy's doing a fist pump. When heaven sends angels, trust and believe they are the most competent angels heaven can amass—they're not to be taken lightly. Some wear wings, but some are God's troops on the ground.

And you will be asked to be someone else's angel, too.

Once in a blue moon, we are called upon to do amazing things. It doesn't happen every day and no warning will be given. But when it does happen, it is your chance to shine your rare fire, the one the universe has chosen to expand the circle of light. The calling might look as simple as donating a winter coat to a homeless shelter or taking a covered dish to a neighbor recovering from an illness. Or it could look as big as buying Christmas presents for a needy family or organizing a neighborhood-watch program. It might even look as insignificant as offering a smile to someone in a wheelchair.

You'll know it's your turn at bat because you'll feel it in your heart. And no one will know if you choose not to answer this call—it's your secret to keep. But you'll know. It will either sit within you like an opportunity lost or it will flourish like peace of mind gained.

This is my truth and I will gladly share with you: When wolves howl, women rise.

And even when you do it all right, even if you're one part Sandra Day O'Connor, one part Mary Seacole, one part Amelia Earhart, one part Misty Copeland and you walk around wearing Mother Teresa's shoes, pain and injustice will still find you.

The universe never takes a break from its fascination with balance. It's how the world evolves. It's how people evolve, too—you can't get to the royalty of your purple until you travel through some red and blue. This sampling of opposites gives you the opportunity to develop a more meaningful and imaginative core.

We live in a world screaming for justice. I could certainly tell you a thing or two about justice. And maybe I will someday. But for now, I want to reassure you that justice always prevails because karma never sleeps—that's probably why she's such a bitch.

There's no doubt that the number-one remedy for wound treatment is justice. It's so much easier to find closure when the person who hurt you is forced to eat a huge slice of karma pie. And they will eat a slice of karma pie, because what we send out always returns to us, but justice might not take place in a courtroom or right in front of our eyes. We may not even know it happened.

We all crave a satisfying end to every tragic story. We cheer when good triumphs. Good always wins, but not always in the way we think it should. Most of us have to learn how to let go and move on without the help of a Disney ending. Enter the beauty of self-love and self-care. When you're busy loving yourself, wounds can heal without any consideration of what happens to the villain.

Justice holds two scales in her hands. One is reserved for the fate of those who hurt us, and the other is reserved for our own fate. It's natural to focus on the movement of the scale that teaches an asshole a lesson, but the truest form of justice is found in the will of the survivor. When we decide that what happens to us is more telling than what happens to the bad guy, we issue our own brand of justice.

I found closure when I stopped letting justice be determined by Cain's fate and instead focused on my own future. Tapping into my own brand of badass was the justice I needed most of all. I can't erase being hunted for thirteen years any more than you can erase how it affected you. I still find myself scanning large parking lots, covering my windows in layers of curtains, and feeling apprehensive whenever I'm in a large crowd. But I'm no longer afraid. I've claimed a perpetual state of groovy with a few kinks thrown in to show I'm a veteran of life.

We all have quirks. I think of the famous sculpture known as the *Winged Victory of Samothrace* who's missing both arms and her head, yet she's still considered a priceless work of art. Quirkiness is valuable.

So how do you go on with life when it seems like darkness got away with hurting you? How do you live your fight song? You let you be you. You live authentically. You let your light shine through the cracks. You carve your own rivers, climb your own mountains, and chase your own dreams. You make the conscious decision to live your own truth. Then you give, you love, and you open yourself up to the possibilities. You become your own best traveling companion.

You let joy happen.

I believe you have everything you'll need to make it in this world. You have shown a profound maturity, resiliency, and determination that I'm only beginning to understand. And you have a natural way of drawing down the sunshine. Hold tight to your strengths—they've saved you before, and they will save you again.

In this letter, I've tried to offer you some useful advice as you begin to navigate your new frontier. I reserved my final thoughts for the ones that I feel are the cornerstones to a warm and peaceful life. Please keep these thoughts in your spiritual locket and consider them the quartz, the amethyst, the carnelian, and the jade of the roads I have already traveled.

Remember that you matter in this world. Tell yourself every day that you are loved and you are worth loving.

Be forever mindful with your thoughts and words—they are the winds sculpting your horizon.

Never let go of hope—it's your walking stick. Without hope, you have nothing to lean on anymore.

Above all else, believe in yourself. Believe in the power of your own art. Believe in the magic of your own light. Believe you have the talent, the skill, the fierceness, and the courage to build your own castle, slay your own dragons, and write your own story.

The world has taught me many things, but the best of all was this: When we believe we can do anything, it comes to pass that we do.

Sending positive energy across the miles and holding you close in thought,

Your Loving Mother

ACKNOWLEDGMENTS

To Sparrow—Thank you for your patience, your remarkable insight, and your never-ending encouragement. Without your faith in this project, I never would have had the courage to share these letters with the world.

To my mother—Thank you for being my first editor. Your willingness to indulge my dream helped shape these letters into words that love, inspire, and heal.

To my editor, Kristy—Your dedication and enthusiasm toward this project were infectious. Your keen eye and bright mind truly brought these letters to life. A thousand thank-yous will never be enough to show my gratitude. It is truly your calling in life to use the art of soulful storytelling to guide the voice of truth.

To Moses—You were the light in the forest. Thank you for quietly showing me the power of your brave and letting me stand safe in your presence.

To the women of the world—We are entering The Age of the Woman. Never before in history have we been so united and so powerful. Thank you for letting me share my journey with you, and thank you for sharing your journeys with me. Silence is the weapon of darkness. When we raise our voices together, we defeat the enemy we call *fear*.

Shine on, sweet sisters, shine on.

CPSIA information can be obtained
at www.ICGtesting.com
Printed in the USA
LVHW111638150520
655691LV00008B/53/J